THE HIGH TECHNOLOGIES AND REDUCING THE RISK OF WAR

Mary Shaw

ANNALS OF THE NEW YORK ACADEMY OF SCIENCES

Volume 489

THE HIGH TECHNOLOGIES AND REDUCING THE RISK OF WAR

Edited by H. Guyford Stever and Heinz R. Pagels

The New York Academy of Sciences
New York, New York
1986

358.17
H638

Copyright © 1986 by The New York Academy of Sciences. All rights reserved. Under the provisions of the United States Copyright Act of 1976, individual readers of the Annals *are permitted to make fair use of the material in them for teaching or research. Permission is granted to quote from the* Annals *provided that the customary acknowledgment is made of the source. Material in the* Annals *may be republished only by permission of The Academy. Address inquiries to the Executive Editor at The New York Academy of Sciences.*

Copying fees: *For each copy of an article made beyond the free copying permitted under Section 107 or 108 of the 1976 Copyright Act, a fee should be paid through the Copyright Clearance Center, 21 Congress Street, Salem, MA 01970. For articles more than 3 pages, the copying fee is $1.75.*

Library of Congress Cataloging-in-Publication Data

The high technologies and reducing the risk of war.
(Annals of the New York Academy of Sciences; v. 489)
"The result of a conference . . . sponsored by the New York Academy of Sciences and the L. W. Frohlich Charitable Trust, which was held May 7-8, 1986 in New York, N.Y."
Includes bibliographies and index.
1. Strategic Defense Initiative—Congresses. 2. Anti-satellite weapons—Congresses. 3. Space warfare—Congresses. 4. United States—Military relations—Soviet Union—Congresses. 5. Soviet Union—Military relations—United States—Congresses.
I. Stever, H. Guyford. II. Pagels, Heinz R., 1939- . III. New York Academy of Sciences. IV. L. W. Frohlich Charitable Trust. V. Series.
Q11.N5 vol. 489 500 s 87-1568
[UG743] [358'.1754]
ISBN 0-89766-373-X
ISBN 0-89766-374-8 (pbk.)

CCP
Printed in the United States of America
ISBN 0-89766-373-X (cloth)
ISBN 0-89766-374-8 (paper)

ANNALS OF THE NEW YORK ACADEMY OF SCIENCES

Volume 489
December 26, 1986

THE HIGH TECHNOLOGIES AND REDUCING THE RISK OF WAR[a]

Editors
H. GUYFORD STEVER AND HEINZ R. PAGELS

CONTENTS

[a] This volume is the result of a conference entitled The High Technologies and Reducing the Risk of War, sponsored by the New York Academy of Sciences and the L. W. Frohlich Charitable Trust, which was held May 7–8, 1986, in New York, N. Y.

University Libraries
Carnegie Mellon University
Pittsburgh, Pennsylvania 15213

Part IV. Perceptions of Soviet Policy

Part V. International Significance of the New Defense Technologies

Financial assistance was received from:

- Boeing Corporation
- The L. W. Frohlich Charitable Trust
- The Richard Lounsbery Foundation
- The Rockefeller Foundation

The L. W. Frohlich Award

In conjunction with this conference series entitled Science and The Human Prospect, a major new biennial award, the L. W. Frohlich Award, is to be given to one or two scientists whose work is related to the topic of the conference. The purpose of both the award and the conference is to draw public attention to the role of science in promoting human survival, the fundamental issue confronting all inhabitants of our planet.

The award itself consists of a medal (shown here), a certificate, and $5,000 to each awardee. In addition, as the major component of the award, each awardee may select two L. W. Frohlich Fellows who will receive a fellowship of $25,000 yearly for four consecutive years in order to continue the research activities begun by the awardee. In this way, the valuable research tradition of the awardee is continued by a young investigator and the majority of the funds go into scientific research.

The award will go to "the scientist whose singular achievements in research hold significant, direct promise for major improvements of human life, the promotion of human survival, and the creation of new economic or educational opportunities." The novel fellowship concept is itself intended to promote the human prospect for survival.

Both the conference topic, on a theme related to human survival, and the awardees are selected by the L. W. Frohlich Awards Committee. The award is jointly sponsored by the New York Academy of Sciences, Columbia University, and New York University, and administered solely by the Academy. The committee consists of eight individuals: two appointed by the president of Columbia University, two by the president of New York University, two by the Academy (which also appoints a chair), and one by the L. W. Frohlich Charitable Trust. The Committee for this year's award consisted of Robert W. Berliner, chair; Quali Al-Awqati, Columbia University; Ben Bederson, New York University; Charles Cantor, Columbia University; Florence L. Denmark, the New York Academy of Sciences; Walter N. Scott, New York University; Richard B. Leather, the L. W. Frohlich Charitable Trust; and Heinz R. Pagels, the New York Academy of Sciences.

The first conference in this series, The High Technologies and Reducing the Risk of War, chaired by H. Guyford Stever of the National Academy of Engineering and Heinz R. Pagels of the New York Academy of Sciences, was chosen by the committee because of the overriding threat to human existence posed by the possibility of nuclear war. It is an ever timely topic. Scientific research has made this threat possible, but may also offer the means of altering and removing it, provided there is the human will to do so.

The resulting conference proceedings are presented in this *Annal.* There is great disagreement among scientists, as well as others, concerning the means of reducing the risk of war. The conference, which included individuals of widely divergent views, reflected these disagreements. Scientists familiar with the new

Top: The L. W. Frohlich Award. *Bottom (left to right):* Heinz R. Pagels, Edwin Land, Charles H. Townes, and Robert W. Berliner.

military systems and several experts on international relations and Soviet perceptions aired their views. There was some heated debate, as is evident from the roundtable discussions in this volume.

The following is a list of conference participants, speakers and chairs, among whom are included many of the major U.S. and foreign strategic thinkers:

David Aaron
Harold M. Agnew
Pierre R. Aigrain
James Blyth
McGeorge Bundy
Shlomo Carmi
Ashton B. Carter
George F. Chapline
Robert G. Clem
Paul Doty
Sidney D. Drell
Joseph Finck
John S. Foster, Jr.
Richard L. Garwin
John H. Gibbons
William T. Golden
Roger L. Hagengruber
Thomas H. Johnson
Thomas H. Karas
Theodore B. Ladd, Jr.
Franklin A. Long
Geraldine Mannion
Michael M. May
Joseph L. Merchant
Frederick A. Mosher
William A. Nierenberg
Heinz R. Pagels
John Pike
J. Mark Pullen
David Z. Robinson
Jack Ruina
Charles E. Schmid
Richard A. Scribner
Frederick Seitz
Robert W. Selden
Marshall D. Shulman
H. Guyford Stever
John Templeton Swing
John Stremlau
Edward Teller
Charles H. Townes
Albert D. Wheelon
Lowell Wood
Gerold Yonas

Although the conference participants were often sharply divided in their views on issues of war and peace, there was complete concurrence about the appropriateness of the 1986 L. W. Frohlich Awardees: Drs. Edwin Land and Charles Townes. Dr. Land was recognized for the work he has done on satellite optical systems which supply important arms limitation and verification information. Dr. Townes was especially cited for his work on the scientific principles that led to the invention of the laser, a device of rising importance in modern communications systems that also has many other commercial and military applications.

The 1986 L. W. Frohlich Award was presented at a dinner given in honor of the awardees on 7 May 1986 at the Bobst Library of New York University. The award was given to Drs. Land and Townes by Dr. Robert W. Berliner, Chairman of L. W. Frohlich Awards Committee, and Dr. William S. Cain, President of the New York Academy of Sciences.

After the awards ceremony, U.S. Senator Daniel Patrick Moynihan addressed the audience on his views concerning recent developments in weapons systems, punctuating his remarks with his customary wit. Although the topic of the conference was one of profound concern, the awards banquet was an event of good cheer and fellowship, even among those who usually disagree. It was a fitting and moving tribute to the distinguished awardees from their colleagues.

Introduction

H. GUYFORD STEVER

Dr. Pagels and I thought that it would be interesting, perhaps, to give a little of the background of the conference subject today.

Science is performed in many different centers in this country, but there is one special kind of activity that peaks in Washington because our federal government is the patron of basic science. For many years I have observed the leaders of science coming to Washington to express to the executive branch and to the Congress their view of the future in the basic sciences which they represent.

Obviously, they want the patrons of science to know what the future offers. There is a uniform optimism amongst the leaders of basic science that the future holds the promise of a great deal of new science. I think that's a very important part of our background here today because whatever we say about the high technology that results from these sciences, it will continue to progress and change the solutions to problems which we have in reducing the risk of war.

It isn't only the leaders in the basic sciences who believe they have a strong and productive future, but also those in derivative sciences such as material sciences, information and communication sciences, and sensor and measurement science, the host of sciences that depend upon physics, chemistry, biology, mathematics, and all the other basic sciences. One can go even farther along that line of reasoning to the high technology products of science.

One of the fruits of science is the improvement of the welfare of our citizens, another the ensurance of national security. The new sciences will continue to unfold and they will affect our peacemaking efforts. The overriding peacemaking effort in the world today is of course the control of nuclear weapons. We have lived with nuclear fission for fifty years. We have lived with atom bombs for forty years and with hydrogen bombs for thirty years. It has been a long time, and although those bombs don't constitute complete weapons systems since other components are needed for military purposes, the focus of peacemaking is on the control of the nuclear weapons.

First we used airplanes to carry bombs, very simple airplanes, propeller airplanes in the beginning, and then jet-propelled airplanes. For the past three decades we have considered ballistic missiles propelled by rockets, first from land bases and then in hardened underground sites and submarine platforms, and now we have returned again to essentially the airplane delivery system in the form of the pilotless bomber.

H. Guyford Stever is Foreign Secretary of the National Academy of Engineering, Washington, D.C. 20007.

Continuingly unfolding high technology has thus influenced how we might deliver nuclear weapons, but the immense destructive power of the nuclear weapon itself is the basis of its importance to military power.

Over that period, of course, we have also discovered that the destructive power of nuclear weapons had effects that we didn't think of in the beginning. In the beginning we had to explain that there was not only the normal physical destruction but also the destruction which came from the radiation fallout. More recently there has been added the possibility of nuclear winters which would come from widespread use of nuclear weapons.

The ballistic missile and the nuclear bomb absolutely transformed the thinking about future warfare into an instantaneous global affair. It has strained our thinking about maintaining peace in the world to handle that concept.

Another line of advanced technology also fitted into this developing picture when space capabilities were developed with earth satellites. Optics and electronics technology enabled us to use these satellites to improve immensely our short-term reconnaissance for military intelligence gathering.

It is interesting also to look back on this period that started fifty years ago. There have been really only two basic strategic concepts used by the superpowers in the world with respect to how one would use those nuclear weapons in peacetime.

The first one was the idea of nuclear superiority and I think we in the United States were the first to embrace that. We thought we could keep nuclear superiority because of our superior technological capabilities and our very fine science, but this idea began to disappear fairly rapidly. In the first place the United States and its allies had atom bombs and nuclear bombs in the forties, and hydrogen bombs in the forties and early fifties. The Soviet Union was only a few years behind. There was a time when we thought we might maintain a nuclear superiority in the world because we had better delivery mechanisms, but that too disappeared with Soviet developments in ballistic missiles.

By the early sixties the other major military strategy emerged to use nuclear weapons capability for a mutually assured destruction or mutually assured retaliation concept. That seems to have been accepted on both sides as the proper way to control nuclear weapons development, but it hasn't controlled it very well.

The number of nuclear weapons has increased steadily and their efficiency, effectiveness, and accuracy and the number of basing schemes and the technologies supplied to make this better has just gone on increasing so that a frenetic stability in a sense has been maintained. Some people believe that total wars have been completely deterred and we are in a satisfactory position with our existing kind of nuclear stability. Others say that a stability that permits ever-increasing numbers of weapons and ways to deliver them in a troubled world is not a very stabilizing concept.

We come to the next line of thinking which brings us here today, and that has to do with defense. Every military weapon advance seems to evoke a defense against it. My first contact with defense against ballistic missiles was in London during World War II in the mid-forties. There was a proposal to shoot down V2s. It was abandoned because a quick examination indicated it just was not effective. In fact, the British War Cabinet's reason for abandoning it was very simple: though they could destroy V2s over London, the number of casualties that resulted from the shrapnel that shot up to shoot them down would about equal the casualties that they would incur if the V2s actually landed in London. They decided that if there were going to be casualties, the actions of the other side should be the cause. It is all in a War Cabinet paper.

Ten years later the same attempt to get defense against ballistic missiles also gained great momentum. In the 1950s a great deal of work was done on ballistic missile defense systems (these defense systems are not something brand new). There were very local ballistic missile defense systems that defended an important city or an important objective such as a missile launching site. There were also space-based systems, concepts which were examined in the mid-fifties and rejected as noneffective either technologically or economically at the time.

The local defense system concept had a longer life and lasted until the early sixties when that too died out also because countermeasures against ballistic missile defense systems seemed to be easier and cheaper to develop.

We now find ourselves in the mid-eighties with the revival of the idea that defense against ballistic missiles can be developed. The Strategic Defense Initiative has, in fact, emerged as a very strong government initiative.

I think it has emerged for a couple of reasons. There are many people who really are completely dissatisfied with the kind of nuclear stability we have in the world today and they are searching for a way out.

It has emerged also because some scientists involved in the technology of weapons believe that there are some new technologies which just haven't been applied and have great potential for making defense systems work.

We will hear a great deal about these issues at this conference. At least two of the technologies that are considered by many not to have been used to their full capability are ground- and space-based laser weapons and computers, sensor, and information-handling equipment for the coordination of instantaneous complex global battle.

There are others who say this is an ideal that we would like to attain, but it is in fact unattainable. They view either the cost as excessive or the technology as not producible.

We are thus already in a peacekeeping process which has been difficult for the leaders of the world to handle. The emerging technologies are makimg it even more complex. The citizenry of the world finds it very difficult to conceive the immensity of the system we are talking about. The manpower, organization, equipment, weapons, research, development, operations, and all of that defeats the imagination of many people. They question the cost, value, dependability, and need. Those who are involved in leadership roles—the leaders of our executive and legislative branches, our military leaders who have to form the military strategy and tactics for the use of the weapons we have, our industrial leaders who will be asked to provide new weapons, our scientific and academic leaders, our leaders in the media—are very troubled by the immensity of the problem of handling the new high technology with the hope of reducing the risks of war. I guess the only solution that is left is for all of us to discuss this problem as much and as often as we can, to try to educate ourselves and others to ensure that technology in the future is aimed more toward mutually assured peace than it is toward mutually assured destruction. This conference grows out of those circumstances.

A number of the speakers today are leaders in the various fields that I have mentioned, many of them in the science and technology areas. I think you will find some disagreement amongst them on what should be done.

On the other hand, the one thing that is true about all the participants here is they too believe that we had better discuss this because of its immense importance to our society today.

Current and Future Military Uses of Space[a]

ASHTON B. CARTER

The civilian space program is a cultural activity, designed to express people's sense of adventure, the progress of technology, and national prowess. Economic or scientific utility is not the standard applied in designing the civilian space program, despite some hopeful talk about growing crystals and performing electrophoretic separations at zero *g*. The military space program is completely different. In our military program, the benchmark of success is not technological advance or novelty, but military capability and related national security.

It is unfortunate that we sometimes tend to carry over to the military space program the mystique that underlies the civilian program. This mystique—reflected equally in urgings that we "must seize the high ground" and that we "must avoid militarizing space"—is not very helpful in perceiving what kind of military space program we need or in managing it.

This talk begins with the premise that however special or dramatic space might appear, it should be regarded merely as another medium for national security activities. We should apply to military missions conducted from space the same standards of cost-effectiveness, survivability, and trade-offs with alternatives that we apply to our other military decisions. The drama can be taken into account after we have gotten our bearings in a more hard-headed military sense. I will not in this paper emphasize arms control as a solution to security problems in space, to the neglect of unilateral military initiatives and acts of self-restraint.

CURRENT MILITARY USES OF SPACE

For the first three decades of the Space Age, the superpowers have found it technically and economically attractive to use space only for the five so-called traditional missions of reconnaissance and surveillance, communications, navigation, meteorology, and geodesy. Let me review these missions very

[a] Parts of this paper were adapted, with permission of the publisher, from: Ashton B. Carter, "Satellites and Anti-Satellites: The Limits of the Possible," *International Security* **10(4)**:46–98 (Spring 1986).

Ashton B. Carter is Associate Director of the Center for Science and International Affairs at the John F. Kennedy School of Government, Harvard University, Cambridge, Massachusetts 02138.

briefly before passing on to the host of new technologies that might in the future greatly lengthen this list of military space missions.

Reconnaissance and Surveillance

Electromagnetic radiation emitted or reflected from terrestrial objects can be detected from space in any of the three wavelength bands to which the intervening atmosphere is transparent, namely, the visible band, certain infrared bands, and the microwave radio band. It follows that these are the bands used for military surveillance.

In peacetime, these remote sensing techniques are used to characterize foreign weapons for U.S. force planning and treaty monitoring and to contribute to strategic warning. Collection of peacetime intelligence is characterized by a leisurely time scale and a benign environment. Naturally one would also like to use these remote sensing techniques for wartime purposes, such as tracking fleet movements, locating rear area targets, sorting out enemy lines of supply and command, monitoring activities at airbases, intercepting field communications, and warning of enemy advances. Though many of the same remote sensing technologies apply to both tactical and strategic intelligence, there are three crucial differences between these two missions. First, battlefield intelligence must be processed and disseminated rapidly if it is to be useful. Second, it is to be expected that tactical sensors of genuine military value will come under attack, whereas peacetime intelligence collection is not directly impeded. Third, space-based sensors, a necessarily global capability, must compete in cost-effectiveness and survivability with other collectors such as aircraft and remotely piloted vehicles that can be brought rapidly to bear in a theater of conflict. These factors make the notion of an "electronic battlefield" orchestrated from space somewhat less compelling than a first thought might suggest.

In the realm of nuclear operations, space is used to detect missile launches and nuclear detonations. Missile warning data permit the safe escape of bombers, tankers, cruise missile carriers, airborne command posts, and, for launch-under-attack (LUA), intercontinental ballistic missiles (ICBMs). Confirmation of detonations on U.S. soil might also serve as a last check on an LUA decision. But the most important use of missile launch and nuclear detonation data would probably be to give decision-makers a clear assessment of what happened, information crucial to responsible action and, under the chaotic circumstances, hard to come by otherwise.

Imagery

The resolution of a given spaceborne optical camera is proportional to its altitude. Thus a photoreconnaissance satellite orbiting at an altitude of 200 km and yielding imagery with one-foot resolution (about the view the human eye gets from the top of a skyscraper) would at 5000 km yield Landsat-like imagery useful for forestry and for *National Geographic*, but useless for most intelligence purposes. Photoreconnaissance satellites are therefore confined to low-earth orbit. Coverage at all latitudes requires polar orbits for these satellites.

Infrared cameras would collect information about the surface temperature of objects on the earth, potentially revealing features obscured at visible wavelengths. Radar images can be formed by illuminating the earth with microwaves and collecting the reflected signals. Radar satellites would provide nighttime and all-weather imagery, since they would supply their own illumination, and microwaves penetrate easily through clouds.

Signal Detection

Satellites can also detect discrete signals in the three atmospheric bands, including microwave pulses from the air defense radar on the ship, telemetry from a cruise missile test vehicle, the visible flash of a nuclear detonation, or the infrared plume of an ICBM launch. If the signal is sharply structured in time, like the flash of a nuclear burst or the pulses of a radar, the emitter's location can be deduced from the differences among the signal's arrival times at several well-separated satellites.

Orbits for signal detection should be chosen to provide continuous coverage of target areas, preventing the opponent from performing tests, sending messages, moving mobile radars, or launching missiles during coverage gaps. Geosynchronous orbits (GEO) offer continuous dwell over mid-latitudes; the U.S. acknowledges stationing warning satellites there. Long dwell times (and coverage of northern latitudes) are also possible from Molniya orbits; the Soviet Union deploys warning satellites in this way. Continuous coverage by several widely separated satellites, permitting emitter location by the time-difference-of-arrival technique, requires a "birdcage" constellation; the U.S. Nuclear Detection System (NDS) aboard the Navstar GPS satellite is in this kind of orbit. (FIGURES 1 and 2 illustrate these orbit types.)

Communications

There are only two ways to communicate information over long distances within seconds: by landline (including transoceanic cable) and by radio. Because the earth is round, line-of-sight radio contact between widely separated points on the earth's surface is impossible. One way to propagate radio waves over the horizon is to bounce them off the ionosphere; shortwave (HF, high frequency) radio propagation in this manner was until recently the U.S. Navy's chief means of communicating with its far-flung ships. But ionospheric reflection is unreliable and cannot support large rates of message traffic. Long-distance communication companies have long placed microwave radio relays on towers and mountaintops for over-the-horizon relay. The communcations satellite is just an extension of the relay principle to higher altitudes and consequently longer relay distances.

Most operational communications satellites (COMSATs) today use ultra-

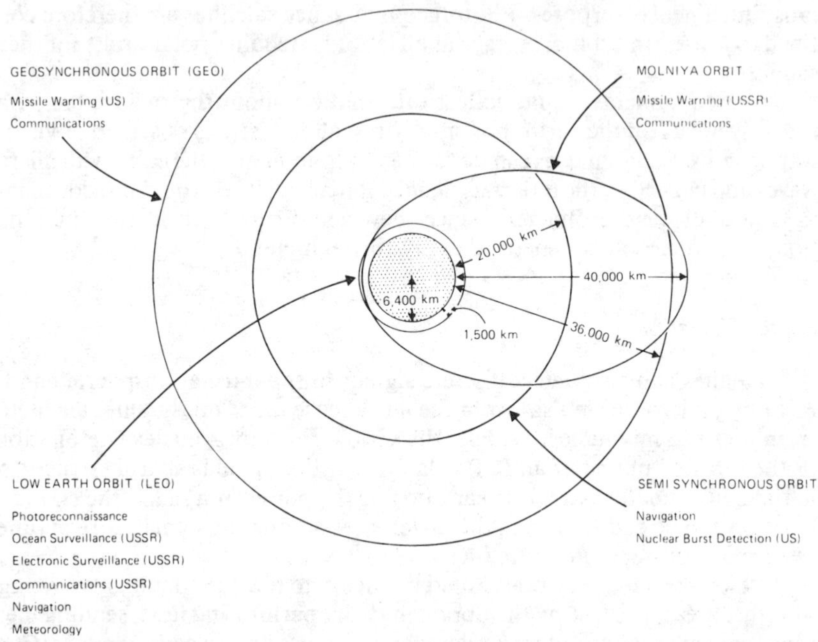

FIGURE 1. The four major orbit types, drawn here to scale, contain almost all military satellites. The LEO region, represented here by a 1500 km (930 mile) circular orbit, is subject to attack by both the U.S. and Soviet ASATs. The U.S. ASAT also has the propulsive capability to attack Molniya orbit, though it will not in fact have that capability in its proposed operational deployment; the Soviet ASAT cannot attack Molniya orbit. Neither ASAT can climb to semisynchronous orbit or GEO. The nature and orbits of U.S. reconnaissance satellites are classified. The supersynchronous region above GEO is little populated today, but its vast reaches offer opportunities for satellite survivability that are likely to be exploited in the future.

high frequencies (UHF) and super-high frequencies (SHF), but extremely high frequency (EHF) systems are under development. The move to higher frequencies for military satellite communication (SATCOM) is motivated by five factors. First, higher-frequency radio waves have a higher limit to their data-carrying capacity than lower-frequency waves. Second, transmitting antennas for higher frequencies can be made smaller without sacrificing performance, since the effectiveness of a transmitter dish is determined by the ratio of its size to the wavelength of the radio waves it is transmitting. Three additional advantages of high frequencies (accompanied by wide bandwidths) for the peculiar needs of military SATCOM are: it is easier to protect higher-frequency links against hostile jamming; covert ("low-probability-of-intercept," or LPI) communication, which does not betray the location of the transmitting ground terminal, is easier with wide bandwidths; and higher frequencies suffer less distortion in passing through an ionosphere disturbed by nuclear detonations.

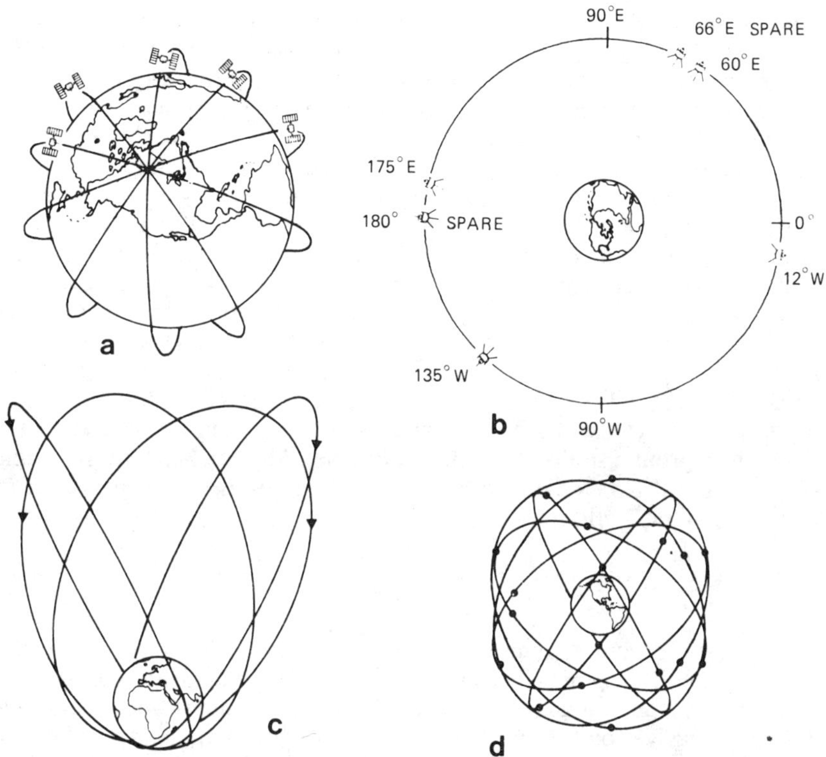

FIGURE 2. Military satellite constellations illustrate the four orbit categories. (**a**) Five U.S. TRANSIT navigation satellites in polar LEO, arranged in five separate orbital planes. (**b**) Four U.S. DSCS communications satellites in GEO equatorial orbit. (**c**) Four Soviet Molniya communications satellites in inclined Molniya orbits, arranged in four planes. (**d**) Eighteen U.S. Navstar GPS navigation and nuclear burst detection satellites in inclined semisynchronous orbits, arranged in six planes.

Laser communication is also coming into use for satellite-to-satellite links and for satellite-to-aircraft links. Ground-to-space laser communication links could obviously be frustrated by clouds.

Military COMSATs are deployed in a variety of orbits. GEO is high enough to allow widely separated ground stations to communicate through a single satellite, and a stationary satellite makes it easy for users to point their antennas. But the polar regions are invisible from geosynchronous equatorial orbit. The Soviets, with many military installations at high latitudes, deploy COMSATs in Molniya orbits. A communications satellite in low earth orbit (LEO) is only visible at any given time from a relatively small patch of earth below. Two terminals within the patch can communicate directly, but widely separated users must store messages on board the satellite when it is overhead, ordering the satellite to "dump" the message when it passes over the recipient. The Soviets deploy large numbers of such store-and-dump satellites in LEO.

Transmitting a message from one hemisphere to another requires an intermediate ground station in view of two satellites, the satellites in turn being in view of the originator and recipient. Likewise, a low earth orbiting satellite that collects its data out of sight of its processing station must have either a local earth station connected by landline or satellite relay to the processing station, or tape recorders to store the data until the satellite passes over the processing station and can "dump" it. Control of complex spacecraft requiring frequent ground commands depends on a worldwide network of earth stations. Suitably located earth stations, in politically stable areas that would also be unaffected by military conflict, are hard to provide. Direct satellite-to-satellite relay links avoid all these problems. NASA's Tracking and Data Relay Satellite System (TDRSS), consisting of a pair of spacecraft in synchronous orbit, will provide essentially uninterrupted relay between satellites at all altitudes and a ground station at White Sands, New Mexico. Satellite cross-links and relay COMSATs are crucial for freeing satellites of their dependence on overseas ground stations.

Navigation

Navigation is not a glamorous mission, but is is essential for supporting reconnaissance, weapon delivery (including submarine-launched ballistic missiles, SLBMs), precision emplacement of sensors and mines, and rendezvous. Terrestrial navigation systems have either restricted coverage (*e.g.*, LORAN) or poor accuracy (*e.g.*, OMEGA). In one satellite navigation method, used by the U.S. Navy's TRANSIT system and its Soviet equivalent, the user listens to how the received frequency of a radio signal changes as the transmitting satellite passes from horizon to horizon, like the wail of an ambulance siren as it first approaches and then recedes. Knowing the satellite's orbit and the pattern of frequency change allows the receiver to deduce its location on the earth's surface. Global coverage points to polar orbits for these satellites; frequent revisits of all locations indicate a number of orbital planes.

Meteorology

Military operations, special operations, and reconnaissance planning all require knowledge of the weather patterns in distant parts of the globe.

Geodesy

This peacetime function has little importance for the ASAT problem, since it would be accomplished by the time hostilities began.

Though they are located in space, these satellites perform the rather mundane functions of a host of other military equipment (reconnaissance aircraft and ships, microwave communications towers, and terrestrial navigation beacons like LORAN). Though these satellites do not carry weapons and do not shoot at anything, some of them can directly support military operations. It therefore seems oddly inconsistent to seek to create a sanctuary in space for this "threatening" military equipment. Why shouldn't satellites be subject to attack like all the other instruments of warfare?

No single answer to this question applies to all satellites. What one can say is that next to these threatening satellites is a class of what I will call "benign" satellites that should *not* be subject to attack. Missle warning satellites exemplify this class most clearly. The much discussed RORSAT, a Soviet radar ocean reconnaissance satellite that tracks multibillion-dollar American carrier battle groups at sea and could direct air attack on them, is supposed to exemplify the threatening category most clearly, though in view of the limitations of the current version we should perhaps say that a future version of RORSAT would make the case more clearly.

In the case of other space missions, it is harder to decide whether they belong in the threatening or benign category, and many fall in between. It is vital to recognize that the designations "benign" and "threatening" inhere not in the spacecraft's mission only, but in the circumstances of its use as well. A benign U.S. photo reconnaissance satellite monitoring a crisis abruptly turns threatening to the Soviet Union when war begins and its daily imagery becomes the basis for air strikes on Soviet supply lines entering the theater. At this point the Soviets will wish to have an antisatellite weapon (ASAT).

If today's military uses of space include a substantial fraction of benign missions, in the future this fraction seems destined to decrease. Many of the potential future military uses of space are clearly threatening. It is natural to want to be able to threaten these satellites in return. Thus arises the basic paradox of antisatellite arms control: to the extent that ASAT development is suppressed and the vulnerability of spacecraft masked, the superpowers will be more and more tempted to deploy threatening spacecraft. And to the extent they do so, pressures will in turn build to set aside the treaty and deploy ASATs.

POSSIBLE FUTURE MILITARY USES OF SPACE

A host of hypothetical future space missions vie for attention and funding. Which of these concepts will actually reach the deployment stage depends not only on technical feasibility (not demonstrated in many cases) and on the value of mission they serve, but most importantly on their prospects for surviving antisatellite attack. Missions that would never be taken seriously if they had to face an unconstrained antisatellite threat will be much more tempting if the threat is constrained. Since some of these missions fall decidedly in the "threatening" category, giving them sanctuary in space could well prove intolerable over time.

Adjuncts to Current Missions

The advance of technology will permit support functions performed from space today to be performed better. For instance, introduction of SATCOM at extremely high frequencies in the U.S. MILSTAR system will allow improved resistance to jamming, low-probability-of-intercept transmission that does not betray the communicator's location or even existence, and better emergency communication through ionospheric regions disturbed by nuclear bursts. Missions performed by terrestrial equipment today might by augmented or backed up by spacecraft. For instance, blue-green laser communications are proposed as a backup to terrestrial and airborne VLF radio for communicating with missile submarines. Space-based infrared sensors could perform the vital job of continuously surveying all orbiting objects, replacing the current network of ground-based radars. Relay satellites like the shuttle-launched TRDSS continue the process of freeing U.S. satellites from dependence on overseas ground stations.

Elaborations to the Nuclear Offense

Four different possibilities can be envisioned in this category. First, space-based sensors might be used to seek out and direct attack on relocatable or mobile targets such as air defense radars, mobile missiles, and mobile (even airborne) command posts. A second elaboration would be a means by which to assess the damage to an opponent from an initial nuclear strike and restrike whatever targets survived. One such scheme would use data from the Nuclear Detection System aboard Navstar GPS to observe detonations of U.S. weapons over the Soviet Union and to "fill in the blanks" where expected detonations failed to occur because of the imperfect reliability of U.S. missiles. Two-on-one targeting of silos and other hardened targets would then be unnecessary. Damage assessment would also support a "shoot-look-shoot" tactic designed to penetrate preferential ballistic missile defenses.

A third offensive elaboration would use satellite navigation to reduce missile guidance errors to tens of feet rather than hundreds of feet, ushering in "usable" low-yield strategic nuclear weapons and even nonnuclear strategic weapons. Satellite navigation could also reduce the cost of Midgetman missiles which must otherwise each carry an expensive guidance system to have silo-killing accuracy. The fourth type of hypothetical elaboration to the nuclear offense comprises the space-based components of all the countermeasurers the offense will need to compete with "Star Wars" defenses. Though these elaborations cannot be specified without specifying the type of defense system deployed, they would be akin to the short-range attack missiles (SRAMs), cruise missiles, stealth and other electronic countermeasures (ECMs), and ICBMs that were the elaborations made to U.S. offense of the 1950s, based upon the high-flying bomber, when the Soviet Union improved its air defenses. In the "Star Wars" case the space-based components of penetration systems might include orbiting jammers, shields, decoy dispensers, and antisatellite weapons.

Nuclear Defense

This includes all the beam and kinetic energy weapons, together with their sensors, discussed in the Strategic Defense Initiative. Orbiting radars or infrared sensors for tracking aircraft, and laser battle stations to attack them, might be components of a future air defense against intercontinental bombers. Lastly, this category includes still-hypothetical sensors for locating and tracking strategic missile submarines through their hydrodynamic, thermal, or other signatures.

Support for Conventional Forces

This is a vast category that ranges from the monitoring of rear areas (akin to peacetime strategic intelligence) to detailed participation in battlefield operations, for example, locating targets, guiding "smart" weapons to them, and relaying voice and data traffic.

Antisatellite Weapons (ASATs) and Satellite Defense (DSATs)

ASATs and DSATs comprise all the paraphernalia of a military competition in space: (1) mines, directed-energy weapons, kinetic energy weapons, jammers, and ECM pods to destroy or fool enemy satellites; (2) defensive escorts for friendly satellites, carrying jammers, decoys, shields, or weapons to fight off ASATs; and (3) space-tracking and identification sensors for ASAT, DSAT, and treaty monitoring.

Space-to-Earth Weapons

Space-to-earth weapons discussed from time to time include beam weapons, orbiting nuclear-armed and conventionally armed reentry vehicles (RVs), and electromagnetic pulse (EMP) generators. Space-to-earth beam weapons have to contend with atmospheric attenuation, which rules out many types, and with the abundant shielding available to terrestrial targets. Nuclear-armed RVs stored in space have never competed in terms of cost, accuracy, or command and control with RVs stored in the noses of ICBMs.

Human Presence in Space

The perennial question of the military utility of staffed spacecraft really should be divided into two questions. First, are there military space missions that can either only be done or be done much better by human beings? Second, do such missions require a continually staffed space station or just a space shuttle capable of periodic visits? A third question is whether the military will find uses for a space station if it is justified, built, and paid for by the civilian space program. This third question is easily answered in the affirmative and is sometimes confused with the first two questions, even though it does not address itself to the true military requirements for staffed spacecraft.

Human beings can perform varied, innovative, and subtle functions that cannot yet be mechanized. It also appears that humans can operate efficiently in space for at least six months without physical harm. But humans require life support, safety, and reentry systems that are expensive and heavy, and they need a habitat spacious enough to keep them physically and mentally healthy. Motions caused by humans moving about in the cabin can impair certain kinds of surveillance. Radiation is also a serious limitation: humans are about 100 times more susceptible to harm than ordinary space equipment and about 10,000 times more susceptible than hardened electronics. Operation in the radiation belts for more than a short period is impossible, and in the polar orbits most useful for earth surveillance, protons from solar flares would expose even shielded humans to radiation doses far in excess of those permitted for terrestrial workers. Staffed military spacecraft would also be very vulnerable to radiation from nearby nuclear bursts and to radiation from distant detonations that were trapped in space by the earth's magnetic field.

Continuous coverage and redundancy are usually more important than complexity for military spacecraft anyway, so many unstaffed satellites would obviously be preferable to a few staffed spacecraft. Satellite repair, replenishment, and assembly, identified by NASA as available from a space station, can also be accomplished from the shuttle. If necessary, the shuttle can be equipped with supplies to allow it to remain in orbit for longer periods than it now can. Since the space station would be in inclined LEO and most military satellites are in GEO or polar LEO, fetching the satellites to be repaired requires orbit transfer vehicles that need themselves to be refurbished on orbit. Repair will not pay for itself unless the number of candidate space systems to be repaired is large. GEO staellites have lifetimes of 7–10 years, after which users usually wish to launch improved models rather than repair old ones.

Photoreconnaissance satellites could profit from periodic refueling, since they use propellant to compensate for atmospheric drag experienced in their low orbits and to adjust their ground tracks for timely viewing of important reconnaissance targets. Assembly of large space structures from many small units transported separately to space has some theoretical attractiveness, but there is as yet no identified military need for it. Assembly, like repair, might be better accomplished from a shuttle than from a space station. For all these reasons, the Department of Defense and the intelligence community greeted the NASA space station rather coolly. Once NASA has made the investment, however, military users are certain to find the station convenient for some purposes.

PRINCIPLES FOR U.S. MILITARY EXPLOITATION OF SPACE

Some of the future military uses of space described above are technically fanciful, and some address military problems of peripheral concern, but an important reason that some of them have not gained popularity or been deployed already is that they have been judged too vulnerable to destruction by ASATs. ASAT limitations might encourage rather than discourage some of these deployments.

ASAT arms control faces two basic problems. First, ASAT attack on some space missions is both tempting and relatively easy. Complex satellites in low earth orbit will probably remain fairly cheap to attack in relation to their cost, and if they are engaged in threatening military activities they will present an irresistible temptation for ASATs. Other arms control regimes have sought to limit activities that were less easy and less tempting. The ABM Treaty conformed to the prevailing technical facts that effective missile defense could not be built. Militarizing the Antarctic and stationing nuclear weapons in space were not tempting enough to stimulate concerns over "breakout" of the treaties that forbade them. Limiting ASATs might mean swimming against the tide of technological advance and short-term military opportunity in a way that limiting these other activities by treaty did not.

The second problem for ASAT arms control is that not all uses of space are benign and deserve protection. Paradoxically, any possibility of sanctuary from attack will probably encourage the superpowers to place more and more threatening satellites in space.

Skirting these two problems will be a challenge for negotiators, and the resulting treaty, if one ever emerges, could be quite complex. It is therefore worthwhile to plot a clear course of actions the United States should take *with or without* ASAT arms control.

Let me close by stating six principles that I think should guide U.S. use of space for its national security:

1. Take advantage of the many means available to improve satellite survivability. The survivability features of satellites in orbit today are not a good indication of what is possible at relatively modest cost. No arms control provisions can protect a satellite whose designer has left it open to "cheap shots." Adequate satellite survivability programs are not an alternative to, but a *necessary precondition* for, effective arms control. Only to the extent that satellites can be made immune to all but elaborate, verifiable threats will ASAT limitations be meaningful.
2. Improve spacetracking and surveillance. In order to alert U.S. satellites to attack, to support attack upon Soviet satellites, and to monitor ASAT treaties, the U.S. will require much better space surveillance than it has today. Much more can be done with available technology.
3. Avoid dependence on vulnerable spacecraft. Space systems assigned wartime roles should have to prove themselves in terms of cost-effectiveness and survivability or not be assigned such roles. Deploying threatening satellites in a way that makes them inherently vulnerable to attack (*e.g.*, in low orbits) reflects bad military judgement. Satellites cannot be protected absolutely by any treaty, and no treaty can survive if such temptations to break out of it are ever-present.
4. Employ survivable backups to satellites. Almost all of the missions performed by satellites can be performed (not as well perhaps, but some-

times adequately and sometimes even better) by terrestrial systems. Thus data relay, reconnaissance, and navigation in the NATO theater can be performed from aircraft (in the nature of some current U.S. programs), remotely piloted vehicles, aerostats, and sounding rockets. Even if backups are not quite as capable as the satellite systems they replace, their existence might have the effect of reducing Soviet incentives to attack satellites in the first place.

5. To the extent possible, segregate on different satellites "benign" from "threatening" missions and nuclear-war-related missions from conventional-war-fighting missions. This will give the Soviet Union the opportunity to respect these distinctions and to exercise restraint in the kinds of threats it poses to "benign" missions like missile warning.
6. Plan to attack Soviet satellites to the extent dictated by U.S. security interests. No ASAT treaty will ban all methods of disrupting all types of satellites. The United States therefore cannot avoid the responsibility to develop a serious and reasonable policy towards attack on Soviet satellites. The U.S. should not forbear to possess ASATs if they are of a type not clearly forbidden by treaty, if using them would have an effect on Soviet military capability worth its cost (and not just fulfill someone's idea of symbolic strength), and if they are tailored to avoid posing a threat to "benign" Soviet satellites to the extent possible. In my mind, these criteria do not justify development of a high-altitude ASAT by the United States at this time, and they also raise questions about the high cost of the current F-15-launched ASAT. On the other hand, the U.S. should demonstrate the ability to give threatening Soviet satellites such as a future generation of ocean reconnaissance satellites and "Star Wars" battle stations a rough time in low earth orbit.

DISCUSSION OF THE PAPER

R. GARWIN (*IBM Thomas J. Watson Research Center, Yorktown Heights, N.Y.*): I think the idea of theater backup capabilities for space-derived functions is very important. It is not always true that these are less capable because they are required to be only local. So, we can do a better job, with higher capacity communication systems and more timely surveillance if we are forced into doing it in the European theater by aircraft, rocket, etc., and if we emphasize that and fund it it can have a very stabilizing effect on the evolution and use of antisatellite capabilities on the other side.

A. B. CARTER (*Harvard University, Cambridge, Mass.*): I completely agree and I overstated it if I said that backups are always less capable. A satellite gives you necessarily, whether you like it or not, a global capability. If you are fighting a theater war that might not be the best way to focus.

We have some programs like the Joint Tactical Information Distribution

System being developed from aircraft for the NATO theater that have exactly these characteristics.

G. YONAS (*SDI Organization, Washington, D.C.*): My impression is that you would be favorable to the notion of some ASAT agreements. Would you make some comment on verification of compliance with such agreements?

A. B. CARTER: I think it is inevitable that, either tacitly or by writing them down, we and the Soviet Union will reach some understanding about how far we are going to go in the antisatellite area. As a practical matter we never do everything that we could do, and we and the Soviets do exercise restraint unilaterally. We will see a lot of that.

So, I think you have to distinguish agreements that are written down and are comprehensive from a wider menu of possibilities which include rules of the road, tacit agreements rather than written agreements, and so forth.

I think the way to proceed if one were interested in written arms control is this. You have to ban what you can be sure you can verify and then ask where those bans leave you in terms of satellite survival. My guess is that with such bans in place, some satellite missions like warning and emergency communications can be made survivable, but that complex satellites in low orbit will remain vulnerable to attack by means that cannot be verifiably banned.

Does that answer your question? I mean, there is no magic formula, Gerry, as you know. Today's satellites are vulnerable to such a variety of subtle problems that there is no way you can write down a treaty for which you could convince yourself that all the means of disruption on the Soviet side could be seen. That is never going to be possible for all satellites. But it may be possible for certain classes of satellites like warning satellites and communication satellites. You don't eliminate the threat to satellites, but you blunt it enough that with unilateral protective actions you can protect some missions.

A. WOLSKY (*Argonne National Laboratories, Argonne, Ill.*): You spoke about the desirability of separating benign from hostile functions, putting them on different satellites. Do the Russians trust their knowledge of our satellites enough not to fear that we cheated?

A. B. CARTER: No, I don't imagine they trust us absolutely and there are certain capabilities that can be supplied to a satellite with very little which is conspicuous about them. For instance, you can put a communications package on all kinds of satellites that have other purposes.

But, for instance, we have traditionally not accompanied our missile warning satellites with the kinds of war-fighting capabilities that we could expect to be very high on their targeting list.

There is not absolute separation. I think you have to treat it case by case. But it's an important principle.

Let me give you another example. Radar ocean reconnaissance satellites which track fleet movements and direct attack are going to be in low orbit whereas a missile warning satellite could be in very, very high orbit. So, there are some natural separations that occur.

Protecting U.S. Space Assets from Antisatellite Weapons[a]

STEVE FETTER AND MICHAEL M. MAY

INTRODUCTION

Over the years the United States has become increasingly dependent on space-based assets to support its military policies. Satellite systems are required to a considerable extent to carry out nuclear operations and to support military forces during a conventional war. Current and future antisatellite (ASAT) technologies may be capable of preventing these systems from carrying out their mission, thereby possibly decreasing the stability of deterrence. This paper explores what can be done to safeguard our space assets.

WHICH SATELLITES TO PROTECT?

There are four types of missions the United States currently performs with military satellites (MILSATs) that are of interest here: communications, navigation, meteorology, and reconnaissance and surveillance.

Communications

The U.S. uses a wide variety of satellites for military and diplomatic communications. These satellites are in geosynchronous orbit (GEO), 36,000 km above the earth.

An advanced satellite communications system called MILSTAR (an acronym for Military, Strategic, and Tactical Relay) is now under development. It is intended to provide command and control communications at all levels of conflict, including nuclear war.

Navigation

The U.S. has two satellite navigation systems: TRANSIT and Navstar.

[a]This work was performed under the auspices of the U.S. Department of Energy by the Lawrence Livermore Laboratory under contract no. W-7405-ENG-48.

Steve Fetter is a Research Fellow at the Center for Science and International Affairs, Harvard University, Cambridge, Massachusetts 02138.
Michael M. May is Associate Director at Large, Lawrence Livermore National Laboratory, Livermore, California 94450.

TRANSIT was developed to aid in the navigation of Polaris submarines. The Navstar system, when complete, will consist of 18 satellites 20,000 km above the earth carrying radio beacons that can be used by special terrestrial receivers to obtain very accurate position and velocity information.

Meteorology

Two Defense Meteorological Satellite Program (DMSP) meteorological surveillance satellites process visible and infrared images of the earth to provide information on cloud cover, temperature, and precipitation worldwide.

Reconnaissance and Surveillance

Under this broad category are all missions that gather the electromagnetic signals reflected or emitted from objects on the earth:

1. Attack warning. U.S. satellites in GEO detect and report missile launches anywhere in the world.
2. Nuclear burst detection. Sensors detect and locate nuclear explosions anywhere on earth.
3. Photoreconnaissance. Satellites in low earth orbit (LEO) take photographs of objects on the earth's surface, permitting treaty verification and intelligence gathering.

Which satellites need protection most, either to maintain deterrence or to perform vital or important functions after the outbreak of conventional or nuclear war? In what cases is it cost-effective to protect the system, and in what cases is it better to perform the mission with earth-based assets (or not perform the mission at all)? Recognizing that the U.S. cannot protect a class of satellites through bilateral agreements while attempting to keep corresponding Soviet satellites at risk, do the benefits from safeguarding the system outweigh the costs of increasing the survivability of corresponding Soviet systems?

These questions are most easily answered when considering systems that are vital to nuclear deterrence, since increasing the stability of deterrence is clearly in the interest of both sides. To the extent that deterrence depends on tactical warning, safeguarding attack warning satellites is especially important. Although tactical warning is also provided by ground-based radars, satellites can detect missile launches 15 minutes before these radars, doubling the time available for decisions.

The ability to communicate orders to the surviving nuclear forces is also essential to deterrence. The weak link in deterrence may be not the survival of sufficient nuclear forces, but survival of the ability to command them. An aggressor is likely to concentrate on the destruction of the command and control systems, especially since the number of these targets is far less than the number of weapon delivery vehicles.

To the extent that the ability to maintain continuous communication between the National Command Authority and strategic and tactical forces depends on communication satellites, these would be among the first targets to be attacked. The ground installations that support these satellites could also be attacked, although they could be made more numerous than the satellites.

Turning to the other military space missions, navigation satellites may be targeted during a nuclear war, so as to deny U.S. bombers and submarine-launched ballistic missiles (SLBMs) accurate guidance information for the destruction of hard targets. This guidance capability is not required to destroy most military, industrial, and population centers. The nuclear burst detection capability may also be a tempting target for the Soviet Union, since it could be used to assess the success of a U.S. strike or the damage from a Soviet strike. But navigation and nuclear burst detection seem to be less vital missions in the maintenance of deterrence.

Meteorological satellites, although very valuable in peacetime and during conventional wars, are less important to nuclear deterrence. Even if weather data are important and these satellites are attacked, weather patterns change slowly over the likely time scale of initial nuclear exchanges.

Photoreconnaissance satellites are similarly valuable in peacetime to monitor compliance with arms control treaties, and during conventional wars and crises. They may become threatening during nuclear war, since they may be able to locate surviving forces for retargeting. If necessary, such missions could be performed by aircraft or fractional-orbit satellites in wartime.

So we find that, of the missions performed by satellites now in orbit, attack warning and command, control, and communications are most essential to maintain confidence in nuclear deterrence. We should on that count endeavor to ensure their survival, perhaps even if, to do so, we must accept agreements that help ensure the survival of the same functions for the other side. Safeguarding these systems should be in the interests of both sides, because increasing confidence in their survivability increases the crisis stability of the nuclear deterrent, thus making preemptive or inadvertent war less likely.

In the case of conventional war, it is much more difficult to determine which satellites should be protected. Attack warning, strategic communications, and nuclear burst detection are irrelevant in this case (unless one is planning to escalate the conflict to the nuclear level). On the other hand, tactical communications, navigation, meteorological, and reconnaissance satellites can aid both sides substantially in targeting enemy forces. The latter systems are force multipliers, and both sides will seek to preserve their own capabilities while denying them to the other side.

In what follows, we focus most of our attention on nuclear-critical U.S. satellites such as attack warning or communications. It should be noted, however, that technology developed to attack other systems could threaten critical satellites, although the high orbits of attack warning and communications satellites (GEO at 36,000 km) serve to make attack on them much more difficult, time-consuming, and costly.

There is an important difference between Soviet and U.S. military satellites for space-based attack warning and communications: many Soviet satellites are in Molniya orbits rather than GEO. These orbits are highly elliptical, with an apogee of approximately 40,000 km and a perigee of 500 km. Satellites in this orbit spend over 90% of their time on one side of the earth, where they function like satellites in high circular orbits. This asymmetry between the orbits of vital U.S. and USSR satellites may present special problems when designing bilateral agreements intended to increase the security of such satellites.

The military uses of space are constantly evolving. The missions described here that are performed by satellites may become more or less important in the future, and entirely new missions may be added that may change the assessment given here.

THE ASAT THREAT

An antisatellite weapon system is any type of weapon system that can be used to interfere with the mission of a satellite. This includes not only the destruction of satellites, but also functions such as the jamming of communications or the blinding of optical sensors. In this section, we examine the capabilities of antisatellite weapon systems that are possible now or in the near future. All of the current weapon systems that have potential or inherent ASAT capability are based on earth. Antisatellite weapons based in space may be possible in the future.

Earth-based ASATs

ASATs based on earth have the potential to be larger and more powerful than ASATs based in space, and also much less expensive, per unit power, to construct and operate. They have the disadvantages of being far from targets in GEO, and of having to cope with the limitations imposed by the earth's atmosphere.

Ground-, Sea-, or Air-launched Missiles

These missiles can be used to attack satellites provided that their range is sufficient to reach the satellite orbit in question. This includes not only missiles intended for ASAT use, such as the U.S. air-launched direct-ascent ASAT now in development or the USSR ground-launched co-orbital ASAT (which has been tested at altitudes less than 2,500 km), but also nuclear-armed intercontinental ballistic missiles (ICBMs) and SLBMs (normal maximum altitude of about 1,400 km without special changes) and the Sprint and Galosh ABMs (150-km altitude).

With special changes such as lighter payload and proper fusing, some of these, including the ICBMs and SLBMs, could deliver ASAT weapons to GEO. These weapons could be nuclear warheads of various yields or conventional homing warheads. ASATs using nuclear warheads have a damage radius ranging from tens of kilometers up to thousands, depending on the yield of the weapon and the hardening of the target satellites. They could damage unhardened friendly satellites. Conventional warheads would have to come much closer to the target, at least within 1 km for a shotgun-type warhead, which is not possible with current inertial guidance systems at these distances.

The speed of such missiles would be about 10 km/s, so it would take at least one hour to reach attack warning and communication satellites at geosynchronous distances by direct ascent. In the case of conventional warheads, mid-course update and terminal homing guidance are required for adequate accuracy. Although a co-orbital approach is much less demanding in this regard, it also takes much longer. Any attack with earth-based missiles is likely to be detected by attack warning satellites, since the boosters would be quite large. There could be sufficient time to discover the purpose of the mission and alert the nuclear forces, hence fulfilling at least some of the attack warning and communications missions of the satellites. Earth-based missiles therefore probably do not represent the most dangerous threat to satellites in GEO.

The situation for satellites in LEO is quite different. Earth-based missiles can reach satellites orbiting 200 to 1000 km above the earth in one-half to two minutes by direct ascent, and guidance technologies have already been proved effective for conventional kill at these distances.

Ground-based High-Energy Lasers (HELs)

Such lasers at certain wavelengths (the atmosphere is transparent to many of the wavelengths between 0.3 and 14 microns) could destroy satellites through heating or through shock. They have the advantage of delivering energy at the speed of light (only a tenth of a second is needed to reach geosynchronous distances from the ground) and the disadvantages of being large and inefficient.

Chemical lasers (*e.g.*, deuterium fluoride), free-electron lasers (FELs), or excimer lasers could be used. It is important to note the differing requirements for damaging one unhardened satellite under test conditions, and attacking hardened satellite systems effectively. If one uses favorable assumptions, a one megawatt ground-based laser ASAT feasible in the near-term, for instance, would nearly double the temperature of a satellite in GEO. Most unhardened satellites cannot survive such irradiation. Yet this does not mean that effective ASATs could be based on such lasers.

The power requirements for a real laser weapon system would probably be at least 100 times greater than what is feasible in the near term, in order to compensate for limited dwell time, greater satellite hardness, and other factors. Optical requirements would also be more demanding. To destroy hardened satellites in GEO, ground-based lasers would necessarily thus be very large installations, with power requirements in the hundreds to thousands of megawatts. It may not be possible to transmit such large amounts of power through the atmosphere without unacceptable beam spreading due to thermal blooming.

Satellites in LEO, however, are much less demanding targets. Most could be destroyed by an ASAT system based on the current state-of-the-art laser, although at large costs and not in a short time.

Space-based ASATs

Weapons based in space can be much closer to and have a clearer view of the target satellites than earth-based ASATs; hence, for a given level of technology, they can be more effective against satellites in any orbit. Space-based ASATs may be more vulnerable, however, and the costs of deploying and maintaining ASATs in space is much greater than on earth.

Nuclear Space Mines

Nuclear space mines can be positioned to follow a target satellite at a sufficiently close range and detonate on command. It should be noted that nuclear space mines used against satellites may destroy or interfere with friendly satellites nearby.

Kinetic-Energy Weapons

Either homing missiles or projectiles fired from guns could be used to destroy satellites by direct impact. Projectiles could be propelled by either chemical or electromagnetic energy (rail gun). A rail gun would have a mass of hundreds of tons and a linear dimension of perhaps 50 m, and would probably not be cost-effective unless it could destroy many satellites, thus increasing the range required for such devices.

Homing missiles propelled by chemical energy could be placed into parking orbits within a few hundred kilometers of the target satellite to allow prompt kill. The size of such a missile would be comparable to that of the current direct-ascent U.S. ASAT homing missile. Such missiles could also carry low-yield nuclear weapons, which would considerably reduce the tracking requirements and be more robust to defensive countermeasures.

Directed-Energy Weapons

Directed-energy weapons based in space can use uncharged particles (photons or neutral atoms) of any energy. Charged particle beams cannot be used as ASAT weapons because the earth's magnetic field deflects them. Candidate technologies are neutral particle beams, the high-energy lasers discussed above, X-ray lasers, and microwave weapons.

Neutral Particle Beams

Neutral particle beam (NPB) weapons are essentially negative ion accelerators that strip off the extra electron afterward. The particle energy is limited by the size of the accelerator; current design concepts produce particles with energies of a few hundred million electron volts. Protons of this energy have a range sufficient to penetrate to the center of current satellites and destroy or damage their electronics. It may be possible to harden electronics, which would lead to a corresponding increase in the necessary dwell time. Even so, NPBs, if they can be constructed in space, might be effective against satellites in GEO. They are the more effective the shorter the range. But since NPBs are unlikely to be cost-effective against a single satellite, their use at short ranges is probably limited.

The power requirements for an NPB can be quite large. Depending on circumstances, 10 to 20 te of fuel would be required to destroy a 1 te satellite. An NPB would have a linear dimension of perhaps 50 m, making it a very noticeable object.

High-Energy Lasers

An HEL based in space could make do with a range considerably smaller than an earth-based laser, but as the range decreases so does the number of targets that can be attacked (although the dwell time per target can be proportionately increased). For example, an HEL 1,000 km from a target satellite in GEO would need less than one thousandth the power of an earth-based laser with the same diameter mirror (space-based mirrors are likely to be smaller), but it could only attack a single satellite, which is probably not cost-effective.

Short-range lasers could be put on highly elliptical orbits that intersect GEO, allowing a single weapon to destroy all satellites in GEO, though over an extended period of time (at least 1 day, probably 1 week). To make space-based lasers less noticeable or identifiable, the mirror must be made smaller, but doing so increases the power requirements, which makes the laser larger. Even accounting for the increased dwell time, a space-based laser would be quite noticeable and identifiable.

X-ray Lasers

Nuclear-driven X-ray lasers have little trouble with energy requirements. (In theory, they could be very effective ASATs, especially if they are exploded where a number of targets are in view.) They are in the research stage and it is not possible to say what can be attained, however. They would require the launching and exploding of nuclear weapons in space.

Microwave Weapons

It may be possible to build a device that uses a nuclear explosion to generate a narrow beam of microwaves. Electronic circuits are probably at least three orders of magnitude more vulnerable to microwave energy than X-ray or particle-beam energy. On the other hand, the destruction of electronics would not usually be noticeable from the outside, leading to uncertainty about disablement of the target. Much more work needs to be done on this concept before further judgments can be made.

In the above discussion, weapon systems size was discussed in terms of their effectiveness relative to U.S. estimates of U.S. satellite vulnerability. Actual Soviet weapons would likely be much more powerful (by perhaps an order of magnitude) for the following reason: for a given threat (X-rays, laser irradiation, bullets, etc.) there is a fairly well-defined threshold beyond which a given satellite system will fail. The defender, who knows the details of the satellite design, can estimate this threshold with some confidence, although there will always be some uncertainty in the estimate of the system's vulnerability; prudence requires that the estimate be lowered, so that one can be confident that the system can survive at this threat level. On the other hand, the attacker does not know the details of the design, and will substantially overestimate the lethal level required to be confident that the target system will be destroyed.

POSSIBLE COUNTERMEASURES AGAINST ASATs

Unilateral Countermeasures

Unilateral countermeasures are actions that the United States or the Soviet Union can take to safeguard satellites without the cooperation of other countries. Since the ASAT threat is undefined, actions should be taken that are effective against a wide range of technologies.

Passive Unilateral Countermeasures

Under this heading come those countermeasures directed towards withstanding or avoiding attack by an ASAT. These may include hardening against expected attack (heating, shock, irradiation, and jamming), evasion (maneuvering, deploying decoys), redundancy (spares in orbit or ready to launch, land-based backups to space-based systems), and moving satellites to less vulnerable orbits.

Hardening can be achieved by some combination of the following: making the working components of the satellite (*e.g.*, solar cells or microprocessors) less vulnerable to heating or irradiation, and/or surrounding the satellite or vulnerable components by an appropriate shield. The measures taken to address one class of threat must be consistent and complementary to those taken for other threats.

Hardening measures such as shields, hardened electronics, and hardened structures can go a long way toward reducing satellite vulnerability, and can also have a favorable cost-exchange ratio against the offense. For example, hardening electronics to 10^6 rad forces long-range NPB weapons to consume an amount of fuel much more massive than the satellite it is attacking. Decreasing the range of the NPB weapon to make it more lethal would require the construction of additional (and expensive) NPB weapons.

Another example is hardening against continuous wave (CW) lasers; measures that increase the hardening of satellites by a factor of 10 may cost about 10% of the total satellite costs, but it would require a laser 10 times more powerful, and much more costly, to destroy that satellite. Hardening against pulsed lasers is a matter of adding mass and eliminating fragile appendages (*e.g.*, putting photocells on the surface of the satellite rather than on booms, or making the satellite operational for a certain time after such booms have been lost).

Cost-effectiveness trade-offs are different with regard to hardening against nuclear weapons or kinetic-energy weapons. The cost of nuclear weapons is not proportional to yield: for example, a 10 or 100 kiloton weapon may not cost much more than a 1 kiloton weapon. Hardening against nuclear weapons can prevent the destruction of more than one satellite by a single weapon, or, in the case of an X-ray laser, decrease the number of satellites a single X-ray laser can destroy. For a given yield, hardening can also force the attacker to come closer to the satellite, thereby increasing warning time and the opportunity for maneuvering.

However, neither a nuclear explosion directed towards the destruction of a single satellite nor, in the case of kinetic-energy weapons, a direct hit by a 1 kg projectile traveling at a relative velocity of 10 km/s can be countered by any reasonable level of hardening. For cost-effective unilateral countermeasures against nuclear or kinetic-energy weapons, one must turn to the tactics of maneuvering, decoys, hiding, proliferation, and use of different orbits.

Maneuvering has capability against some threats. Maneuvering will work against terminal homing missiles as long as the satellite can escape the fairly small "basket" of the homing system. It should work against a nuclear-armed earth-based missile without homing capability. On the other hand, if the ASAT missile is space-based only 1,000 km from the satellite, the fuel requirements for maneuvering would be excessive (on the order of the mass of the satellite). Maneuvering does not help at all if there is no warning, as would be the case with directed-energy weapons or close-by space mines.

Decoys have some limited applications. Decoys may be deployed before attack or under attack. If decoys are deployed before an attack, the attacker has time to examine them. The decoys therefore must be realistic and expensive. This cost could be reduced by having decoys mimic inactive on-orbit spares, but it still would be substantial. With the time available to the attacker, the defender could never have complete confidence that the decoys were effective. On the other hand, if warning is available, cheap decoys could be deployed at the moment of attack, but this strategy will only work with nonnuclear homing missiles; ballistic missiles are not smart enough to be fooled by decoys, and directed-energy weapons give no warning.

Proliferation is another possibility. If one could increase the number of hardened satellites by a substantial factor, one would, at the very least, force the ASAT system to become obvious. But proliferation alone is not cost-effective: if an ASAT system is cost-effective against some number of satellites, it will also be cost-effective against twice that number. The advantage may go to the defense, however, if it is possible to replace complex, expensive, multi-purpose satellites with many simpler, cheaper, single-purpose satellites.

Another potentially effective passive countermeasure is to move critical satellites into less-crowded orbits. These non-GEO orbits have several advantages: (1) ground-based ASATs missiles would take much longer to reach higher altitudes, increasing the time available for warning or maneuvering; (2) the power requirement of ground-based lasers is proportional to the square of the satellite altitude, so that a target at 10 times GEO would require a laser power 100 times greater; (3) supersynchronous orbits are not unique as GEO is, making the orbit less crowded and the identification of potentially hostile satellites much easier; and (4) satellites in supersynchronous orbits are more difficult to track from the ground, which can frustrate ASAT attacks.

Basing satellites in high orbits has the following disadvantages: First, the cost and complexity of satellites and ground stations will increase somewhat because of tracking requirements (satellites above GEO orbit more slowly than the earth revolves), and because transmitting power and/or receiver sensitivity would have to compensate for the increased distance. Second, the resolution of reconnaissance and surveillance satellites, such as attack warning satellites, decreases with distance. Third, the cost of launching satellites into orbits higher than GEO will be greater, since up to 18% more fuel is required for a given payload mass. Note that the number of satellites necessary to perform a mission need not increase, but that the size, power requirements, and cost of each satellite would probably be substantially greater.

There is time to complete a program of passive countermeasures. Typical U.S. military satellites have lifetimes of 5 to 10 years. Although some current satellites cannot withstand even a relatively mild ASAT attack, there is sufficient time to take unilateral measures to increase greatly the survivability of future systems, since it would take the Soviet Union at least 10 years to design, test, and deploy an advanced prompt-kill ASAT capable of threatening critical satellites in GEO.

Passive countermeasures, especially hardening, can go a long way toward lessening the vulnerability of satellites. They also cause effective ASAT systems to become large, expensive, and detectable. They are not sufficient by themselves to ensure survivability, however. There is no perfect passive countermeasure, nor are there perfect substitutes for space assets. Secure, redundant land links would not satisfy all strategic requirements and would be very expensive for the U.S. (less so for the USSR). In the case of attack warning, it would mean relying on half the current warning time, or giving up reliance on tactical warning altogether, which would require a new strategic posture.

Active Unilateral Countermeasures

In this section we discuss countermeasures that threaten the attacking ASAT system. This would mean deploying one's own ASAT to either deter attack or to destroy the opposing ASAT. The latter systems are sometimes called DSATs (defensive satellites), but it is not clear what the technical difference is between systems that are designed to kill satellites and those that kill ASAT satellites. A basis for a valid distinction might be that DSAT systems would only be able to attack over a very limited range and are associated with a certain satellite system. In this case, DSATs would be seen as strictly defensive, since they could not attack the opposing ASAT system unless they advanced within range. Although this may be practical against ASAT space mines or missiles, such defenses would be worthless against directed-energy weapons unless the range of the DSAT was at least as large as that of the opposing ASAT.

Depending on the balance between active and passive measures, space-based ASATs could give an advantage to preemption and therefore create instability in a crisis situation. If both sides depend on satellites to perform crucial deterrence functions, and both sides also deploy ASATs to threaten the other's satellites (as well as their ASATs), then substantial benefits could accrue to the side going first. This is essentially the same argument that is used when evaluating vulnerable land-based ICBMs: If both sides have valuable but vulnerable weapons, each will fear preemption by the other, and will therefore be tempted to preempt himself. A crisis or accident (collision with space debris) could trigger a satellite war and measurably raise the probability of terrestrial war.

Active countermeasures are also likely to destabilize the arms race for similar reasons. If ASATs are practical, then so are DSATs, which could also function as ASATs, leading to a measure-countermeasure arms race.

These arguments apply especially to space-based systems; if ASATs are earth-based and do not rely on space-based components, then ASATs could not attack other ASATs, and ASAT deterrence may be crisis stable, though it will still add a component to the arms race. An example is the U.S. ASAT under development, which can reach targets anywhere in LEO but cannot easily be preemptively destroyed. Even if ASATs can be made invulnerable to preemption, ASAT deterrence may not work if the Soviets valued the destruction of our satellites more than the survival of their own. This may be the case with preemptive attack, where attack warning, strategic communications, and navigations satellites would be much less valuable to the attacker after the missiles are launched.

Bilateral and Multilateral Agreements

If both sides have a stronger interest, at least in peacetime, in safeguarding their space assets (or some part of them) than in maintaining a capability to destroy the other side's, and if unilateral measures taken to safeguard these assets force ASAT systems to be expensive and detectable, then verifiable bilateral or multilateral agreements to limit ASAT technologies or deployments may be possible and may be perceived by both sides to improve the security of both nations. For this to occur, a policy decision must be reached on both sides to the effect that such factors as enhanced crisis stability, decreased arms expenditures, and enhanced second strike effectiveness outweigh the deterrence or wartime advantage of holding satellite systems at risk.

Measures taken unilaterally to make satellite systems survivable will make arms control seem advantageous, both because they serve to increase the cost and decrease the effectiveness of ASAT systems, and also because they drive ASAT systems to larger dimensions and power requirements so that bans and other restrictions are more likely to be verifiable. Two basic ASAT arms control measures may be considered: operational agreements (*e.g.*, keep-out zones), and restrictions on development, testing, and deployment.

Keep-out Zones

These represent a way to increase the distance between satellites and potential ASATs through formal agreements to maintain a certain separation between the satellites of different nations.

An important argument for keep-out zones is that there appear to be only two effective defenses against space mines, whether nuclear or directed energy or perhaps even conventional, because of the short range and rapid engagement which is possible. First, the space mine can be attacked whenever it is verified to be a space mine or when it comes within an engagement window. Second, we can try to deal with the problem through the type of agreement envisioned in the paper.

As an example of a structured agreement, the United Nations could partition certain zones of space, with adjacent zones perhaps being allocated to allies. The most crowded and vital orbit, GEO, is already organized to prevent communications satellite (COMSAT) interference. GEO could be divided into 360 one-degree zones 740 km wide. With proper design (*e.g.*, the U.S. having at least three adjacent zones) potentially hostile satellites could be kept at least 1,000 km away. Even a very large nuclear explosion would not be certain to destroy current hardened satellites at this distance. Missiles stationed in parking orbits 1,000 km away should be detectable and identifiable, and warning time would be available, possibly enough to assess the threat and relay the message to earth. Keep-out zones also aid to some degree in reducing the threat from one-on-one directed-energy weapons, since such weapons will have to be fairly large if stationed thousands of kilometers from the target.

Other orbits could be divided into 360 spherical shells 1,000 km thick starting at 13,000 km above the earth and going out to the moon's orbit of 380,000 km, allocated in a manner identical to the 360 zones of GEO. This would include the orbits of Navstar and the Soviets' Navstar-like navigation systems. Space inside 13,000 km and outside the moon's orbit would be unregulated. No elliptical orbits need be permitted in supersynchronous, though friendly passage could still apply here or in semisynchronous.

Structured keep-out zones may impose restrictions on satellite missions. It is current practice for satellites to drift several degrees above their mean positions, which would be impermissible with keep-out zones a few degrees wide. Satellites could be kept on tighter orbits, though this would require more fuel. Narrow keep-out zones should allow the allocation of GEO zones in a manner consistent with its current use (*i.e.*, present U.S. satellites would be located within proposed U.S. keep-out zones).

There are alternative, less rigidly structured possibilities. Spheres of, for example, 1,000 km radius could, by agreement, be made keep-out zones for certain satellites. Foreign satellites would be prohibited from entering this sphere without permission. This would appear to allow only 130 or so protected satellites in GEO, but the actual upper limit would be several times larger, since satellites of allied nations could be stationed within each other's zones, and since slightly inclined (3°) orbits or orbits 2,000 km inside or outside of GEO would be permitted. Such agreements would work better in semi-or supersynchronous orbits where crowding is less of a problem.

Foreign satellites would be allowed the right of friendly passage, subject to certain restrictions, such as a maximum number of transits per day. Satellites from other nations wishing for some reason to share a keep-out zone could be subject to inspection before launch. Counter-rotating GEO satellites and intersecting elliptical orbits pose a problem and might have to be limited or banned.

Keep-out zones could be actively defended, though the problems raised above for active unilateral countermeasures would apply. Self-defense systems could not be added to current satellites, since the weight and power requirements of such systems are likely to be far greater than the satellite it is protecting. In addition, the operation of some DSAT weapons could destroy a nearby satellite. A separate DSAT satellite, very much resembling the ASAT systems described above, would be needed. Destroying a nuclear warhead at a range of 1,000 km, for example, would require a very large NPB or laser. DSAT weapons may not be able to defend the satellite at all if the nuclear weapon is salvage-fused and can be maintained close to its quarry.

Molniya orbits present a special problem for keep-out zone agreements of all kinds, especially because of the asymmetry between the U.S. and the USSR in the number of satellites in this orbit. Satellites in Molniya orbits come as close to the earth as only 500 km at perigee in the Southern Hemisphere. The value of keep-out zones is greatly diminished for Molniya orbits, because earth-based ASATs would be much more effective against them. Air-launched ASATs such as the current U.S. ASAT can attack these satellites at perigee, since they can be launched from the Southern Hemisphere, though to destroy an entire satellite system one would have to wait for all satellites to pass through perigee, which would take up to 12 hours.

Bans on Testing and Deployment

Bans on testing large (>1 MW) ground-based lasers in an ASAT mode and on the testing and deployment of large mirrors in space can ameliorate the prompt threat from earth-based systems. Such a ban is likely to be verifiable, since lasers this powerful would be large structures, and would probably be located in relatively cloudless regions, permitting observation with surveillance satellites.

The remaining prompt ASAT threats, space-based kinetic-energy and directed-energy weapons, could be eliminated by a ban on their development, testing, and deployment in space (nuclear weapons are already banned from space). Such a ban should be verifiable since the weapons in question could probably be identified, and since they would require testing in space to be reliable, which could be detected.

A side benefit to a ban on ASAT testing would be the reduction of space debris. It has been estimated that the planned U.S. ASAT tests could double the total amount of debris in LEO. A more extensive ASAT testing program against real satellites might make whole regions of space unnavigable. Other unexplored side effects could exist. ASATs could be tested against balloons, which might decrease somewhat the amount of debris generated, but not completely, since such balloons are likely to be heavily instrumented. Even the debris accumulating in orbit in the absence of ASAT testing, such as paint chips and pieces of exploded boosters, are suspected to have damaged several satellites in the past few years.

VERIFICATION OF COMPLIANCE WITH AGREEMENTS

Compliance with a keep-out zone agreement could be monitored in several ways. Satellites identified as having no ASAT capability (by inspection or agreement) could be identified with radio beacons. The ability to detect satellites without beacons would still be required in order to detect cheating; this could be accomplished by radar and/or infrared space surveillance satellites. Certain individual satellites could be equipped with such systems to monitor their own keep-out zone.

Improved space tracking and surveillance systems are usually proposed in connection with ASAT arms control. These systems can cut both ways, in the sense that a sophisticated space surveillance system can form the basis for an ASAT system as well as safeguard existing satellites, much as large terrestrial radars can form the basis for an ABM system as well as an early-warning system. The ABM Treaty prohibited large radars that were not on the perimeter of the nation and looking outward, in order to prevent quick treaty breakout. Just as in the ABM case, the construction of large space surveillance systems may cause concern about compliance with an ASAT treaty.

It may be possible to limit space tracking systems to the mission of verifying compliance with agreements, so that such systems would not be capable of missions that threaten these agreements. For instance, keep-out zones could be monitored by infrared sensors (radar requires too much power) on board the protected satellite, rather than by extensive networks of dedicated satellites, which could easily be the basis of an ASAT weapon system.

If dedicated surveillance satellites are required, one possibility is sensors in counter-rotating GEO, perhaps operated by an independent third party. This would allow a single surveillance satellite with a range of a few thousand kilometers to observe every satellite in GEO once every twelve hours, and be in view of a particular satellite for perhaps 15 minutes during this time. Such a system would be very good for discovering obvious ASAT threats in near-GEO orbit, but not space mines or kinetic-energy weapons disguised as normal satellites. Even so, only ten such surveillance satellites might be needed to prevent the simultaneous destruction without warning of any given set of satellites, since at least one third of the satellites would always be under surveillance at any given time.

Dedicated surveillance satellites of limited range could also be paired with certain critical satellites to provide continuous monitoring of the satellite keep-out zone. One could have a few long-range surveillance satellites to monitor all space out to GEO, but such systems could also be the basis for an ASAT or ABM system, while the other systems mentioned could not.

Nuclear weapons (and therefore nuclear space mines, nuclear homing missiles, and X-ray lasers) are already banned by the Outer Space Treaty. At present, it is not possible to verify such a ban. In theory, one could inspect satellites before launch or while in space to detect gamma radiation from the fissile materials. This may or may not be politically practical. From a technical point of view, the question of radiations from nuclear reactors would have to be dealt with. The threat from nuclear space mines might be sufficiently defused by keep-out zones, provided that the space surveillance system is sufficiently capable. If space mines are equipped with small missiles to propel them into the keep-out zone they will be more readily detectable, which should allow a few minutes for attack warning.

Verifying a ban on the testing of ground-based lasers in an ASAT mode is, in principle, fairly straightforward. As noted above, lasers powerful enough to pose a threat to high-altitude satellites will be very large. The U.S. has shown the ability to locate much smaller lasers. Ground-based lasers are at fixed locations, and can only be tested during cloudless periods, when space surveillance of the lasers is also possible. By posting surveillance satellites over the laser sites, one should be able to detect, by the scattering of light as the beam passes through the atmosphere, whether the laser is being tested in an ASAT mode. In addition, if a comprehensive space surveillance system is available, the optical signals of all large space objects could be monitored, which would make it possible to determine if they were being illuminated by a laser.

It is also possible to verify a ban on space-based lasers and particle beam weapons, since such weapons would have to be large and distinctive if sized to attack satellites several thousand kilometers away. The destruction of satellites by kinetic-energy weapons can also be verified by space tracking and surveillance systems.

IMPACT OF ASAT LIMITATIONS

What impact would the bilateral agreements described (coupled with unilateral actions to make the satellites as survivable as economically practical) have on the military policies of the United States and the Soviet Union? The most obvious effect would be to deny both countries the ability to destroy high-altitude satellites, both those that are essential for deterrence (attack warning and communications), and those that may not be (navigation and nuclear burst detection). The development of new technologies, such as earth-based HELs, would be allowed, but they could not be tested in an ASAT mode. Space-basing of such technologies would be banned together. Limitations on the testing or deployment of systems already developed, such as the low-altitude ASAT systems developed by both parties, and systems with inherent ASAT capability (ICBMs, and ABMs), are not considered in this paper.

The agreements considered in the previous section would impose restrictions on many military missions that are not now performed in space, but could be, such as ballistic missile defenses (BMDs). A BMD composed of directed-energy weapon systems that are powerful enough to destroy thousands of missiles during a few minutes (boost phase) or tens of thousands of reentry vehicles (RVs) over tens of minutes (mid-course phase) will almost certainly be a threat to satellites in semisynchronous and GEO orbits. Such systems could be more effective ASATs than ABM weapons, because the ASAT mission can be performed at the moment of one's choosing, and satellites are in general softer targets that travel on predictable paths.

It is true that the distances involved in attacking a satellite in GEO are much greater than in attacking a missile: roughly 36,000 km versus 1,000 km (1,000 km is a commonly assumed orbit for space-based laser battle stations). Since the intensity of a laser decreases as the square of the distance, the flux at GEO will be over 1,000 times less than that on a booster. Satellites can be made almost as hard as boosters, thus for equal dwell times satellites in GEO should be safe, even though the system is potent against missiles. The Strategic Defense Initiative Organization supports high-orbit ASAT arms control measures, the motivation being that many of the sensors necessary for strategic defense would be placed in high orbits.[b]

Dwell times cannot be expected to be equal, however. ABM systems will have to shoot successfully at 1,000 (boost-phase) to 10,000 (mid-course) objects per minute, whereas ASAT systems would only need to attack at most 100 satellites in a few minutes, say about 10 per minute. (Satellites could be proliferated or send out decoys, but then so could missiles.) In addition, many more laser battle stations can participate in the ASAT attack than in the ABM defense: in the ASAT case, nearly all could, while in the ABM case, less than one tenth could. These two considerations give the ASAT attack an advantage of at least a factor of 1,000 in dwell time, and nullify the effect of the added distance. In fact, a defense system would probably be more potent as an ASAT because satellites are more difficult to harden than boosters or RVs, and an attack can usually be coordinated better than a defense and can occur at a time of the attacker's choosing. Earth-based laser ABM weapons should be particularly effective against satellites, since in most such schemes the laser energy is reflected from mirrors in GEO.

[b] See "Limited ASAT Gains Backers," *Science* **231**:331–332 (24 January 1986).

In conclusion, directed-energy systems capable of boost-phase or mid-course ballistic-missile defense would threaten the high-altitude space assets that the agreements discussed above seek to protect. Countermeasures may or may not change this situation. Moving to deep space orbits, for instance, could be effective. In addition, a defense based on technologies with limited range (small homing missiles launched from space platforms, for example) might not have much effect on satellite systems. The interactions between defenses and space systems security will have to be considered very carefully.

Although one cannot protect present and currently planned satellite systems through restrictions on ASATs and deploy a BMD at the same time, this does not mean that ASAT arms control is impossible while research continues on BMD. Resolution of this question depends on whether demonstrations and field experiments that may of themselves provide some ASAT capabilities are deemed necessary to the BMD research and development program. If for some significant period of time these demonstrations and field tests are not deemed necessary, ASAT limitations could in theory at least be agreed on for that period. In the final analysis, however, developing a BMD and ASAT arms control are probably incompatible. It is unlikely that either country would willingly forego the ASAT option if the other had plans to deploy space-based BMD components, since ASATs may be one of the most effective countermeasures against such a system.

CONCLUSIONS

The attack warning and communications satellites based in geosynchronous orbit are important for the maintenance of deterrence. These satellites, along with the Navstar navigation satellites, are intended to perform vital functions at the outset of, or during, a nuclear war.

Although current earth-based weapons do not pose a threat of prompt destruction to high-altitude satellites, a variety of future technologies could be so employed as antisatellite weapons. These include earth-based lasers and space-based nuclear mines, kinetic-energy weapons (rail guns and homing missiles), and directed-energy weapons (particle beams, optical lasers, X-ray lasers, and microwave weapons). These potential ASATs would be potentially identifiable, at least in its testing phase, assuming a range of 40,000 km for ground-based weapons and 1,000 km for space-based weapons. Keep-out zones could put a limit on the minimum range of space-based weapons.

Satellites can be hardened to the effects of nuclear weapons, continuous and pulsed lasers, and NPB weapons at a favorable cost-exchange ratio. For example, increasing the hardness against continuous lasers by a factor of ten increases satellite cost by perhaps 10%, whereas the cost of the laser required to overcome the satellite in the same amount of time increases by a much larger factor.

Moving satellites into supersynchronous orbits may be an effective countermeasure against potential ASATs by making some less effective (earth-based missiles and lasers) and others easier to identify (space-based mines, kinetic-energy and directed-energy weapons).

Keep-out zones could be a useful countermeasure against some space-based ASATs. They can ameliorate the threat from space mines, reduce the threat from homing missiles, and force particle beams and lasers to become large and therefore identifiable. Keep-out zone compliance can be monitored by infrared sensors mounted on critical satellites.

Active defense of satellites or of keep-out zones may not be crisis stable. Each side may fear preemption and require a hair-trigger posture to prevent both satellites and ASAT satellites from being destroyed. Active defense would probably also lead to a measure-countermeasure arms race as each side attempted to make their satellites and ASATs invulnerable to the other's ASATs.

Bans on testing (and in some cases deployment) of new technologies in an ASAT mode complement keep-out zones in limiting the threat from earth-based as well as space-based ASATs. Large-scale testing of an advanced ASAT would be observable, so a ban would be verifiable.

Limitations on ASATs are not likely to be compatible with the deployment of a strategic defense with space-based battle stations. Although such battle stations would have to operate over a much larger distance when used in an ASAT mode, the scale of an ASAT attack is so much smaller than that of a missile defense, and so many more battle stations can participate in the ASAT attack than the missile defense, that a successful BMD (other than terminal or other limited-range defenses) would be a potent ASAT.

DISCUSSION OF THE PAPER

H. Agnew: I want to make two points. One is a suggestion quite different from what Mike has mentioned. The emphasis Mike had with regard to survivability, unilaterally or otherwise, was to make your satellites a long ways from the other individual satellites. I would suggest that a key trick of terrorists, which is on our minds today, is the use of hostages, which means that you place your satellites very close to the other invididual satellites. By close I mean within a couple of hundred meters and by doing that it makes it quite difficult for him to destroy your satellite without running a risk of destroying his satellite.

At the same time you could incorporate in your satellite an active means of destroying the satellite if you ever wanted to. It is sort of a combination do-all if you are of that mind, but, I think the idea of having your satellites close to each other could improve the security of both nation's satellites.

There is one other comment I would like to make, more with regard to Ash's paper. I believe that we have to face up to the fact that what we need in space in satellites are power levels, electrical energy levels, much greater than what we have available today. We can no longer be content with power levels in the tens of kilowatts.

SP 100 under Gerry Yonas at the 100 kilowatt level is certainly a step in the right direction, but we really need power levels in the hundreds of kilowatts and once you have done that I think it is much easier to harden the satellite dust because in my opinion the solar cells are the most vulnerable. They are large and they are quite soft compared with what I think you can do with the nuclear system. When you realize that a nuclear system, an active nuclear system the size of let's say 20–25 square meters can be in the range of one hundred plus kilowatts it allows you the option of much faster mobility. The solar cells do not allow themselves to take very much in the way of acceleration.

So I think two things: increased power levels will enable you to vastly increase the hardness, and the idea of working close to another satellite has distinct advantages.

M. MAY (*Lawrence Livermore National Laboratory, Livermore, Calif.*): These are additional points. The only comment I will make on the second one of Harold's points is that I have seen advanced work on materials to make solar cells, which if they are deployed and bear out their promise, would make even solar cells difficult to destroy without coming pretty close with a lot of power.

G. YONAS: (*Strategic Defense Initiative Organization, Washington, D.C.*) First of all I would like to make a comment on the extension of Harold's idea about being close and there is nothing closer than if we actually share the ownership of that satellite.

Then, a question to you Mike and that is, I think you had a hidden assumption in your comments about the fact that a good booster killer is a terrific satellite killer. That was an assumption rather than proof and I think it has yet to be shown whether this is true. The question is, do you think it has been technically shown that you can't harden a satellite much better than you can harden a booster?

M. MAY: I tried to outline what I thought were the main factors involved. I didn't do it very well because of the time limitation. Let me say another word about it.

There are several factors which go into the lethality of a weapon against either boosters or satellites. One is the power or flux, how many watts per square centimeter can be delivered. Another is the time available, the time in which the target is in view. Another one is the hardness of the two targets not now, not today, but ultimately after the hardening measures have been taken.

Those are three of the more important determinants of the capability of lasers against the two kinds of targets. Synchronous satellites are much further away from lasers that are based either on the ground or in near-earth orbit that works in favor of the survivability of the satellite. The flux goes down with the square of the distance.

On the other hand, and compensating that effect, I believe in most cases satellites in distant orbits will be in sight of the lasers a much greater fraction of the time, and the lasers will have far fewer satellites per minute to deal with than they would have boosters per minute. That goes in the other direction.

The numbers I put in the analysis, which was quite preliminary, made those two factors come out roughly even, leaving the question whether satellites or boosters can be made harder. That's a difficult question to answer. There is a penalty for hardness both in boosters and in satellites. You have to look at the cost of that penalty in detail.

Antisatellite Weapons and Space Warfare

ALBERT D. WHEELON

INTRODUCTION

Previous discussions of antisatellite weapons (ASATs) have been held in hypothetical environments. What *if* the Soviets used their existing co-orbital antisatellite weapons or improved them? What *if* the United States continued development of its airplane-launched antisatellite missiles and thereby threatened Soviet low-altitude satellites everywhere? The debate of such issues was necessarily theoretical because no such weapon had ever been fired in anger and because it seemed unlikely that they ever would be, short of general war. When I accepted the invitation to address this conference, I expected that this would be another conference of theorists.

Three striking events have changed our perspective in the last 100 days. The space shuttle Challenger was lost on 28 January 1986 after 24 successful flights. The entire shuttle fleet is now grounded for an undefined period. A Titan 34D failed on 18 April 1986 in a launch from Vandenberg. This was the second consecutive loss, and the Titan family is also grounded for an indefinite time. On 3 May 1986, a Thor Delta rocket carrying a weather satellite failed after launching from Florida, and the remaining handful of Deltas must be considered suspect. Only the Atlas Centaur rocket has not suffered a recent failure, and there are only a few of these vehicles left.

Three different launch failures present a genuine crisis for the United States. We are unable to launch new satellites or replace those now in orbit. This frustrating situation may last for several years. It reminds us how dependent we are on the spacecraft now in service, and emphasizes the importance of preserving those satellites on which we have come to rely so strongly. This brings home to us the importance of maintaining at all costs our pathway to space.

If the Soviets were to use their antisatellite system to destroy the few satellites we now maintain in low earth orbit, we would be unable to replace them for several years. During those years, we would have to conduct our affairs in almost total ignorance of Soviet activities. This would be an extremely dangerous situation and would turn the clock back to 1960.

As we meet here today, we are reminded of the very great importance of the matter at hand. We are impelled to think hard about unpleasant possibilities, and about what we can do cooperatively or unilaterally to enhance our national security.

Albert D. Wheelon is Vice President for Operations at the Hughes Aircraft Company, Los Angeles, California 90045-0066.

TARGET ACQUISITION

Let us begin by recognizing that it is an easy thing to locate satellites. Communication satellites must emit large quantities of wideband electromagnetic radiation just to do their job. One need only listen and use direction finding to locate them. Navigation satellites must transmit characteristic signals to be useful and they also can be so located. Warning, weather, and reconnaissance satellites must send their data back to earth by electromagnetic waves to fulfill their mission. They can all be located through these transmissions. Radar satellites are surely the simplest to locate because they must transmit very strong signals to receive useful echoes.

Even if satellites did not radiate or used sophisticated signal waveforms to hide their transmissions, they can be located by several means. The first is through passive infrared acquisition. Because a modern satellite dissipates several kilowatts of electrical energy, it is a bright infrared source against the cold background of outer space. This remarkable contrast was observed by the Infrared Astronomical Satellite, which had to process out the strong infrared signatures of earth-orbiting satellites. Even if this infrared radiation could be suppressed, a satellite can be tracked by microwave radar or laser reflections out to synchronous orbit.

Because satellites travel in predictable orbits about the earth, it is possible to forecast their movements for long periods of time, unless large orbit maneuvers are executed. Such maneuvers are very expensive because of the large impulse that is required to change direction of a satellite that is traveling at speeds of 10,000 to 25,000 feet per second. A reasonable basis for proceeding is that the U.S. and USSR can each know with high confidence where almost every earth satellite is and where it will be.

DESTROYING SATELLITES

The destruction of satellites does not require nuclear weapons. Nor does it require the high-power lasers being discussed in connection with the Strategic Defense Initiative (SDI). Because satellites travel through space at very high speeds, it is only necessary to stand in their path to destroy them. It is possible to intersect the trajectory of a satellite in several ways. The Soviet system places a satellite in an orbit similar to that of the target, catches up with it, and explodes a warhead to destroy its quarry. The current American approach is similar to skeet shooting: a crossing trajectory of interceptor and target is used.

Remarkable advances in terminal guidance now make direct hits feasible, so that no explosive warhead is required. This technology was demonstrated during the last two years by the Homing Overlay Experiment against a ballistic missile and by the Miniature Homing Vehicle against a satellite target. This new technology is relatively insensitive to the type of orbit in which the target is flying, and makes obsolete much of the theoretical ASAT discussion of the past two decades.

Of course, one can effectively disrupt satellites without driving into them. Communication and listening satellites can be overwhelmed by strong ground radio transmitters. This option has been available for twenty years but apparently never exercised. Optical systems can be spoofed or burned out by pointing ground lasers at them, a practice that may or may not have been explored experimentally. Finally, radar satellites such as those in the Soviet system can be confused by skillful transmission of spurious echoes.

Electromagnetic pulse effects (EMPs) on satellites from nuclear detonations is a much celebrated topic. While EMPs may be the side effect of general nuclear war, it is unlikely that nuclear weapons would be used prior to that event simply to put satellites out of action. This is especially so when less dramatic and alerting techniques are available. Electromagnetic pulse flooding of a fleet of satellites does have the advantage of attacking many targets with one weapon. Its effects vary strongly with range, however, and depend critically on the level of nuclear hardening actually employed in each satellite, levels which are unknown a priori.

The conclusion must be that present earth orbiting satellites are quite easy to confuse or disable. One need not resort to nuclear weapons or directed energy weapons systems to put them out of action. They survive today by the forbearance of the major powers.

GROUND STATIONS

If one is concerned about the vulnerability of one's satellites to ASAT attack, one should be equally concerned about the vulnerability of their ground control stations to sabotage or direct attack. It has been periodically noticed that our most important military space activities are all controlled by a single ground facility near Sunnyvale. This single point failure has been identified and a backup facility is being constructed near Colorado Springs.

This concentration is more a matter of convenience than necessity. Economy of scale arguments are repeatedly advanced to show that it is cheaper to add the people and computers that control a new satellite to the existing facility than to establish a new facility. Such an argument serves the needs of the existing institution, but it leads to dangerous single points of failure for our space systems. It is not even clear that it is sound economically. All commercial satellites are controlled by small, individual ground stations that serve two or three operating spacecraft. Since commercial operators are especially sensitive to economic pressures, their unanimous decision for separate control stations would seem to undercut the economy of scale argument.

The conclusion is that one can create small individual control centers for almost every satellite. And one can do so at no increase in cost. The incentive to do so is to proliferate the control stations so that the ground segment is no more vulnerable than the space segment. This is a unilateral measure that either side can take at reasonable cost to protect its space assets.

LAUNCH SYSTEMS

The world's way into space is provided by a small number of launch vehicle families. The U.S. has focused its launch tasks on the space shuttle, which takes one to an altitude of 150 miles. To go higher, one must use integral propulsion built into the satellite or one of the family of standard upper stages: IUS, PAM-D, and Centaur. Although there have been intermittent problems with these stages, more fundamental concern has been aroused about our exclusive dependence on the shuttle.

The Thor Delta and Atlas Centaur vehicles have been undergoing a phaseout in order to make way for the shuttle. The Carter Administration agreed to commit all defense satellites to the shuttle, thus completing the exclusive launch arrangement NASA had sought. This monopoly grant has been a policy of national tragedy. It has pandered to the demands of a single agency rather than the good of the country. It was perfectly obvious to thoughtful people that the shuttle would eventually suffer an accident, and that when it did, the entire fleet would be grounded. This has now happened in a far more dramatic and tragic way than anyone imagined.

Two years ago, the Reagan Administration reversed the previous policy of exclusive dependence on the shuttle and authorized the Air Force to buy a new series of Titan rockets, known as Complementary Expendable Launch Vehicles. The first of this new series will become available in 1988, just as the present inventory of Titans is exhausted. Were it not for the two recent failures of the Titan 34D, one could rest confident that all critical defense payloads could be launched indefinitely with the Titan family.

We have been, however, newly reminded that our insurance policy also has failings. The country stands in triple jeopardy because of the recent failures of the shuttle, Titan, and Delta. These failures are our fault, but they remind us how dependent we are on launchings from the bases in California and Florida.

The Soviet Union is constrained to launching satellites from its two historic sites in Plestsk and Tyuratam. They have stuck to proven rockets and have not tried to comingle the important job of launching satellites with the development of a manned space program. Although they launch their rocket boosters more frequently than we do, presumably to compensate for shorter satellite lifetimes, their absolute launch rate is small. Both countries depend on a trickle of launchings to establish, replace, and enlarge their fleet of satellites.

France and its European partners have established the Ariane family, which are launched from an equatorial site in French Guiana, as a commercial service. They launch four to eight times a year, primarily to put communication satellites into synchronous orbit. The Japanese built the Delta under license and launch small satellites into synchronous orbit twice a year. The Chinese have developed the Long March rocket series, which they are now offering to other nations as a launch service.

The world is thus dependent on a half-dozen launch systems, based at as many launch sites. Even taken together, they cannot launch rapidly. This slow pipeline represents a single-point-of-failure vulnerability to both the U.S. and USSR. It is unlikely that launch operations could be shut down intentionally by either party short of general war, but the current American situation raises grave concern over the possibility of self-inflicted wounds.

LOW-ALTITUDE REGIME

The altitude range of 100 to 500 miles is filled with satellite systems of high value. This is where the U.S. space shuttle operates. It is where the Soviet manned satellites now travel, and where the U.S. space station will fly. This is the staging orbit that will be used by manned missions beyond the earth.

Both the U.S. and USSR operate reconnaissance satellites in such orbits that pass over the North Pole. These satellites are vital to the U.S. and increasingly important to the Soviets. Their rising dependence was made clear during the 1973 Middle East showdown and the Falkland crisis, when they rapidly launched reconnaissance spacecraft to cover developing events. The Soviets operate their nuclear-powered radar satellites that are used to locate American naval elements in similar orbits.

Low-altitude orbits are also used by several weather satellites operated by the National Oceanic and Atmospheric Administration (NOAA) and the Air Force. Single satellites that observe the earth's surface, its agriculture, and its natural resources are now operated at such heights by the United States (Landsat), France (Spot), and probably the Soviets. The Japanese plan to launch similar spacecraft to monitor the ocean surface.

The number of satellites in this layer is probably twenty on any given day. The central theme here is high value. The shuttle, space station, and reconnaissance system are extraordinarily expensive and valuable.

It is an easy matter to attack such satellites, if there is the incentive and will to do so. The United States established two ASAT systems in 1963 and kept them in place for almost a decade. One was based on the Nike-Zeus ABM system at Kwajalein. The other used Thor intermediate-range ballistic missiles (IRBMs) on Johnson Island. Both systems depended on nuclear warheads. Both counted on the low-altitude target satellite passing quite close to those islands, which introduced a substantial delay in the attack capability.

The Soviet ASAT was first tested about the time that the U.S. dismantled its two systems in 1967. It depends on launching a killer satellite into an orbit almost identical to the targets. The ASAT then closes in by guided maneuvers and detonates an ordinary explosive warhead near the target. This system enjoys only modest success: it has had 11 failures in 22 tries.

The U.S. began the development of a modern ASAT in 1977, in conjunction with a renewed negotiation approach to ASAT arms limitations. The concept was to use a two-stage 2600-lb rocket launched by an F-15 fighter aircraft. The aircraft would position itself ahead of the target satellite, and loft its rocket so as to meet the target in low earth orbit. Terminal guidance is provided by an infrared sensor and is so accurate that it kills the target simply by running into it. The system was flight-tested three times in 1985, once against an orbiting target. From these successful tests, it is clear that the United States has a powerful and versatile new weapon system that can eliminate low-altitude Soviet spacecraft.

In principle, one can maneuver low-altitude satellites to avoid ASAT attack. This requires the satellite to expend fuel to supply the orbit adjust impulse, and forces the orbital activities program to be rewritten for the new orbit. This cannot be done very many times. Such corrections may complicate the operation of current ASAT vehicles, but probably will not defeat a determined attack.

There is a significant disparity between the United States and the Soviet Union in the low-altitude regime. We have coalesced our national technical means around a very few satellites of extraordinary capability that have long lifetimes. The Soviet uses a much larger number of shorter-lived satellites. As a result, we seldom launch and they launch often. Because ours is an open society and theirs is closed, we necessarily attach greater importance to data returned by these spacecraft. A terrible asymmetry is thus established in which we depend heavily on a few satellites that can be attacked successfully by the operational Soviet ASAT system. Our ability to replenish such assets is now compromised by the shuttle and Titan failures. We now are in an extraordinarily vulnerable position vis-à-vis the Soviet ASAT capability.

What inhibits ASAT use over the long pull is the fact that each side holds the other in pawn. Mutual forbearance is imposed by the large value of the targets and the low cost of attacking systems, a record-setting cost-exchange ratio. In a very real sense, our low-altitude systems are each held hostage by the other party.

MEDIUM-ALTITUDE REGIME

This is the volume of space around the earth between 500 and 22,000 miles. It is used almost exclusively by the U.S. and USSR, and primarily for military satellite systems. This is where the numerous GPS navigation satellites fly in a variety of orbit planes. Soviet Molniya communication satellites, used for both military and civilian service via the Intersputnik Consortium, operate here in highly inclined individual elliptical orbits. American satellites operate in similar orbits. The number of spacecraft operating in this large volume is probably near 40.

These satellites are easy to track because they emit signals characteristic of their mission. One can attack them individually by launching an interceptor into the same orbit and then let the terminal homing system produce a direct hit. Whether this happens immediately or years later simply defines it as an "interceptor" or a "space mine." Whether the attack is prompt or delayed, it is possible to destroy a satellite in this region with high confidence.

What is far more difficult is to destroy all the satellites in this region. This is especially the case as the numbers increase. To sweep the region requires many one-on-one attacks. This is likely to be an impossible undertaking since each interceptor must be placed in the unique plane and orbit of its target. Preparation for such a sweep would almost surely be apparent.

One can counter such attacks by providing proximity radars on the operating satellites that sense the approach of an interceptor. With this data, the satellite itself can take evasive action so as to keep the interceptor at a safe distance. Providing detection and evasive capability to satellites operating in the region will cost payload and performance, but will greatly impair the attacker's ability to mount a coordinated attack on many satellites.

SYNCHRONOUS REGIME

The most important regime in space is the geosynchronous orbit. This is where virtually all communication satellites operate. It is also the residence of ballistic missile warning satellites, systems that contribute a great deal of strategic stability. In contrast to lower operating zones, this regime is remarkably confined. All the satellites fly in a single plane and all fly at the same altitude. The large three-dimensional volume of medium-altitude systems is thus replaced by a one-dimensional ribbon 150,000 miles around. Although the charm of this orbit is its synchronization with earth's rotation, it also has the disadvantage of imposing a strict confinement in space, which makes it extraordinarily easy to attack satellites in this arc.

Many flags fly in the synchronous ring. Civilian communication satellites are operated there by the following nations: the U.S. has 29, Canada 6, Japan 3, India 1, Russia 16 (assuming a single satellite is operating at each of the orbital positions coordinated with the International Frequency Registration Board), Indonesia 3, China 1, France 1, Australia 2, Mexico 2, Brazil 2, and the Arab League 2. Three international organizations operate there also: Intelsat with 110 member nations has 15, Eutelsat with 26 member nations 2, and Inmarsat with 45 member nations 5. At different frequencies, the U.S. military operates 12 communications satellites, the United Kingdom 1, NATO 4, and the Soviet Union an unknown number.

In addition to these communications satellites, four weather satellites in synchronous orbit provide synoptic coverage under the auspices of the World Weather Watch. The point of my brief audit is to remind ourselves that the entire world has a vital stake in the stability of the ribbon in space.

It would be easy to locate and attack any one of these satellites in synchronous orbit. Once one enters the orbit, all the satellites appear stationary. In fact, operators go to considerable trouble to station-keep their communication satellites very precisely so as to avoid electromagnetic interference with one another. As a result, they present "sitting duck" targets to an interceptor moving around the ring.

None of the civilian satellites are provided with defensive measures and none are likely to add such features. However, the military warning satellites need not keep station precisely and could perform evasive maneuvers if they were equipped with warning radars and suitable propulsion. The move-countermove game for these high-priority warning satellites is relatively easy to analyze.

I believe that a strong stability has set in at synchronous orbit. It is based on two realities. The first is the importance that the superpowers place on their communication and warning satellites. The second is the large number of international and national spacecraft located there, each vital to the user. To wage war in this orbit would bring the whole world down on the aggressor. If it comes to that, our defensive and offensive moves are easy to define. We can evade attack on our spacecraft and launch our own interceptors to go after Soviet assets. This sounds like a no-win game for both superpowers, and the world at large.

NEGOTIATIONS

Formal negotiations on ASAT control between the U.S. and USSR were proposed in 1977, begun in 1978, and broken off by the U.S. in 1979 in response to the Soviet invasion of Afghanistan. The Soviets then took their case to the United Nations, without great effect on either the U.S. or world opinion. The Soviets alleged that the shuttle program was a military threat, although they must have known that this was a lie. During the early years of the Reagan Administration, the Soviets encouraged attention to the ASAT problem, generally in the direction of banning such weapons completely.

The President's March 1983 SDI proposal tended to complicate consideration of ASAT matters by superimposing a much larger issue onto the use of space. There is no question that an SDI vehicle could kill a satellite far more easily than an ICBM. An ASAT, however, cannot kill an ICBM. The problem is not symmetrical. Much effort has gone into trying to separate the issues, largely without success.

In Soviet eyes, SDI significantly enlarged the scope and urgency of ASAT discussions. During the 1984 presidential campaign, the Soviets worked hard to force the U.S. to the ASAT bargaining table. As a precondition to such meetings, they insisted on no American ASAT testing. In the end, they refused to meet in Geneva when it became clear that the U.S. would not delay its initial testing of the F-15/MHV system. The Soviets have abstained from further tests of their own ASAT system for the last two years in an effort to put pressure on the U.S. to forgo its own development.

My view is that our vital interests are best served by avoiding attacks against satellites. I believe that the Soviets will come to the same conclusion, if they have not already done so. Soviet dependence on space systems is increasing relentlessly. The rest of the world has a compelling interest to avoid hostilities in space. The present situation is best described as mutual deterrence, or as I prefer to say, *mutual forbearance*.

Had we not persevered in developing our own system, the USSR would have enjoyed a unique capability to threaten our high-priority, low-altitude systems. Having checked that move, we return to a mutual stand-off. It is vitally important that we complete the development of our ASAT system.

If these low-altitude ASAT systems are extended to medium altitude and the synchronous orbit, it would not change the calculus of forbearance. It would be expensive and produce further anxiety. However, the symmetrical possession of such weapons is not the central issue. The point is that both parties have so many imporant satellites in so many different orbits that it is impossible to draw down either side's capability in a short time.

If this assessment is right, we can approach ASAT negotiations with considerable calm. I see a striking similarity between space activities and embassy installations. Each is a hostage to the other party, each serves a useful purpose, and each has a tradition of immunity.

The purpose of an ASAT treaty would be to codify the truce that already exists. If the stability of mutual forbearance is confirmed, we can probably forge an agreement that reflects the present stability. We could agree not to extend the present low-altitude ASAT systems to higher orbits. In doing so, we will calm each other's fears. More importantly, we will calm the fears of the rest of the world, which has a large and increasing dependence on satellites in synchronous orbit.

We can provide detection and evasive subsystems to our high-priority satellites to make them substantially less vulnerable to attack. We can also construct backup satellites, ground control stations, and launchers, so that a surgical strike on our key assets can be quickly repaired. By doing so, we can enhance the worth of a treaty and discourage Soviet attempts to develop secretly a capability to disable our most important spacecraft. Such measures would strengthen any treaty understanding by making it less tempting to cheat.

My conclusion is that an ASAT treaty is a near-term opportunity, if it can by uncoupled from SDI. It does not depend on trust. It is guaranteed by enlightened self-interest. Our greater dependence on space is a correct assessment. It need not, however, stand in the way of negotiation if we are prepared to match Soviet threats at each level of escalation and by doing so discourage their progress. The window of opportunity to conclude such an arrangement may be short-lived.

DISCUSSION OF THE PAPER

H. AGNEW: I was impressed by your dissertation that really the vulnerable parts are not the satellites because of their redundancy, but, the ground stations. Has any thought been given to let's say our government providing a subsidy to the multitude of private stations that are growing up to fulfill that as a backup role? They have everything except perhaps the receivers and the right band spread. It would seem to me it would be very cheap and very prudent to do such a thing. Has this been considered?

A. WHEELON (*Hughes Aircraft Company, Los Angeles, Calif.*): There is a presidential telecommunications task force whose job is to try to make commercial communications usable in time of stress.

If you go out and look at people's backyards you see six-foot dishes that receive television from commercial satellites. There are a million and a half of these antennas and that number doubles every two years. If any one of the 26 commercial satellites were to survive, the President would have television access to a significant cross section of the population—those million and a half individual receivers. Many of them are hooked up to auxiliary power because they are on farms.

Thus we have an effective way to keep in touch with the American people after a war if we could just put a few improvements into the commercial satellites. It makes good sense to do so and you don't have to buy very much additional equipment to make it a powerful adjunct to stand-alone military assets.

There is a precedent for doing so. It is the federal program whereby we subsidize the airlines to put special structural features into civilian aircrafts so that they can be used to carry military cargo in case of war.

Too often the military has thought they must carry the whole burden of communications. In fact, they are a small part of the communications infrastructure. If we could just find a way to do a little anticipatory adaptation, the situation of the world would be best served.

M. STENZLER (*Discover Magazine*): You briefly touched on this point. I would like to ask a question. In light of your claim that the U.S. ability to place satellites in orbit is severely hampered as illustrated by the most recent failures, which you mentioned in your talk, what is the viability in the short term of launching U.S. satellites using either European Space Agency rockets or the Japanese rockets?

A. WHEELON: The Ariane rocket is offered as a commercial service. A number of American companies have proposed to launch on the Ariane rocket.

NASA has notified the people who had made launch arrangements on the shuttle that it may not be able to honor those. If it does honor those commitments, it doesn't know when it can do so.

Meanwhile, people who have an urgent need to get into space for continuity of services have gone to Ariane and negotiated launch agreements. That's taking place in a free market situation and the Europeans are being helpful in trying to accommodate those things that must get up in the short term.

In general, the military satellites cannot be carried by the Ariane, both because of its volume restrictions and its payload restrictions.

The Japanese are flying a booster they built on license which is basically the kind that we used in the early seventies. It has a very limited payload and volume capability. They launch very infrequently and are in no position to offer much help. It is just too tiny a rocket to be useful.

Thoughts on the ASAT Issue

JACK RUINA

Thinking about whether we should or should not try to limit antisatellite weapon (ASAT) activity by agreement reminds me of a story of two people who went to a rabbi to adjudicate their differences. The rabbi heard out the first one and said, "I think you're right." Then he listened to the other person and said, "I think you're right." An observer objected, "But rabbi, they can't both be right." To which the rabbi retorted, "I think you're right too!"

The previous papers suggest why we cannot call upon our old prejudices and views about arms control in general to guide us in the matter of ASAT limits since the ASAT issue is really more complex. Many sensible papers written about the pros and cons of an ASAT agreement end up waffling a bit, never clearly saying either that we need to ban all ASAT activities or the opposite, that any ASAT restriction would be a serious loss to us. There is good reason for a bit of indecision.

To start with, the matter of ASATs and arms control is not a central arms control policy issue when compared with such issues as antiballistic missiles (ABMs), deep reductions in offensive arms, or even a comprehensive ban on nuclear testing, and certainly not when compared to U.S.-Soviet relations generally.

On the central arms control issues, when dealing with nuclear weapons per se, people tend to have strong convictions toward the extremes. Either they focus on the risk of any exchange of nuclear weapons and therefore oppose any addition to nuclear capability, or they focus on the Soviet nuclear threat and stress the need to seek security by keeping pace with existing or anticipated Soviet capabilities. Positions on arms control issues here become simple and unequivocal. We must preserve the ABM Treaty or abrogate it as quickly as possible. We must take the initiative in ridding the world of nuclear weapons or we must be sure to respond to every Soviet nuclear development. We must stop nuclear testing or we cannot consider such a step as long as we maintain nuclear weapons in our military arsenals. Whereas there is general agreement that the nuclear arms race is madness and also that the Soviets are a threat to U.S. security, strong disagreements relate to how to balance the concerns about each of these issues.

But no one has strong emotional reactions to military satellites, which are not all that different from civilian satellites. Nor do military satellites perform missions all that different from other military equipment. They are used

Jack Ruina is Professor of Electrical Engineering at the Massachusetts Institute of Technology, Cambridge, Massachusetts 02139.

in a variety of roles (communications, meteorological observation, photography, navigation, etc.) which do not arouse deep convictions or prejudices.

Although the appeals to avoid "militarization" of space are enticing, we must realize that space is already militarized and has been from the very beginning—with reconnaissance and communication satellites—and no one should be upset about that.

Space has not yet been "weaponized." That is, neither side (to my knowledge) has orbited operational weapons of destruction and in fact we have a treaty prohibiting orbiting nuclear weapons. One can see the appeal in trying to keep weapons of any kind from space and in going one step further by not developing or testing any weapons, ground- or space-based, that are intended to destroy satellites. The rationale for this is as follows: Let's prevent this dimension of warfare from developing. We have not gone very far in developing and testing antisatellite capability, so let's close the door here before it gets out of hand.

The other side of this issue is equally compelling. If satellites are of value to a potential military opponent, why is it not fair game to develop a capability to negate whatever benefit they may provide to the enemy? Developing systems to destroy enemy aircraft and enemy communications and reconnaissance devices are all in the nature of military preparedness, so why should ASAT development be off-limits? If an enemy's satellites are intended to do us harm, why not develop means to destroy them when and as needed?

The matter is made more complex by the fact that some of the adversary's military satellite assets are beneficial to us and should not be threatened: satellites that provide hot-line services, early warning of missile attacks, surveillance needed for arms control, and more.

We can be certain that the military will increasingly exploit satellite technology, but it is not at all clear how important and how indispensable the use of satellites will be in conventional warfare a decade or so hence and particularly whether endangering satellite operations for both sides provides either with a net gain. Satellite technology, ASAT technology, and also concepts about the use of both satellites and antisatellite systems in military operations are changing rapidly and predicting their future roles is necessarily uncertain.

Taking irrevocable (or hard to revoke) steps either by strongly limiting ASAT activity or rapidly developing operational ASAT capability will necessarily be done with great uncertainty about the role of satellite technology in conventional warfare a decade or so hence. One can hardly be certain now whether either promoting ASAT activity or limiting ASAT activity will result in a net gain for us militarily. It is no wonder that there is waffling on the ASAT issues.

Drs. Wheelon and May have comprehensively described the antisatellite systems that we have. In low earth orbit we can destroy satellites quite easily without exotic technologies such as directed-energy weapons, and ground- or space-based rail guns. Indeed, any terminal ABM system capable of exoatmospheric operation has inherent antisatellite capability. In principle, a system that can shoot down ballistic missiles outside the atmosphere can also work against low-earth-orbit satellites. The recent successful Homing Overlay Experiment was designed to be an ABM experiment, but was just as effective as an antisatellite experiment. Incidentally, although acclaimed as an early SDI success, it was designed long before President Reagan thought about SDI or maybe even about becoming President. No one is proposing to ban tests of so-called conventional terminal ABM systems, so naturally both sides can advance straightforward antisatellite technology for low-earth-orbit intercept.

I would like to mention here one of our ASAT programs in the early 1960s, the SAINT program. At the very time the SAINT program was getting underway, the U.S. was beginning to get some excellent information about the Soviet Union from our satellites. We therefore had the gnawing sense that we should not fiddle around too openly with this technology because it might encourage the Russians to do likewise and thereby threaten a key and irreplaceable U.S. military asset. On the other hand, the Soviets were clearly active in pursuing space technology for military purposes and no one knew what space-based threats we might have to face. Remember this was the immediate post-Sputnik era and people's imaginations ran quite wild about what the 10-foot-tall Russians were up to. The compromise was not to build hardware but to study the problem, so waffling here is nothing new.

With ASATs we are talking about nonnuclear kill. If you use nuclear weapons, the ballgame is very different; satellite destruction is easier but consequences of use are far more serious. No one wants to start a nuclear exchange just to destroy a satellite. We are talking about a possible military operation in Libya, the Perisan Gulf or some such place where the Soviets might be using satellites in an important military role. Should we now develop the capability to negate whatever military advantage satellites may be offering them? Although we do not want to forgo such a capability, we should also be wary of initiating or intensifying a satellite-ASAT race with the Soviet Union. The reality, as Ash Carter's presentation made very clear, is that we cannot have it both ways; that is, have an advantage when there are hostilities and yet accept some controls and regulation of ASAT activities.

It would be great if we could instantaneously invoke substantial capability during a war and just keep it hush-hush until then.

But there are some U.S.-USSR asymmetries that must be considered here. First, the U.S. is much more involved in worldwide operations than the USSR, so that the great advantages that satellites offer for worldwide communication are more important for us than for them. Second, we are ahead in space technology per se and in its exploitation and have thereby become more dependent upon it than the Soviets. Third, reconnaissance satellites have allowed us to penetrate the Soviet systems with its great secrecy, a need we have to a far greater extent than the Soviets have in relation to the U.S. All this suggests that we had best shy away from ASAT activity rather than risk Soviet reciprocation against our satellites.

Deep down, however, many people realize that the ASAT question raises the specter of a technology race of a different character from what is involved with nuclear weapons. Let me explain. If we have or did not have the technological advances offered by MX, would the nature of the U.S.-USSR confrontation be very much different? Would Moscow or Kiev be safer if we used lower rather than higher yield-to-weight bombs? Nuclear weapons are so destructive and so numerous that "improvements" are illusory fine tuning. But when it comes to satellite-ASAT technology, you are dealing with a race in which advances in technology are of fundamental importance. And that is a race where the United States has a clear lead that it can maintain, and would understandably be reluctant to forgo.

So what about ASAT limits or bans? To my mind, the best alternative is self-restraint. Whatever benefits the development of ASAT capability now offers is not enough to compensate for the costs to us when the Soviets develop the equivalent capability. For that reason I differ from the other speakers; I would have preferred no F-15 program. I do not think it offers a net gain to our security, but it is not a a great step forward in ASAT capability either and matters can probably be kept under control even after the F-15 system is deployed.

The next best alternative is to develop what Michael May and others have called rules of the road, something like not going into the other guy's bedroom without knocking. Don't deploy a satellite with explosives and move it five meters away from the other fellow's satellite, he won't like that. The third alternative, trying to negotiate limits on ASAT programs with the Soviets, is just too complicated. It would entail negotiation of details, irrelevant arguments about capabilities, and overemphasis on questions of verification that, if anything, are likely to stimulate rather than limit ASAT activities. Past negotiations in other areas have often had this effect.

To my mind, the best we can do for now is to avoid provoking an unnecessary ASAT race from which we have more to lose than gain.

DISCUSSION OF THE PAPER

R. GARWIN (*IBM Thomas J. Watson Research Center, Yorktown Heights, N.Y.*): There is nothing wrong with these Ariane II incompatible goals, but we shouldn't base our national security on our ability to achieve them simultaneously. With all of the wisdom and information we have had this morning we have had a couple of incompatible goals stated.

One, for instance, is the ability to destroy when we want to the Soviet radar ocean reconnaissance satellite or other military-aiding capability in space.

The second goal is the ability to deter Soviet attack on our satellites.

When we destroy their satellite we will no longer be deterring satellite attack.

The benefit mentioned about our advantage in destroying satellites is a very minor one. If I can use a very small cheap bullet to shoot you and you have to use a bigger more expensive bullet to shoot me, that's not nearly the advantage that I get from using space in a military sense. That's where our advantage lies, not in destroying the other guy.

Finally, two of the speakers, Wheelon and May, mentioned the difficulty of destroying all satellites simultaneously. That's true now with expensive visible attacking weapons, but it will not be true if the Soviets put effective weapons into space when we will have to develop small inexpensive and visible space mines which, in fact, will give us the capability of destroying every Soviet satellite simultaneously because we will be in position all the time and you can look forward to the day that they will have the same ability here.

Emily Post only works in a society of law. If you have a society with no law at all manners don't count so much.

F. LONG (*Cornell University, Ithaca, N.Y.*): One of the things which Jack talked about which pleased me was forbearance; a fancy way of saying that is to say arms control begins at home. In fact, I hope in the next couple of days we will see a number of cases where unilateral measures like, for example, forbearance will make sense.

The SDI Perspective: Transition and Technology

GEROLD YONAS

Although most public opinion polls reflect overwhelming support for strategic defense by the general population, there is a wide divergence of opinion concerning the Strategic Defense Initiative (SDI) among scientists, policy analysts, and politicians. I hope that you will listen carefully to the wide range of opinion on the SDI, think about it, and form your own judgement based on facts and not speculation, or even worse, prejudice.

Interestingly, as recently as 1982 over two thirds of the American population was unaware that it is defenseless against ballistic missile attack, and quite concerned when informed of the truth of the situation.[1] This state of mind was brought vividly to my attention when a woman came up to me after a public speech and chastised me for being unaware of the fact that there were defensive missiles near her farm. She was surprised to learn that those missiles could only be used to retaliate, and not to defend.

The President and the Secretary of Defense have emphasized the importance of examining the technical potential for moving away from our present posture of defenselessness against ballistic missiles. In the President's famous speech of 23 March 1983, he challenged the technical community to look at advanced technologies that may, in the future, provide increasing capabilites for defense against ballistic missiles. As a result, we are now engaged in a focused, and accelerated research program. This is not a deployment program, but a research and technology program to provide the necessary basis for a future president and congress to make an informed decision regarding the deployment of defenses.

If a future decision leads to the deployment of defensive systems, our objective will be to do so in cooperation with our allies and the Soviet Union. If new defensive technologies prove feasible, and meet our criteria (which I will discuss shortly), we will want to begin a jointly managed and cooperative transition to a new balance in which we place greater reliance on defensive systems for our protection and that of our allies. Such defenses will enhance deterrence by creating excessive complications for any aggressor's first strike

---

Gerold Yonas was Chief Scientist and Acting Deputy Director of the Strategic Defense Initiative Organization, Washington, D.C. at the time this conference was held. He is currently Vice President of the Titan Corporation, 9191 Towne Centre Drive, San Diego, California 92122.

planning, thereby lessening the chance of a first strike ever being seriously contemplated.[2,3]

Successful SDI research and the development of defense options would not lead to abandonment of deterrence, but rather to the enhancement of deterrence.[4] Deterrence requires that a potential opponent be convinced that the risks and costs of aggression far outweigh the gains. The widespread discussion of deterrence has focused almost entirely on only the potential costs. This view holds that the terror of nuclear weapons is such that their very existance in itself deters war. But deterrence can also function if one has the ability, through defense and other military means, to deny the attacker the gains he might otherwise have hoped to realize.[5]

We believe that the strategic balance could be made more stable by greater reliance on defenses. Effective defenses could so complicate a potential attacker's planning for a first strike that such an attack could not be seriously contemplated and deterrence would thus be significantly enhanced. Our intent is to shift the deterrence balance from one that is based primarily on the ultimate threat of devastating nuclear retaliation to one in which defenses play an increasingly important role. We believe that the latter more defense-oriented approach to deterrence could provide a far sounder and sensible basis for a stable and reliable strategic relationship.[6]

Although not required, we would prefer that this shift be accomplished in a cooperative strategic environment. It would be in the context of a cooperative, balanced, and verifiable environment that reflects a balance of offensive and defensive forces in ways that reduce existing nuclear arsenals while enhancing security and stability.[7]

Should SDI prove successful, what we have in mind is a jointly managed transition, one in which the United States and the Soviet Union would together phase in new defenses in a controlled manner while reducing offensive nuclear arms. Such offensive reductions would help enhance stability during a transition by decreasing concern that the growth of defenses could support, rather than discourage, a first-strike strategy. Furthermore, the reductions would simplify the task of defense, thereby offering both sides increased security at lower costs.[8]

In Geneva, at the nuclear and space talks, the United States seeks to discuss the offense-defense relationship and to explore with the Soviets how a cooperative transition toward a more defense-reliant arms control regime could be accomplished, should defensive technologies prove feasible.[9] Our arms control team is pushing forward in Geneva to come to an understanding with the Soviet Union regarding the relationship between offense and defense. We are trying to demonstrate that the U.S. goal is not superiority. Our goal is not to place the Soviet Union in a position of fear in any way, or to threaten them with a first strike. Rather, our objective is to achieve mutual and deep offensive reductions, reductions that would help end fears of first strike, and, if the SDI proves successful, would contribute to the transition to a more stable deterrence posture based on a defensive capability to deny an attacker its objectives.

Some noted commentators have maintained the view that arms control and strategic defenses are incompatible, and that the absence of defenses constitutes the necessary basis for successful offensive arms control. We believe that such a view is mistaken. Indeed, the history of the Strategic Arms Limitation Talks (SALT) and the Strategic Arms Reduction Talks (START) demonstrate that this view is mistaken.

In 1972, the United States signed the Antiballistic Missile (ABM) Treaty. The United States proceeded from the assumption that the limitation of defenses in the ABM Treaty would be the basis for further negotiations which would lead to significantly reduced offensive weaponry. The theory was simple: If both sides had survivable retaliatory nuclear forces at about the same level of capability, and both sides were otherwise defenseless, then neither side would have an incentive to strike first, *i.e.,* the situation would be stable. If one side were to strike first, it could never hope to escape the effective retaliation of its adversary.[10-13]

The purpose of offensive limitations was to reduce the first strike threat to retaliatory forces, thereby ensuring stability at equal levels of capability. It was expected at the time that the ABM Treaty would provide the necessary basis for achieving such offensive reductions within two to five years following SALT I.[14]

Unfortunately, that has not proved to be possible. During SALT II and the 1982-1983 START negotiations the Soviets showed little readiness to discuss meaningful limits on or cuts in offensive arms. Instead, strategic arsenals have expanded greatly since 1972. The number of warheads on Soviet strategic ballistic missiles today is four times the number when SALT I was concluded. The Soviet capability to destroy hard targets (such as U.S. ICBM silos) promptly has increased by a factor of more than ten. In short, despite the ABM Treaty and the absence of U.S. defenses, the Soviets have deployed the most worrisome element in the strategic relationship—a ballistic missile force capable of threatening virtually the entire U.S. fixed land-based portion of our retaliatory forces. This result is just the opposite of what was expected to be the result of the 1972 ABM Treaty and SALT I and II negotiations to control offensive arms.[15]

The point is that following the ABM Treaty, and in the absence of U.S. defenses, the Soviet Union pursued a vast increase in those types of destabilizing capabilities necessary to threaten ICBMs promptly, while the U.S. did not. We have learned a history lesson from our almost two decades of negotiations, and now believe that increased reliance on defenses for deterrence will establish a more effective basis for offensive arms control. We believe this for three reasons:

- Effective defenses will degrade the value of ballistic missile forces, thereby rendering them more easily controlled and reduced.[16]
- In the context of very deep offensive reductions, or even should all nuclear arms be eliminated, the technical knowledge required to make such weapons would remain, and we would need to deal with the danger of cheating or exploitation by irresponsible elements. Nonnuclear defensive systems would serve that purpose.[17]

- The aggregate of Soviet offensive and defensive activities since 1972 is persuasive evidence that they did not endorse their own vulnerability or accept the concept of stable mutual deterrence on which we believed the ABM Treaty to be premised.[18] The Soviet Union spends some ten times more than do we on defensive programs overall;[19] it spends as much or more on strategic defenses as it does on strategic offensive programs.[20] The Soviets have been engaged for many years in research and development efforts examining laser weapons, particle beam weapons, radio frequency weapons, and kinetic energy weapons for ground-based and space-based strategic defenses. These are some of the same technology areas against which the Soviet Union has mounted a massive propaganda campaign. Soviet work in these areas is clearly in applied research and development, not merely in basic research as they would have us believe.[21] The point is that the Soviet Union clearly has not endorsed the notion of mutual vulnerability as the basis of stability, and is very interested in acquiring a defensive capability. An arms control regime that focuses on the reduction of offensive forces and the deployment of defensive systems would permit the Soviet Union to achieve the damage-limitation capability it has so long sought, and for which it expends much of its strategic budget. But within the context of mutual U.S. and Soviet defensive options, it would not be at the expense of the U.S. and our allies.

What is wrong with the Soviet defensive effort? Frankly, nothing if the U.S. also has defenses and both sides have reduced their offensive weapons. I don't think any of us would want to create any type of unbalanced situation. Even though we do not seek superiority, we certainly would not want to see ourselves in a position in which the Soviets were able to gain any meaningful level of superiority in the strategic arena.

I often hear the suggestion that the defensive transition under consideration has been reduced to the goal of defending ICBMs. Our program is not emphasizing defense of just missile silos. In fact our research program is looking at very effective comprehensive defenses, so effective that there would be no military reason for the Soviet Union to launch a ballistic missile strike at us or our allies.

A very effective defense would require that significant progress be made in a number of technological areas such as surveillance, computers, software, space transportation, materials and techniques for increasing the effectiveness while miniaturizing and lowering the cost of interception by both kinetic energy, and by that I mean smart weapons, and directed energy, or speed of light weapons.

At the same time we find some opponents of the program saying that if we do anything it should be to look into far more simple approaches to defense such as protecting limited targets. One such proposal for a limited defense, offered by one critic, is to bury nuclear devices in our soil. If we see the Soviet missiles coming, we could detonate these preimplanted nuclear devices so a cloud of dust is lofted into the air, destroying Soviet reentry vehicles as they run into this cloud. I question whether this, in the end, could ever be a safer and more useful method of providing security for the country.

What has the U.S. really done in initiating the SDI? To begin with, the President did not request a development or deployment program but asked us to pursue a prudent research and technology program across a very broad spectrum. The President first asked us to make a plan, and I was actively involved in that planning process from the beginning in the summer of 1983. We then began pursuing that plan under the auspices of a single organization—the Strategic Defense Initiative Organization (SDIO)—and under the direction of General Abrahamson we carefully built up our effort from less than $1 billion per year in 1983 to a funding level of $2.7 billion in this fiscal year.

It is important to remember that the SDI was not a program that was created rapidly out of thin air. There were many activities already underway in bits and pieces through the Department of Defense, in the areas of surveillance, advanced computer studies, interceptor experiments and software programs to name a few. But this research was disconnected and did not focus on a single goal under a single manager. It was restrained, incomplete, and inconclusive. We were not satisfied that even our minimal expenditures were providing an adequate hedge in the face of the vastly larger and determined Soviet defense program.

We are now pursuing a coordinated effort in a wide range of technologies and are moving toward a centrally focused goal. We are not merely looking at this program as a technological challenge such as the Apollo program or the Manhattan Project. The SDI must deal with the technological challenge of working against a determined and capable opponent. Here we find both good and bad news. The bad news is that the Soviets, if they refuse a cooperative transition, will be working hard to find countermeasures to any deployed SDI system. The good news, however, is that the Soviets must rely on the same laws of physics and chemsitry as we, and if we find convincing ways to overcome these countermeasures we should be able to demonstrate that fact to them.

Nevertheless, we can't put ourselves in a position of giving them a veto over a possible defense as it must satisfy our needs even if they choose not to forgo the full set of possible countermeasures. It is thus important to realize that the SDI must, from the very outset, be driven by possible Soviet countermeasures. We have therefore worked very hard within the SDI to put together a countermeasures group whose job it is to "think Soviet." In order to explain this more fully, let me first answer the question, What are countermeasures?

Possible counters to the SDI could include attempts to confuse or overwhelm the defense by greatly increasing the apparent number of attackers. They could employ large quantities of decoys designed to look like attacking objects and make the attacking objects look like decoys. The Soviets could attempt to outmaneuver our first layer of defense by completing the booster burn time very rapidly to get past the defense. They could also try to outshoot the interceptor platforms, or attempt to blind the sensors before they can alert the interceptors. We are considering these and other countermeasures and our task is both to invent believable counters to the defense and solve the problems they pose.

These countermeasure studies then play an essential role in executing programmatic decisions about SDI technologies, to decide which technologies to accelerate, which to continue, and which to drop. In making these decisions, we have adopted specific criteria to guide us along the path of technologies which, *if* implemented, would be effective as well as stabilizing.

First, we want to avoid crisis instability. We don't want to encourage the Soviets by our actions to initiate an offensive step. In order to achieve crisis stability, the components of a future defense system need themselves to be survivable against an attack. If, in a crisis, the Soviet Union believed that it could successfully defeat our defense by attacking its deployed components, then the deployment itself could be destabilizing. If defense systems were made survivable however, this type of instability could be minimized. I should emphasize that survivability in this context means retaining the ability to fulfill the mission, not the survival of each and every element of a defensive system.

The second criterion is that technologies have to be militarily effective. That is, they must enable the defense to counter sufficient attacking ballistic missiles and their warheads as to eliminate their military utility.

Finally, these technologies must be able to create powerful disincentives against Soviet efforts to overcome the defense through countermeasures or the simple proliferation of ballistic missiles. To accomplish this, defenses must be inherently flexible, or what we call robust. By this I mean that the defensive system will have to have growth potential so the Soviet Union would see that if they tried to deploy countermeasures, our defensive technologies could stay ahead of and be easier to implement than their offensive countermeasures.

The mechanism we have employed to carry out an SDI design is to employ top-level system analyses called architectures. An SDI architecture should be looked upon as more of a city plan than a design for a specific building, factory, or road. The city plan is necessary to describe the relationship between the various components so that they may come together to form a functional city. In this same way, SDI architectural designs are being carried out by experienced aerospace system engineer teams to examine the ways in which different systems in different tiers of a multilayer defense will operate together in the face of determined countermeasures. These architectures generally involve multiple tiers of defense so that ballistic missiles and their warheads not intercepted by one tier can be intercepted by others. A multilayered defense will provide us with the greatest probability of interception and in this way will lead to a defense that is so effective that the opposing side is likely to be deterred from launching an attack in the first place.

As previously noted, we have to construct our SDI architectures in light of the Soviets developing realistic offensive countermeasures. For instance, we are told time and again that all the Soviets have to do to defeat our defense is to replace their existing missiles with fast-burn missiles, which might burn out in the atmosphere in about 1 minute rather than the present time of about 5 minutes. This quick burnout would make it very difficult to have adequate time to intercept a burning booster when it is valuable, visible, and vulnerable. However, when one looks at what the missile is trying to do, namely, deliver a large and complex set of objects into space and hit a particular set of targets with great precision, and in addition, be able to deploy many decoys to confuse our interceptors, then replacing Soviet missiles with fast-burn boosters is likely to be a major task. It certainly is not going to happen overnight. Such a task might take decades, would be extremely difficult and costly, and would extract a price in offensive capabilities.

Other countermeasures might be used, but it is not clear how easily the Soviets can implement them or at what cost. In fact, many types of decoys cannot be deployed while the missile is still in the atmosphere. What the Soviets could gain in being able to penetrate one part of the defense makes it very hard for them to penetrate the next layer of defense, and that is the idea behind multiple layers of protection. When the Soviets look at the likelihood of being able to defeat a very effective multilayered defense that could be deployed in the same time frame as many of the countermeasures, it is not clear that it would appear useful to them.

In order to study the means the Soviet Union might employ to counter or reduce an SDI system's performance, we have provided for an internal competition between the "blue" (U.S.) and "red" (Soviet) teams. The job of the red team is to design techniques to confuse, overwhelm, and even attack the blue team's defense. This continual internal competition is one of the key characteristics in positing the characteristics of a successful SDI architecture, and is absolutely essential for considerations of an effective defense.

I would now like to discuss the different areas embodied in the SDI. When you see, hear, or read about the SDI in the media, you frequently note the emphasis on glamorous death beams or ray guns. One of the most important, but often overlooked, areas of SDI research however is in the apparently less exciting area of sensors. These are the so-called eyes and brains of a defensive system and are therefore some of the most important technical elements in the entire program.

Nearly half of our money for the next five years is going to be invested in this aspect of our program. Sensors could be placed in space either in low or high orbit, on aircraft, or on the ground and would not only warn us, but provide detailed information of a threatening attack against the U.S. or our allies. A surveillance system composed of sophisticated sensors is essential in order to detect the threat, characterize its nature, and provide the necessary information to enable well-informed and trustworthy decisions in very short periods of time.

This surveillance system could have widespread implications for other activities where we need real time information to control large and very complex systems. For instance, I could envision advanced sensors playing a role in a global surveillance and data management system completely revolutionizing air traffic control. This surveillance and information technology may also have tactical applications, providing us with increased knowledge of the buildup of conventional forces that could pose a threat. We will increasingly find in the future that whenever we are faced with the need for collecting and processing information in order to make rapid decisions, we will employ such advanced sensor and data handling systems.

One example of this sensor technology receiving increased emphasis is that of infrared sensors that would enable us to "see" objects in space by the heat they radiate. Such a sensor would employ a telescope to collect the radiation from distant targets, mosaics of thousands or even millions of tiny detectors, to create a precise image of a warm object such as a missile booster, and miniature computers attached to each of the detectors to process the data and transfer it instantaneously to an imaging analysis computer. Infrared technology is not only playing a vital role in target detection and tracking, but is also the present basis of many of our homing target interceptor concepts.

Today we have the capability of detecting an attack against us, but our only reponse would be to retaliate by offensive means. The defensive system we now envision would permit us to do a lot more with this information. It would allow us to use the information obtained by a surveillance system to point beam weapons or guide interceptors in attacking and destroying the threatening attackers.

Two years ago we demonstrated our first ability to detect as well as intercept in space a threatening object hurtling toward its target in the final test of the Homing Overlay Experiment. This experiment successfully demonstrated that we have the ability to launch a homing projectile propelled by a rocket into space, look out across space and seek out a very small object (a reentry vehicle traveling 5000 meters per second), maneuver into collision path, seek it, and destroy it. This experiment, which was a very significant demonstration of our advanced technology, showed that we could, in essence, hit a bullet with a bullet.

Currently we are looking into ways to miniaturize our technology for interception in order to develop new techniques for manufacturing extremely small, lightweight, low-cost, but smart rocket-launched projectiles to carry out intercepts in space from launchers located on the ground or in space.

In addition to detection and interception, a successful interceptor system must also be able to deal with Soviet countermeasures designed to confuse the defense sensors using such techniques as deploying multiple lightweight decoys, or hiding the real RVs in a cloud of chaff, or debris. Potential defense solutions to this problem include the use of directed energy weapons such as particle beams based in space or lasers on the ground to "tap" the various attacking objects in order to determine which objects are real and which are decoys. Such technologies would not have to destroy all of the detected incoming objects, but would allow us to determine with a high degree of certainty which of these objects should be intercepted and destroyed.

An example of one of these speed of light technologies that is receiving increased emphasis is the ground-based laser. The major technical issue we confront here is that we must transport the beam without it being diffracted and diffused by the atmosphere. Recently we carried out a very successful experiment in which we demonstrated for the first time that we could create a clever optical system, which in essence could take the twinkle out of the stars. The cause of the "twinkling" of stars on a clear night is the high-altitude atmospheric turbulence that perturbs the starlight before it reaches the ground.

We have now demonstrated that it is possible to transport a specially prepared laser beam through the atmosphere without this diffracting effect. In addition to solving the problem of laser beam propagation, we are experimenting with technologies necessary for the development of very powerful advanced lasers placed on the ground. Here also we have been making very important strides. One particular type of laser, called the free-electron laser, has been making rapid progress and is one of the leading contenders for the ground-based laser portion of our program.

We have also made significant advances in the area of lethality and hardening. This extremely important part of our program has unfortunately been poorly understood by the public. It does not command a large fraction of our budget but is critical in evaluating the robustness of our defenses. It involves the red team trying to harden their offensive weapons so as to increase their survivability against a defense. In this part of the program, we employ models of Soviet missiles or their components and attack them with kinetic or directed energy weapons in order to determine their degree of hardness against our defense interceptors.

The recent experiment at our high-energy laser facility in White Sands, New Mexico, in which a laser was used against a model booster, yielded important information on the extent to which boosters could withstand laser attack.

Critics of the SDI program said that since the laser was actually in a nearby laboratory, and the booster was tied down to a test pad, and because the flight and propulsion loads on the booster were simulated and it was not a real laser weapon, that the experiment was not valid. What these critics do not understand is that this test was never meant to be a laser experiment at all, but instead was a test of the booster in order to compare our previous theoretical calculations on booster hardness with real data. We are carrying out these hardening and lethality studies in all areas—microwaves, lasers, particle beams, kinetic energy weapons—and they are proving to be pivotal in our evaluation of weapon concepts.

If one considers the full range of program elements, one finds that there are a large number of seemingly peripheral support or indirect areas that will nevertheless be pivotal to creating an effective defense. One critical area that has been inadequately publicized is space transportation. Just deploying any SDI system that is largely dependent on space assets will require us to find an entirely new method of transportation that will call upon technology that goes far beyond the space shuttle.

We are also emphasizing a second support area that, in general, limits our ability to make giant technical gains: the basic area of advanced materials. The SDI program is developing materials that are light yet very strong, able to withstand high temperatures, and wear resistant. You may say that such a combination of properties will be impossible, that such materials would be extraordinarily expensive. We are discovering, however, through the use of advanced composite materials, that the combination of the properties of rather ordinary materials that are interwoven together can give us new engineering materials that have the properties we ultimately will need.

A third support area that is benefiting every day from not just one investment, but from widespread commercial applications, is miniaturization and dramatic increases in speed and cost effectiveness of computers. We are seeing that through such techniques as parallel processing; computers are shrinking from large racks, down to small desktop models, to a few circuit boards. Our final goal is to have a giant computer reduced down to the size of a baseball or even smaller! In addition we will require that these computers be able to withstand a severe space and radiation environment, so we are developing new manufacturing processes that build into new electronics the needed radiation tolerance.

Obviously the computer hardware provides only part of the brain power for a defensive system. We will also need to have instructions to tell the computers how to do their job, the so-called software. It is clear that we will need new technologies for specifying the software requirements and engineering the actual production of the software. It appears as though the software required for a complex, multilayered defensive system will be enormous; some estimates are that it will be the largest software system ever developed. Nevertheless, in size alone it is not that far in excess of the existing capabilities of the switching systems that are used by the telephone company.

The number of lines of code does not, however, tell the whole story since our software must be flexible, expandable, and most of all, testable. This tesing wil help us deal with the vital issues of coordinating the hardware, software, and the human decision planning process. Because of the vital nature of this software development task, we are rapidly proceeding with the development of a national facility that will allow us to begin exploring system battle management and control early in the research effort as opposed to waiting until after the hardware for the system is developed, as in many past programs.

I am sure you realize that there are many complex issues spanning the entire breadth of the program that will have to be answered before we can make a decision to move forward beyond research to development and possibly deployment. We know that the eyes and the brains, the issues of transportation and materials, and the task of specifying and managing the battle are just or even more important than the beam weapons we hear about so much. At the same time we must continue to be mindful and successfully deal with potential, but not unrealistically imagined, countermeasures so as to create the environment for significant advances in offensive arms reduction. An aggressive and creative red team is going to be just as important to meeting our goals as our blue team. It is only through such a thorough and rigorous process that we can really satisfy the President's challenge to the technical community.

I feel very confident now, given the rate of progress we are making every day, that we can fulfill our mission to provide the necessary information to make that fateful decision, based on a hard set of facts and not speculation.

REFERENCES

1. SINDLINGER. July/August 1982.
2. NITZE, P. Survival, May/June 1985, p. 105.
3. NITZE, P. Current Policy **794**: 2.
4. D.O.S. Special Report no. 129, p. 5.
5. NITZE, P. Survival, May/June 1985, p. 100.

6. NITZE, P. Philadelphia speech. Current Policy **751**: 2
7. MCFARLANE, R. Current Policy **670**: 3.
8. NITZE, P. Current Policy **751**: 3.
9. NITZE, P. Current Policy **810**: 2.
10. NITZE, P. Current Policy **751**: 1.
11. NITZE, P. Current Policy **810**: 1.
12. NITZE, P. Current Policy **711**: 1.
13. D.o.s. Special Report no. 129, p. 1.
14. NITZE, P. Survival, pp. 102-103.
15. NITZE, P. Current Policy **751**: 1.
16. ABRAHAMSON, J. Defense 84, August, p. 3.
17. NITZE, P. Current Policy **751**: 1.
18. NITZE, P. Current Policy **751**: p. 1.
19. D.o.s. Current Policy **730**: 3.
20. MCFARLANE, R. Current Policy **670**: 2.
21. NITZE, P. Current Policy **810**: 2.

DISCUSSION OF THE PAPER

UNIDENTIFIED SPEAKER: I have two brief questions, one systemic and one technical. First, what is the minimal effectiveness you can have to have a militarily useful system, in other words, deny the other side a militarily useful mission?

The technical question is, Do pulse lasers give you an advantage over continuous wave lasers in terms of interaction with the atmosphere and so forth?

G. YONAS (*Strategic Defense Initiative Organization, Washington, D.C.*): The first question is how good does the defense system have to be to deny the objectives of the attacker.

We've looked at various kinds of exchange analyses and if the goal of the attackers is to precisely strike certain military targets, then you have a system that is very effective and effective means more than . . . I hate to say the number, because it will wind up in the *New York Times* in big print. (There's almost nothing I can say that won't wind up in that regard). Very effective means it is going to cost him many more times what he has already invested, to regain the capability he had originally.

So, that's a matter of statistics. For instance, if you look at his ability to effectively strike specific targets today, and then, you put in a multitiered defense system, some of the calculations show that a rather low level of effectiveness forces him to invest ten or twenty times more than he has already invested to achieve that original level of military effectiveness.

UNIDENTIFIED SPEAKER: Is 85% low or high?

G. YONAS: It doesn't sound so bad to me. On the second question, a thermal laser may have to burn through an ablator that is added to the external booster skin to protect it from laser attack. On the other hand, a pulsed laser produces an impulsive load that crushes the booster and the level depends on the structural strength. They are totally different kinds of kill and it may be that the kind of kill that is most effective is the combination of thermal and impulse by having a repetitive impulse that actually bores its hole through the protective material and prevents it from being protected either by a thermal ablator or some kind of structural improvement.

N. LONG: In light of what you said about cost-effectiveness and the importance of cost-effectiveness vis-à-vis what it cost the Soviet Union to overwhelm the system, could you comment on General Abrahamson's reported change in the ground rules for Paul Nitze's requirements to affordable which seems like quite a different ballgame from the one you were talking about?

G. YONAS: Well, it seems to me that this notion of cost-effectiveness can get into a question of rhetoric. If General Abrahamson said affordable and now the question is why he did not say cost effective, I think it is beginning now to be a discussion of semantics.

Let's go back to the fundamental issues. What are we really trying to do?

We are trying to have a system that is so effective it discourages an offensive response, that discourages proliferation, that makes this kind of defensive technology something that becomes more attractive to the Soviet Union than responding offensively and that's the motivation, that is the requirement, and this argument over semantics is not very useful. The real issue is motivation, convincing the Soviets to back away from further offensive investments, to start to move to mutual offensive reductions and to build up defense.

M. M. SHERRY: Dr. Yonas, you speak about the systems requiring radiation hardness for their operability. In your short-range laser slide you mentioned, if you could clarify that slightly, counter error. I am just relating to the Pulitzer-Prize-winning article of 7 March 1985 in the *New York Times* which documented that these electron laser systems when they are not being used on outgoing nuclear rockets in their boost phase would be able to be used against soft ground targets such as groups of people or buildings. You spoke of the rocket gun. We can put our minds to the task of building better implements of death. However, it is being proved to us today that these nuclear and radiation systems are very dangerous to the preservation of human life.

Do you feel you are devoting yourself to what our country stands for?

G. YONAS: Absolutely. Let me explain why I believe that this kind of research should be carried out and why I feel very strongly about this basic hope and belief that we both share, that we should be striving for technologies or investments or national security that protect life and don't threaten life.

Today we have weapons for mass destruction. We have nuclear-tipped missiles that can be used to destroy. We can both destroy ourselves in a very short time with relatively low costs and very great ease and as we proceed further with more and more information all we have in our hands to respond with is the threat of retaliation. That is what we have today.

What we are trying to do is to provide anti-weapons, weapons which cannot as you describe create mass destruction. You are saying, Is it conceivable that some kind of a space-based laser would cause a loss of human life?

I think there is no question that that kind of thing is just as real as the question of whether an automobile or a rock or a laser be used to harm human life in some limited sense. The point is these technologies would be militarily ineffective in terms of this notion of mass destruction compared to what we have today, namely nuclear-tipped ballistic missiles.

I don't see any military effectiveness against ground targets from any of the technologies that we are looking at.

M. M. SHERRY: We are in 1986 now. We have experience behind us that has proved that whenever our country has developed the state of the art in inflicting death on humanity the other side has always matched us. We invented the atomic bomb. We invented the hydrogen bomb. Cannot we learn from our experience before it is too late?

G. YONAS: From what I can see there is no militarily effective way to use these kind of space weapons against ground targets. That's an extremely important consideration and when you understand that and you compare that with the alternative, namely reliance on threat of retaliation, I think you would begin to see why many of us in the program feel that this program is logical and ethical and is the right kind of research to pursue at least in terms of understanding whether or not we can go down this road.

New Technologies and Ballistic Missile Defense Systems

SIDNEY D. DRELL

President Reagan's call to science and technology to give us a shield against the threat of nuclear annihilation is not new. Every president upon entering the White House has looked for something better than deterrence, something better than living as mutual hostages under the threat of nuclear annihilation, only to face up to reality and recognize that in the face of the enormous destructive potential of thermonuclear weapons, deterrence is a condition that cannot be avoided in a heavily armed nuclear world.

The earlier debates concluded, first, that the effort to build an effective nationwide antiballistic missile (ABM) defense to defend people, not just concrete and weapons, was futile; it can't be done in a heavily armed nuclear world. Second, the effort to develop such a nationwide ABM shield could be destabilizing as both the U.S. and the Soviet Union developed and deployed not only competing ABM systems, but also offsetting offensive forces to overpower, evade, or attack and disable the opposing ABM system. It was acknowledged that we couldn't escape deterrence by technical fixes alone. We had to learn to manage the competition peacefully.

This earlier conclusion led to the ABM Treaty of 1972, which is of unlimited duration and is in force today. It stands as an early milestone of efforts by the U.S. and the Soviet Union to avoid nuclear war. It defines the common premises of our effort to achieve stability and reductions in nuclear armaments, and to avoid nuclear war, working together despite our fundamental differences and political confrontation. Along with six of the seven Secretaries of Defense in Republican and Democratic administrations who served for more than 18 of the 20 years between 1960 and 1980, I continue to believe that the ABM Treaty contributes to our security and to lowering the risk of nuclear war. Although there have been disappointments in reducing, or even limiting, the level of arms since the treaty was ratified in 1972, I would certainly not abandon it before, or unless, something superior and practicable has been established as being available.

It is of course proper to ask anew in 1986: Do the technical advances of the past 14 years, as prodigious as they have been, offer us new and better prospects for dealing with the nuclear threat looking ahead now into the fu-

Sidney D. Drell is Professor and Deputy Director, Stanford Linear Accelerator Center, Stanford University, Stanford, California 94305, and Co-Director of the Stanford Center for International Security and Arms Control.

ture? Even if it is unrealistic to escape from deterrence, as most now realize, will strategic defenses enhance deterrence as is currently alleged?

I support addressing this question with a prudent, high-quality research program in strategic defense technologies, one that is designed and prosecuted in a manner that maintains a full range of technological options and is consistent with the widest security objectives of the United States, including full compliance with U.S. treaty obligations, and in particular the ABM Treaty in 1972. The only realistic framework for such a program is one that is based on a full recognition that we have not yet established which technologies are feasible, we have not determined their costs, survivability, and effectiveness against countermeasures, and we do not know whether deployments can be verifiably regulated.

I am not by any means a naysayer or pessimist when facing technical challenges, but we should be realistic in assessing the enormously difficult challenge to achieving an effective defensive system in the face of enemy countermeasures. As one example, consider the problem of discriminating real warheads from decoys as they fly together in large numbers above the atmosphere. There are several means, including nuclear weapons in various deployment modes and nonnuclear hit-to-kill projectiles (such as the one tested in the Homing Overlay Experiment), by which the defense might kill warheads or reentry vehicles (RVs), in mid-course. Most of these means seem potentially reasonable as components of military systems, provided their targets can be uniquely identified. However, no solution is presently in hand to this problem of how to tell RVs from decoys, which has been with us since the original Nike-Zeus ABM concept of the late 1950s.

This year the Strategic Defense Initiative Organization (SDIO) recognized that both passive and simple active discrimination are inadequate for the mid-course phase and has now turned to the concept of interactive discrimination, that is, lasers or high-energy neutral particle beams fired at objects to produce observable changes depending on whether they are hitting a heavy RV or a light decoy. These changes would then be identified by other passive sensors. These are, however, no more than theoretical concepts at present. Furthermore we lack essential data as to the conditions any such systems would encounter in an environment disturbed by multiple nuclear explosions. There are order-of-magnitude uncertainties in critical factors such as the density of electrons or the flux of radiation at different wavelengths. Nor can we gain such direct data about what the environment would be like following multiple nuclear weapons detonations without resuming the atmospheric testing of nuclear weapons, in violation of the Limited Test Ban Treaty of 1963.

This is just one example of the revolutionary, or as yet unforeseen, advances that will be required before an effective nationwide defense can be achieved against a determined adversary and his available countermeasures. Consider also the challenge of boost-phase intercept which is a crucial new ingredient of the envisaged strategic defense. This is the first of three or four successive tiers or layers of the defense concept that is proposed. It is designed to destroy most of the attacking missiles over the enemy's own territory within seconds after they are launched, that is, during the boost phase while their engines are still accelerating them up into space. It is considered an essential component of any defensive system able to respond effectively to an unconstrained threat, as stated in the official Department of Defense report to the U.S. Congress in April 1985.

Suffice it to say that as interesting or intriguing as the concept of boost-phase interception may be, its prospects, whatever they may be, lie well in the future, orders of magnitude beyond today's technology and sensitive to countermeasures available to the offense. In particular, a boost-phase defense must start and complete its mission in seconds. At most a few minutes are available to engage today's missiles during boost, but the technology to shorten the total burn time to less than one minute already exists.

This means that the interceptors will have to be predeployed in spacc, or they will have to get there very, very quickly. If they are in space their numbers must necessarily be very large, since only a small fraction of them will be on-station within range of Soviet launch areas at any one time. They will be more vulnerable than the missiles that are their targets, as they move in predictable orbits like ducks in a shooting gallery. Edward Teller in Congressional testimony (to the Senate Armed Services Committee, 2 May 1983) and in *Popular Mechanics* (July 1984) has rejected the idea of space basing of defensive battle stations because of their expense and vulnerability. I agree.

These disadvantages of space basing have suggested that we look to the possibility that the interceptors be based on the ground, poised to pop-up into space upon notification of enemy launch. The only practical device, compact and light enough for doing that, is the X-ray laser pumped by a nuclear explosion. There is no law of physics which says this cannot be done in principle, but at present our physical understanding of the potential of such devices is much too primitive to draw any definite conclusions. We are still learning basic physical facts about them. Significant advances into new regimes are required. Moreover consider the necessary operational concept: since the earth is round and one cannot peer over the horizon to see a rising booster, such a system would have to be based on submarines, close to the Soviet shoreline, and able to repond instantaneously following the launch of an attacking missile.

We also should remember that the laws of physics are not secret. They cannot be classified, and the possibilities of such lasers are well recognized by Soviet scientists. They have discussed these concepts in their literature as have American scientists in ours. As we well know from experience, they will build such devices if we do, probably not very long after we start, and surely long before we have a full operational system of our own. It is ironic, but not surprising, that this widely heralded technology which first triggered so much interest in "Star Wars" is de-emphasized by the Administration's stated goal of developing a nonnuclear defense system. In fact, its most practical application could well be as an antisatellite weapon (ASAT) against an opponent's Star Wars defenses, should we go ahead.

This illustrates another technical problem of defense: It will rely necessarily on space-based sensors for eyes and ears, even if the weapons themselves are not based in space. These will then be vulnerable to ASATs. As we develop strategic defenses, however, ASATs will be a ready by-product, unavoidably so since their task is simpler. Therefore developing the SDI will lead to ASATs that will be threatening to the space-based assets of the SDI.

Other schemes for accomplishing boost-phase intercept have been proposed, but all share one or both of the difficulties of having potentially vulnerable components (namely, large orbiting mirrors in space necessary in order to deflect the light from a ground-based laser back down onto the booster, or high-energy particle beam accelerators in space), or of being ground based and having precious little, if any, time to get up in space in order to destroy boosters before they deploy their payloads.

Because of these operational issues, and in the face of countermeasures by a determined and uncooperative opponent dedicated to defeating it, there will still remain great problems in deploying a nationwide defense system even if the expensive reasearch and development program of the Administration achieves all of its ambitious technical goals. Furthermore, we must be able to maintain high confidence in such a system and its ability to accomplish the enormous task of battle managment in a very short time, although it can never be tested under realistic conditions such as an environment disturbed by nuclear explosions. To anyone who has experienced the turn-on of a high-energy accelerator, such as at SLAC or Fermilab, this appears to be not only an enormous, but a preposterous requirement.

One cannot compare these awesome requirements with those faced by the Apollo program to put a man on the moon, an analogy which has been drawn to point to other great challenges which have been met by science and technology. Putting a man on the moon was solely a technical challenge. The moon couldn't shoot back, or run away, or dispense moon decoys, or turn off its lights. Even so, recall how many lengthy holds we witnessed during the countdowns for the moon shots, or, for that matter, for the space shuttle flights. Such holds will not do for a defensive system which has barely seconds to spare, and no privilege of saying "Hold your attack. I'm not ready. Please wait a few minutes—or hours!"

In the face of such severe technical and operational difficulties that must be mastered and cannot be avoided, I see no prospect of building an effective nationwide defense now or of achieving one in the foreseeable future, unless the offensive threat is tightly constrained technically and greatly reduced numerically as a result of major progress in the U.S.-Soviet political process and dialogue. The challenge of Star Wars, then, is not only a technical one, nor even an awesome operational one. It is also, perhaps foremost, a political challenge to succeed in limiting offensive forces while simultaneously developing defenses to stop them. And when I think of that challenge I am reminded of the statement, attributed to Albert Einstein, "Politics is much harder than physics."

The importance of this arms control framework is apparent as one looks ahead toward possible deployments of defensive systems. As Paul Nitze remarked in a speech to the Philadelphia World Affairs Council on 20 February 1985, if the SDI research program of the Administration is fully successful in developing new technologies that satisfy the two criteria of survivability and cost-effectiveness, then a decade or more from now we can look forward to entering a transition period during which defensive weapons will begin to be deployed in conjunction with offensive forces. This would be a "tricky" enterprise. Moreover, Nitze said, "We would see the transition period as a cooperative endeavor with the Soviets. Arms control would play a critical role."

Evidently, we will require an arms control regime in order to get anywhere with defensive deployments. Thus, the strategic defense programs in the coming decade must not contribute to dismantling our current treaty achievements.

This is very important and I will reemphasize it. The effort to change from an offense-dominated to a defense-dominated policy requires, at the outset, restraints in offensive countermeasures. The technical situation is such that the necessary restraints can be achieved at this time only through progress in arms control. Therein lies our most pressing need; and furthermore U.S. and Soviet research in defensive technologies must not be allowed to lead to the dismantling of existing treaties.

One cannot rule out on the basis of physics alone that at some future date the cost-exchange ratio between offensive and defensive forces may favor the defense. At present, however, such a favorable exchange ratio has not been established. Nor has it been established that we know how to build survivable defenses. In the absence of meeting these two criteria we face the prospect outlined by Ambassador Nitze in his address on 20 February:

> The technologies must produce defensive systems that are survivable: if not, the defenses would themselves be tempting targets for a first strike. This would decrease, rather than enhance, stability. . . . New defensive systems must also be cost-effective at the margin—that is they must be cheap enough to add additional defensive capability so that the other side has no incentive to add additional offensive capability to overcome the defense. If this criterion is not met, the defensive systems could encourage a proliferation of countermeasures and additional offensive weapons to overcome deployed defenses, instead of a redirection of effort from offense to defense.

Beyond technology we must also address policy problems such as the transition to a defensive policy. The question still remains how to maintain a strategic and arms control stability en route to a defensive policy even should the technology lead to prospects for survivable cost-effective defenses. Is there a stable strategy for deploying effective defenses, one which does not lead to high risks of conflict as a result of instability during the "tricky" transition period? I have seen no persuasive study that defines means for making such a transition.

In the face of these technical and political factors that I have described, how do we answer the big question: What should we be doing in strategic defense to meet U.S. national security needs as broadly interpreted?

In very broad terms, a prudent program[a] should explore a full range of technologies in order to protect us from surprises. It should also provide for

[a] The description of this program that follows draws on a report prepared by a workshop of the Stanford University Center for International Security and Arms Control entitled "Strategic Missile Defense: Necessities, Prospects, and Dangers in the Near Term" (1985).

near-term as well as long-term options should they be needed. This will help deter the possibility of a Soviet breakout from the provisions of the ABM Treaty by making it clear that we are prepared to respond. As to the means for carrying out this program, I believe that at present it is far too early to consider large-scale technology demonstrations that could raise serious issues of compliance with the ABM Treaty, and thereby jeopardize our wider security interests, without contributing usefully to our understanding of how to reach our goal of an effective defense system.

Almost all of those few technologies that appear to be ready for demonstrations are not forbidden by the ABM Treaty. These include low-power pointing and tracking experiments, upgrades in the capabilities of early warning sensors, large-scale integration of small mirror elements, and atmospheric compensation experiments.

Field testing of some of the most difficult and yet-to-mature technologies, such as directed energy weapons systems or space-based kinetic kill vehicles of light weight with miniaturized guidance and control upon which various proposed defenses might rely (especially boost-phase defenses), is clearly forbidden by the treaty.

In addition to their political costs, the premature promotion of such technologies to the demonstration and test phase can be very harmful to attainment of any particular technical goal in strategic defense. A considerable body of evidence has shown that early demonstrations of new technologies have two deleterious effects. First, they tend to freeze the technology being demonstrated before it is fully mature and thus guarantee less than full capability. Second, they are expensive and tend to absorb money from the associated research and development program (because of cost overruns) and thus eliminate the possibility of better solutions. Large-scale demonstrations in space or against targets in space may be good public relations but currently they are bad science. Therefore, unless we succeed in creating a new approach to effective nationwide defense, the U.S. program should be compatible with, and in fact should seek to enhance, the effectiveness of the ABM Treaty.

Within these broad guidelines there is important work to be done in each of three categories:

1. So-called traditional or conventional ABM weapons, which we take to mean the fixed, land-based nuclear-armed interceptor rockets and radars originally envisioned and considered explicitly by the ABM Treaty in 1972.
2. Directed energy (laser and particle beam) weapons.
3. Supporting technologies necessary for advanced systems integration and for support of missions closely related to ballistic missile defense.

What follows is a brief description of the work that can and should proceed in each of these three categories.

Conventional ABM Weapons

The principal goals of a research program in "traditional' ABM weapons are (1) to develop and maintain a research and development base of evolving state-of-art conventional systems capability, and (2) to develop and test penetration (pen-aids) against the system to maintain confidence in the effectiveness of the U.S. offensive deterrent.

These two goals must be addressed as a joint effort. Together they require development and operation of a test facility where high-quality research on conventional terminal defense systems and advanced offensive pen-aids can be pursued. The provisions of the ABM Treaty permit development and testing of fixed, land-based system components of this type and the current U.S. test site at Kwajalein Island is the natural locus for such an effort. Since conventional ABM weapons now constitute the only candidate strategic defense system that is based upon tested, integrated, and proven system components, the threat of U.S. deployment of these systems is credible, and could be instrumental in deterring a Soviet breakout. I disagree with the decision to terminate all such work in the SDI program.

Directed Energy Weapons

This category of research includes what are usually referred to as laser technology and X-ray lasers, as well as other exotic concepts. Since all these technologies are as yet highly speculative, or far from mature, a research program should maintain a proper diversity of activities. Some priority choices, however, can and should be made.

Laser Technology

Chemical infrared (IR) lasers have been proposed for predeployment in space to accomplish boost-phase kill of ICBMs. A space-based defensive system that depended on such lasers would have a considerable number of serious disadvantages, for example, the need for very costly redundancy in order to maintain laser satellites on station at all times, the high cost of vast energy stores in space, and, above all, a tremendous vulnerability to direct attack by several means that have highly favorable cost-exchange ratios to the offense. These factors make such laser battle stations in space completely impractical, and chemical IR lasers should be eliminated from consideration as ballistic missile defense weapons.

At this time, free-electron lasers appear promising as high-intensity shorter wavelength sources. High brightness alone, however, may not be adequate in practical applications if such systems ultimately require very large, expensive, and vulnerable high current accelerators as energy sources. For laser weaponry future work should concentrate on increasing the capabilities of free-electron and ultraviolet (UV)/visible lasers, particularly ground-based ones, to ascertain whether they offer any credibly effective potential.

High-energy ground-based lasers will certainly provide some military capability in antisatellite weaponry. For this reason, the security implications of such capabilities should be carefully considered. In contrast to their ASAT application, ground-based lasers operating as part of a defense system will also require large mirrors of very high optical quality to relay their upwardly aimed beams back to target. The most frequently described system envisages a relatively small number of very large mirrors in high earth or geosynchronous orbits to relay the beam to an array of many smaller mirrors in low earth orbit from which they are directed onto target. Achieving high reliability and maintaining survivablity of such a system present major challenges.

X-ray Lasers

Nuclear-driven X-ray lasers, which have primarily been discussed in terms of defensive weapons applications, could well have a considerably greater potential for employment in support of offensive operations.

If the moderately high brightness levels that have been discussed publicly are achieved, X-ray lasers could be used as ASAT weapons. Still another possibility is that they might be integrated into offensive weapons systems like submarine-launched ballistic missiles (SLBMs). They could then be launched as part of a first strike, and used to "pin down" or destroy ICBMs that are being launched in response to the strike. This may be called a "preboost phase" defense. All of this makes it clear that there can be no such thing as a purely defensive system, contrary to what has been alleged on behalf of the SDI.

There is currently very great uncertainty regarding the performance levels of X-ray lasers that can be reached or maintained against countermeasures. If very high brightness levels are achieved, they could be the basis of a potentially effective defensive layer. Since the Soviet Union is likely also conducting research and development in this area, the United States has a strong incentive to understand what performance levels are actually achievable. Basic physics issues of X-ray lasers remain to be understood. The development of X-ray lasers and other refinements in nuclear weaponry could, of course, be stopped by a Comprehensive Test Ban Treaty, or by a less ambitious agreement that substantially lowered both the number and maxiumum yield of nuclear weapons tests. Such measures could also greatly aid Soviet and U.S. diplomatic efforts to limit the proliferation of nuclear weapons to still more nations of the world.

In the absence of such treaties, it is clearly most prudent for the U.S. to pursue a high-quality research program on X-ray lasers. It should be clearly understood, however, that an efficient X-ray laser, should it prove to be feasible, might also prove to be the single most effective counter to defenses that depend on space-based assets. On the basis of technical judgments as well as political considerations, I believe that a serious attempt to eliminate, or further constrain, underground tests of nuclear weapons would be more clearly in our national security interests that would be a continued program of active testing.

Supporting Technologies

Among the tasks that are included in this category are mid-course discrimination technology, improvements in warning and acquisition sensors, space survivability, fast-burn boosters, battle management; and aircraft and cruise missile defense.

Mid-course Discrimination Technology

I have already described the importance and difficulty of this task.

Improvements in Warning and Acquisition Sensors

The sensors on which the defense systems rely for warning of attack, as well as for quick analysis of the size of the threat (attack assessment), must provide large amounts of timely, high-quality, accurate, and reliable information. Independent of defensive weapons programs, there is a great need for effective early warning and attack assessment capabilities.

Space Survivability

A broad research effort should be made to examine the survivability of all space-based assets to the full range of credible threats. An understanding of space survivability issues will, of course, be critical to understanding the feasibility of many advanced defensive weapons systems and to understanding possible threats to intelligence, warning, and communications systems. Two specific possibilities must be addressed within the framework of such an effort: space mines and ASAT systems.

Space mines are long-lived satellites which may contain either conventional or nuclear explosives. Such satellites could be designed to maneuver within range of other satellites to kill them. These devices therefore provide a simple, inexpensive response to hostile deployments of space-based weaponry.

Also of interest is the potential relationship between ASAT capabilities and ABM systems. Since satellites in low-altitude orbits move at nearly the same speed and in the same range of altitudes as long-range ballistic missile warheads, many ABM system concepts would also have high capability against satellites. We must thus resolve the difficult dilemma that many ABM developments will also advance threats to satellite platforms (*i.e.,* the eyes and ears of a defense, if not its weapons themselves) that are crucial to its successful operation.

This also raises the possibility that space-based defenses could engage each other. Hence, the extent to which ASAT and ballistic missile defenses are actually coupled, and the importance of this coupling, must be examined further and clarified.

Fast-Burn Boosters

A potentially straightforward countermeasure to a great variety of boost-phase or postboost-phase attacks by a strategic defense could be the employment of fast-burn boosters. Consequently, the U.S. should establish a research and development base for evaluating hardened fast-burn boosters and rapid RV deployments, both to allow us to evaluate the effectiveness of such Soviet programs to counter U.S. boost-phase defense concepts and to prepare us with appropriate and timely counters to possible Soviet threats to U.S. missiles in boost phase.

Battle Management

Any large and complex defensive system will need to be able to acquire and handle enormous amounts from data sensors, to analyze the data rapidly, and to commit the appropriate systems components to the engagement. This demanding set of data-handling and logic tasks is referred to as battle management. A multitiered nationwide defense will require improvements in technologies needed for battle management so great that they may appropriately be characterized as revolutionary.

Aircraft and Cruise Missile Defense

Studies on the feasibility and desirability of installing defenses against air-breathing weapons are needed as a matter of balance. Otherwise, if the United States were actually to succeed in providing nationwide ICBM defense, it would be in the embarrassing position of having a defense against what are currently the most numerous and threatening carriers of nuclear weapons but no defense at all against the others.

The Need for Oversight

A program proceeding from research to development can and will remain vital and responsive to its objectives only if it is continually challenged to do so. Too often in such programs the necessity of demonstrating favorable cost-exchange ratios against opponents is forgotten or conveniently kept well in the future.

To prevent this, two critical advisory bodies should be established.

The first would be a "red team"—or team of devil's advocates—to provide analysis of the offense and of countermeasures, and to evaluate the offense's cost-effectiveness in defeating the defense. This red team should have a charter independent of the management of defensive weapons research and development. A close connection should be established between the red team and the intelligence agencies, for their mutual benefit. The red team would thus receive more realistic and detailed accounts of Soviet capabilities; the intelligence community would be assisted in focusing its efforts on U.S. needs for intelligence on what the Soviet Union is doing both in defensive and offensive countermeasures.

The second critical advisory body would be a senior-level, independent oversight panel that would examine work on defensive research and development and report at a very high level in the Administration. The panel should comprise both experts in the various technological and military specialities and former public officials in defense and arms control matters. This panel should maintain knowledge of the technical and programmatic status of work on defensive weapons that is sufficiently detailed for the panel to advise the government on the setting of priorities. The panel should also conduct periodic reviews of the research and development to ensure that the work remains in close harmony with U.S. overall strategic goals and policies (in both the military and arms control realms).

I emphasize the importance of creating such an oversight panel. The Administration and the Pentagon SDI office have stated their intentions to conduct the research and development on defensive weapons "in a manner fully consistent with all U.S. Treaty obligations." However, the 1985 report on SDI submitted to Congress in April has the strong flavor of what the chief SALT I negotiator, Ambassador Gerard Smith, has called "an anticipatory breach of contract."

The 1985 report exploits inevitable verbal ambiguities in the 1972 treaty to pursue the new technologies. For example, Article V of the treaty forbids development, testing, or deployment of "ABM systems or components" which are space based or air based. In the 1972 ratification hearings before the Senate Armed Services Committee, Ambassador Smith defined the prohibitions on development as starting when "field testing is initiated on either a prototype or breadboard model."

At issue is how far one can go in disaggregating components into subcomponents in order to claim compliance. Is it within the bounds of the agreement to test an airborne or space-based sensor against a warhead, as long as it lacks a direct communication link to the ground? Is it consistent with the treaty for an airborne or spaceborne missile interceptor to be tested against a satellite, just not against an ICBM warhead? Or may it be tested against a warhead, as long as it does not carry its own target-tracking system? Can one develop space-based high velocity interceptors (kinetic kill vehicles or rail guns)?

This is a current issue of major importance. In the fall of 1985 the Administration adopted a more liberal interpretation of Article V of the ABM Treaty, contending that it did not apply to the development and testing of new technologies. It agreed, however, that for the time being the SDI program would remain under the more restrictive interpretation that heretofore had been adopted and used as a restriction on the program. More recently both General Abrahamson, Director of SDI, and Richard Perle, Assistant Secretary of Defense for International Security Policy, have suggested the need for more liberal interpretation as the SDI program proceeds. In testimony before the Strategic and Theater Nuclear Subcommittee of the Senate Armed Services Committee, General Abrahamson said on 25 March 1986 that otherwise "we would not likely be able to make an intelligent decision to develop SDI." Assistant Secretary Perle said that is was "highly likely" that we would adopt the liberal interpretation which Gerard Smith has said would "make a dead letter of the Treaty."

Conclusions

In conclusion, I summarize the actions the U.S. should take that will meet our national security needs, which include enhancing prospects for success in arms negotiations and reducing the risk of war:

1. Reaffirm our commitment to the ABM Treaty of 1972. It defines the common premises of the U.S.-Soviet effort to avoid nuclear war and to achieve arms reductions, and thus serves our national security goals.
2. Organize and support a prudent, deliberate, and high-quality research program on defensive technologies within the ABM Treaty limits. The availability of such technology, together with the real possibility of American countermeasures, can contribute to discouraging the Soviets from deploying defensive systems in violation of the treaty, minimizing the adverse effect of such a potential Soviet "breakout" if it should occur, and protecting us against technological surprises.
3. Recognize that, at the present primitive state of many of the new technologies, it is far too early for us to undertake large technology demonstrations.
4. Form a strong red team to challenge the defense program concepts against potential Soviet countermeasures. Any deployed defensive system will have to be effective against a determined opponent who can resort to a wide variety of countermeasures in order to defeat, deny, evade, destroy, or otherwise overpower the system.
5. Enact legislation in Congress with the explicit provision that the research and technology program must proceed by means that are fully consistent with the ABM Treaty. I believe that the FY86 funding level of $2.75 billion is more than adequate for a strong research program that makes appropriate priority choices in developing new technologies. I have grave doubts, both on technical and strategic grounds, that significant acceleration or expansion of ABM research and development is warranted or prudent.
6. Form a senior-level, independent oversight panel of experts and former public officials in defense and arms-control matters. This panel should advise the government at the highest levels on the setting of priorities. It should also conduct periodic reviews of the program to ensure that the work remains in close harmony with the overall strategic (both military and arms control) goals and policies.

A deliberately paced U.S. research effort on strategic defense, organized and pursued with clearly stated goals and means, abiding by the ABM Treaty, and in accord with these six recommended actions should not only serve our security well at a reasonable cost (not very different from what we have been spending in the recent past). It should also give the Soviet Union, itself engaged in research and development on strategic defenses, no real reason to feel the need for additional offensive or defensive forces in response. A U.S. effort with better planning, explanation, and diplomacy might moderate Soviet concerns, and their perceptions, which now regard the U.S. program as threatening their deterrent capability, menacing strategic stability, and defeating the prospects for arms control. It would, of course, also be of enormous value for the Soviets to take some reciprocal steps to explain some of their troubling actions, including in particular discussion of the Krasnoyarsk radar. More openess in this dialogue would be immensely valuable.

The impact of such clearly defined and constrained activities on the ABM Treaty should be nil in the near-term and mid-term. Genuine success in creating a new approach to effective nationwide strategic defense would indeed present a challenge to the ABM Treaty. If this should occur, it would do so well into the future, and regardless of which side would succeed in developing the defensive system. In such an eventuality, the U.S. would need to conceive and negotiate a new arms control regime that would successfully integrate offensive and defensive forces.

Finally, it is important for us all to recognize that the path to a safer world cannot be paved by technology alone. This path will have to be paved initially, and for a large part of the way, by progress in diplomacy and arms control. Strategic defenses can aid our quest for a safer world only if they are pursued within an arms control framework that limits further weapons buildups and countermeasures. I see no prospect of building an effective nationwide defense now or of achieving one in the foreseeable future unless the offensive threat is tightly constrained technically and greatly reduced numerically. This will require major progress in the U.S.-Soviet political process and dialogue.

DISCUSSION OF THE PAPER

F. LONG (*Cornell University, Ithaca, N.Y.*): You mentioned two significant advisory committees, a red team and a senior oversight panel. An interesting question is, Do you envisage those as being within the government, benefiting by accessibility to classified information but suffering from all of the inhibiting things that go into being an advisory committee?

S. DRELL (*Stanford University, Stanford, Calif.*): I think they both have to be within the government. To be useful the red team is going to have to have access to very delicate information, intelligence information. I understand they are beginning the formation of a red team in the SDI program. When it gets to be strong enough so that one can know that it is truly independent, it will have earned our confidence. I hope that is happening.

I heard a red team briefing recently. It has a budget that is growing. Gerry Yonas can tell us more about it. I think it is coming along. It may fill the need, but I do not know yet how tightly it is incorporated into the organization.

As far as the oversight panel, that is a more delicate problem. The ideal would be, of course, to have the Administration create something like a Scowcroft panel with a rather broad involvement of very competent people of integrity. If that is not in the works to be created by this Administration, then the only alternative I can see is for Congress to create such an oversight mechanism; but the ideal would be for it to be within the Administration at a very high level.

B. IGWEBUIKE (*Long Island University, Brooklyn, N.Y.*): I would like to know the actual provisions of the ABM Treaty of 1972.

S. DRELL: Well, the treaty of 1972 has many articles and subsections and I can't recite them all for you. What is important for this discussion is that both the United States and the Soviet Union, aside from the very limited deployments, which I won't talk about, are permitted to do ABM test work at two sites. For the United States these are at White Sands, New Mexico, and Kwajalein in the Pacific. Sary Shagan is one of the sites in the Soviet Union. Just now I forgot the name of the second one. At these sites testing of fixed land-based ABM systems—nonmobile or rapidly reloadable—is permitted.

Article V of the Treaty forbids the development and testing of components for space-based, land-mobile, airborne, and sea-based systems. Staying within that provision through appropriate restraints in the reasearch on new technologies is what I talked about as being important.

W. TROUSDALE (*Wesleyan University, Middletown, Conn.*): Could you make a couple of comments on what you said at the end, particularly on what is the effect of the current SDI efforts on current arms control negotiations and over the next couple of years?

S. DRELL: Well, that is a good question. What is the impact of the current SDI program?

First of all, what we have actually done so far has been totally within the treaty provisions. However, some of the rhetoric about SDI has sounded like we are headed towards a quick deployment decision. General Abrahamson has described the program as on a fast course headed toward an early 1990s deployment decision. When Ambassador Nitze talks about it, as he did last month, he says we don't know enough to even think of being able to make such a decision before the mid-1990s.

So, in terms of actions, it is a treaty-consistent program. In terms of stated goals, they sound rather more ambitious.

Now, what is the effect on negotiations or on the future? Let me put it this way. It could be the greatest and it could be very harmful. If we insist with no compromise that we can do whatever we want to under the new "liberal" interpretation of the treaty which says that Article V does not apply to the new technologies, then I am sure the treaty will further erode and will be lost in short order.

It is in trouble already because the question of the Krasnoyarsk radar, which the Russians haven't adequately explained, has to be resolved.

On the other hand, you can also take the point of view that we have now created, by a master stroke of politics, the consummate bargaining chip, the "quintessential bargaining chip" in the words of Jim Schlesinger. We now have a program which will force the Russians to compete in advanced technology, not merely numbers of missiles; and they don't like that. If they don't like that, then the Soviet Union will have to sit down and work out with us what is allowed research and what is forbidden development work under the ABM Treaty. We have room for give in that compromise to get them to reduce their large MIRVed offensive ICBMs which we don't like.

The U.S. and the Soviet Union have to get at each other's basic fears and resolve them. The SDI could be a very effective bargaining chip if we reaffirm the rigorous interpretation of the ABM Treaty, clarifying its application to new technologies: Where does one draw the line between forbidden and allowed activities? To resolve the Soviet concern, we require really significant reductions in the MIRVed ICBM threat.

I would like to think that we have, potentially, a real opportunity; but I don't know when, or if, we are going to use it.

Can the SDI Reduce the Risk of War?[a]

GEORGE F. CHAPLINE

If the Strategic Defense Initiative (SDI) is interpreted as a program to render ballistic missiles carrying nuclear warheads "impotent and obsolete," I believe the answer to the question posed in the title of this paper is almost certainly yes. This answer does not presuppose that such a defense is both technologically possible and economically affordable. The technological and economic feasibility of a defense against ballistic missiles has been widely debated, but actually only after a vigorous program of research could one possibly decide whether a defense against ballistic missiles is technologically possible, economically affordable, and cost-effective at the margin. A more appropriate topic for current debate would be the a priori strategic desirability of such a research program.

As has been eloquently pointed out by McGeorge Bundy and David Aaron (see papers in this volume), one might legitimately question whether it is really necessary to supplement our current nuclear retaliatory capabilities with ballistic missile defense. In the long run, though, I believe that there are potential problems with the idea of maintaining peace through nuclear deterrence. To my mind, the most serious of these problems is the possibility that an insane political leader could come to power in the Soviet Union (or the United States for that matter). An insane political leader might not be deterred by the specter of nuclear war in the same way as the current leadership of the Soviet Union and the United States. Of course, getting rid of ballistic missiles would certainly not eliminate all means of delivering nuclear weapons. But it does seem reasonable to expect that without the extremely short flight times of ballistic missiles to contend with there is more time to consider options and act in the most rational way.

What about the claim that a defense against ballistic missiles would be "destabilizing." It should be kept in mind that what really counts is whether a ballistic missile defense reduces the risk of nuclear war. Since no one knows what factors dominate the probability of nuclear war, it is hard to see how one could claim that ballistic missiles defense is destabilizing in the sense that it would actually increase the likelihood of nuclear war.

If the United States deployed ballistic missile defenses, it is possible that for some period of time the United States might enjoy nuclear superiority.

[a] This work was performed under the auspices of the U.S. Department of Energy by the Lawrence Livermore National Laboratory under contract no. W-7405-ENG-48.

George F. Chapline is affiliated with Lawrence Livermore National Laboratory, Livermore, California 94450.

It does not seem plausible to me, however, that this would induce the Soviet Union to launch a first-strike attack against the United States. The cost to the Soviet Union of a Soviet first-strike attack would clearly be greater with ballistic missile defenses than it is today. If the cost today is sufficiently high to deter war, it is not clear what significance can be attached to "destabilization." Naturally, this situation would change if the Soviet Union perceived that the United States was preparing a first-strike attack.

Against the dubious claim of destabilization must be weighed the obvious advantages of a defense against ballistic missiles: (1) greatly reducing the military effectivenss of a surprise first attack, (2) limiting damage in the event of nuclear war, and (3) forcing the adversary to spend money on defensive rather than offensive weapons. The first advantage would especially hold true if the numbers of offensive missiles were greatly reduced. Indeed, one is tempted to suggest that one should not even contemplate drastic reductions in offensive missiles in the absence of strategic defense.

This point brings up the charge that any defensive system could simply be overwhelmed by building more offensive missiles. The answer is that it certainly does not make sense to deploy a defensive system that can simply be overwhelmed. Indeed, this is why terminal defense schemes for missile silos do not make sense. Such defenses can in all known cases be overwhelmed by assigning several warheads coming at few-minute intervals to the task. The Strategic Defense Initiative, however, is based on a layered concept for defense that enormously increases the leverage available to the defense. In particular, one can use one's resources to defend certain targets selectively, *i.e.,* particularly military or civilian targets. Because the attacker does not know which targets are being defended, he cannot concentrate his resources on those targets. Thus the advantage goes to the defense.

An example of a defensive system exploiting this advantage would be a fleet of interceptor rockets carrying X-ray laser weapons based at the ABM site in North Dakota, which would be permissible under the ABM treaty. Because of their long range, these X-ray laser weapons might be used to defend any target in the continental United States. It is clear that no matter how many offensive missiles were used in the initial attack, one could always ensure on a cost-effective basis the survival of some targets. It is also clear that one could slowly increase this capability to provide protection for most civilian as well as military targets.

How likely is it that this scenario could be implemented? I believe it will be some time before the technical feasibility of schemes like the one just described can be determined. On the other hand, the time is ripe to debate the strategic desirability of ballistic missile defense.

Will "Star Wars" Work?

JOHN PIKE

The most important question about the Strategic Defense Initiative (SDI), popularly known as "Star Wars," is "Will it work?" This question really consists of three separate questions. First, will it work at the gadget level? Can we build the individual devices that would go into a ballistic missile defense system? Second, will it work as a system? Can we tie all of those gadgets together into a reliably functioning system that will cohere, and will the system continue to function in the face of things that the Soviets might do to degrade the system's effectiveness? And third, will it work as a national security policy? Does it make military sense, and do the advantages of this strategy outweigh the disadvantages and problems it might create?

It is very important to differentiate among these three different ways in which the SDI might "work." One problem in the debate over the SDI has been the tendency to equate workability at the gadget level with workability as a strategy, to assume that if we demonstrate a rocket that can intercept a warhead, or a laser that can shoot down a missile, then Star Wars must necessarily be a good national security policy. It is far from clear, however, that technical virtuosity can be equated with political wisdom. Although there is an important techincal component to SDI, esoteric arguments over how many lasers can dance on the head of a pin must not be allowed to obscure the much more important political problems of the program. These political issues are simple, and straightforward, and constitute the main problem for the President's program.

The SDI is potentially the most dangerous weapons system of the nuclear age. If the United States continues with the Star Wars program, it will lead to a massive escalation of the offensive arms race, increase the risk of nuclear war, and make any negotiated arms control impossible. The President's vision of a magic shield protecting our people is an illusion, and although he promises that Star Wars will be a nonnuclear defense, in reality the program is highly reliant on new types of nuclear weapons.

THE CONCEPT OF SDI

The basic idea behind the SDI is that of a layered defense that would attempt to intercept ballistic missiles at each point in their trajectory from shortly after the time that they are launched until just before they reach their targets.

John Pike is Associate Director for Space Policy at the Federation of American Scientists, Washington, D. C. 20002.

This layered approach builds on previous antiballistic missile (ABM) systems that used one or two layers. By adding additional layers, the SDI seeks to improve the overall effectiveness of the defense. Whereas two layers that are each capable of intercepting 50% of incoming warheads would intercept only 75% of the warheads, four such layers would intercept almost 95% of the warheads. Additional layers could further reduce the leakage of warheads through the defense.

The SDI system would initially attempt to intercept ballistic missiles during their boost phase, the first phase of a ballistic missile trajectory during which it is being powered by its engines. During this phase, which usually lasts between 3–5 minutes for an ICBM, the missile reaches an altitude of about 200 kilometers, whereupon powered flight ends and the missile begins to dispense its reentry vehicles. The defense would also attempt interception in this post-boost phase when the missile's warheads and decoys are released into space.

Interception in these phases is attractive because the number of targets is small (only a few thousand), and the rocket's hot exhaust makes the targets easy to track. Interception in this phase would use space-based lasers, particle-beam weapons, railguns (a sort of electric cannon), or small interceptor rockets fired from space.

The defense would also attempt to intercept warheads during the mid-course phase, which is the phase of a ballistic missile trajectory, lasting about 20 to 25 minutes, where the missile has released its warhead and decoys and is no longer a single object, but a swarm of reentry vehicles (RVs), decoys, and debris falling freely along pre-set trajectories in space. During this phase the warheads and decoys would be attacked by projectiles fired by railguns. In the late mid-course phase the warheads come into range of ground-based interceptor rockets.

Finally, the defense would use ground-based rockets to attack warheads during the terminal phase of their trajectory when the reentry vehicles reenter the atmosphere at an altitude of around 100 kilometers. This phase generally lasts only 30–100 seconds. Terminal phase defenses in the SDI are limited to area defenses of cities. Defense of hardened military targets would be a final defense, but the SDI does not include technological efforts intended for this type of defense.

WILL IT WORK AT THE GADGET LEVEL?

Will the SDI work at the gadget level? Yes, although there are clearly a number of gadgets that have been debated over the last three years that probably will not, and therefore probably do not make a great deal of sense. There is increasing convergence between the SDI Organization and its critics that many of the technologies that were critized early on probably do not look very attractive. A year or two ago there was a lot of discussion of chemical lasers in space, or railguns or imaging sensors, but you do not hear very much talk about those any more. The technical deficiencies that the critics identified two and a half years ago with these technologies have finally been acknowledged by the SDI Organization.

The SDI technical debate has largely focused on the number of space-based lasers that would be required for the boost-phase layer of a defense. Unfortunately this debate is in danger of degenerating into a dispute over how many lasers can dance on the head of a pin. What is at issue is not conlcusions but rather assumptions. There is no unique "correct" number of laser battle-stations needed as the first line of defense. Given a plausible range of assumptions about system characteristics and Soviet countermeasures, any number between 50 and 5000 can be derived.

Furthermore, at the gadget level, these are not going to be miracle weapons; they are going to obey the laws of physics, and those do impose some limitations on what the weapons can and cannot do. For instance, many of these weapons, such as X-ray lasers or neutral particle beam weapons, perform fairly well in the vacuum of space, but less well when they run into the atmosphere. Many of these weapons would therefore be effective above the atmostphere, but would be ineffective at shooting at targets inside the atmosphere. This has important operational consequences that impose limitations on how well the devices would work.

Finally, the people who are working on these gadgets are not wizards. They're just ordinary people. They are the same people who build the rest of the gadgets our military uses. Today many of the SDI gadgets are still only in the advanced-artist's-concept stage. Thus estimates that are made of how long it will take to build the first test model, how much it will cost, and how well it will work are understandably optimistic. Complicated technology at the cutting edge of the state of the art always takes longer, costs more, and does not work quite as well as the artist promised.

Nonetheless, despite engineering deficiencies, the limits of physics, and the fact that the same people who build the rest of the military's machines are also going to be building these with all their limitations, for the sake of argument, and probably in fact, the gadgets that would go into the SDI probably can be built. We can hit a bullet with a bullet.

WILL IT WORK AS A SYSTEM?

The real question concerning Star Wars, though, is not hitting a bullet with a bullet, but stopping a shotgun blast with a shotgun blast. The problem is not intercepting a single warhead, but intercepting hundreds or thousands or tens of thousands of warheads. This question of whether it will work as a system really consists of two different but related questions. First, can all of the gadgets be brought together to function as a coordinated system? And second, will the system continue to function in the face of Soviet countermeasures?

Bringing the gadgets together into a workable system is not clearly going to be an easy task. One of the most difficult aspects of this problem is writing the computer programs, the software, that are needed to coordinate the system's sensors and weapons. Estimates are that the software would probably require between ten and one hundred million lines of code. That is literally a document that is ten to one hundred million lines long—two hundred thousand to two million pages of computer code. For the system to work perfectly, and to work reliably, this massive document would have to be written without a single misspelled word, without a single comma out of place, and without a single mistake in grammar or syntax. Everyone recognizes that this is not going to happen.

You can get around this problem by writing the program, putting it in the computer, and then testing the system. But if a single computer is running the entire system, the only way you can effectively test it is with a full-scale simulation of World War III, that is by firing thousands of rockets at it and attacking it with missiles and lasers. But since the software would perform differently depending on the precise sequence of events that it encounters, it would be necessary to simulate World War III several times, perhaps every afternoon over a period of several years.

There is growing recognition that such a vast volume of error-free software cannot be written, and that realistic testing of such a system is not a realistic option.

The alternative is a decentralized system with lots of little computers that are running small pieces of the defense. Such a system could be tested, and software errors in part of the system would not necessarily affect the rest of the system.

But this means that the system is no longer coordinated. The battle that is being fought in one area is not going to have much impact or influence on the way the battle is being fought in another area. The capacity of the defense to respond to structured attacks would be diminished. Warheads could get through on part of the system and be ignored by the next part of the system. The defense could compensate by adding more of everything, but then the system becomes increasingly expensive.

Finally, it is unclear, given the way the SDI Organization is currently developing the system, whether the software that is being written will in fact be usable. The people working on the software question have recommended that the SDI should write the software first and then find the gadgets that can work with that software. The best known recent example of the problem that results from not following this software-first approach is the Sergeant York DIVAD air defense gun, which was recently cancelled. The Army took a quite reliable tank chassis, put on it a well-proven gun and attached a radar that had been in operational service for over a decade, and then went to the computer programmers and said, "Write us some software that can tie these three things together." After over five years of doing that the computer programmers were still unable to design software that could make this machine shoot at other things besides latrine fans.

WHAT ABOUT THE SOVIETS?

So clearly there are going to be difficulties in tying the system together. The problem, however, is that the Soviets are not going to be cooperating with us. There are a number of things the Soviets can do to reduce the effectiveness of the system.

The most obvious and straightforward countermeasure to a strategic defense is simple proliferation of offensive forces. A defense that might be highly effective against 10,000 warheads could prove totally worthless if confronted with 30,000 warheads. The SDI Organization's own estimates suggest that a very probable Soviet reponse to the SDI would be to increase their existing seven and a half thousand warheads on ballistic missiles to perhaps as many as forty thousand ballistic missile warheads by the end of the century.

The Soviets could further complicate the life of the SDI planner by throwing in a number of decoy warheads that the system would also have to deal with in some fashion. Decoys have the potential to be a very troublesome countermeasure against defense sensors during the mid-course. One of the most effective is a balloon decoy (similar to a weather balloon), which could be made to look like a warhead, thus increasing the number of targets that the defense would have to cope with. If warheads are hidden inside balloons, the job of defense becomes even more difficult. Originally the SDI had estimated that the Soviets might employ perhaps 300,000 decoy warheads. Now the estimates are something on the order of five million decoy warheads. Dealing with these decoys is clearly a very difficult task.

The number of boost-phase weapons required is a function of (among other things) the time available for interception and the vulnerability of the missiles to directed energy weapons. One attractive option for the offense is to reduce the duration of the boost phase of its missiles. Current liquid-fuel missiles such as the SS-18 or the Titan II have a boost phase that lasts about 5 minutes. Solid fuel missiles such as the SS-24 or the MX have a boost phase of about 3 minutes, and a number of studies have conlcuded that high-acceleration ICBMs can be built with a boost phase of a minute or so.

Halving the length of the boost phase would double the number of lasers or other weapons that the defense would need to deploy. Further reductions in the length of the boost phase are possible, using so-called fast-burn boosters. These missiles achieve the velocity needed for intercontinental ranges while at very low altitudes, too low for most space-based weapons to be effective. Such fast-burn boosters require special high-acceleration solid rocket motors and special coatings to protect against atmospheric friction. But the technology required to build fast-burn boosters is very similar to that required for ground-based ABM interceptor rockets, and both the United States and the Soviet Union could build such boosters by the end of this century.

Additional countermeasures to directed energy weapons include hardening or armoring the surface of the booster. Spinning the booster would have the effect of spreading the energy of a laser beam over a wider area, further reducing its effectiveness. Other countermeasures to lasers include discharging a stream of coolant onto the surface of the missile while it is in the atmosphere, and dispensing aerosols to surround the missile when it is above the atmosphere in order to diffuse directed energy beams.

Finally, the Soviets could directly attack the system. Space-based weapons that could intercept ballistic missiles would be equally capable of intercepting other space-based weapons. And our space-based weapons floating a few hundred miles over the Soviet Union will clearly be vulnerable to all types of weapons that would be on the ground. The question of whether these space lasers are offense or defensive weapons could in large measure just depend on who shot first. By taking the offense with the laser one could shoot the other side's laser defenses into smithereens.

For all of those reasons, although SDI will probalby work at the gadget level, at the system level if it works (and it probably will), it will do so imperfectly and not all the time. That is the growing consensus among those who examine these questions. With the possible exception of the Commander-in-Chief himself, no one is talking about a perfect defense that will make it impossible to detonate nuclear weapons in the United States.

WILL IT WORK AS A STRATEGY?

But the most important question is: Will it work as a strategy? Former Secretary of Defense James Schlesinger has noted that there are basically two types of ballistic missile defense systems, those that are desirable but not feasible, and those that are feasible but not desirable.

In the category of desirable but not feasible belongs President Reagan's vision of the perfect astrodome defense of the population. This is what he's selling. When the President gets on the television or the radio or gives an interview, he is trying to sell the American public on the notion that if World War III happened we could all take our lawn furniture into the backyard and open a can of beer or pour some lemonade and watch a laser light show for about five minutes, and no warheads would land and everybody would be OK.

Everyone recognizes that this is not one of the options. The real question is: Are less than perfect defense systems desirable?

What is the good of these less-than-perfect defense systems? First, although leaky defenses cannot prevent damage to the United States, they could help limit damage. A goal of limiting damage to the United States immediately poses the question of what an acceptable level of damage is. Are 20 million dead an acceptable outcome from a nuclear war? Would our ability to limit American casualities to perhaps 20 million influence our political behavior in crises or in peacetime in any significant way that would differentiate it from the way we would behave today? Probably not. Even if we could limit American casualties to 20 million dead, a debatable point, what possible political goal would be worth the risk?

We could defend our retaliatory forces. We could close the window of vulnerability. Many people really are not very concerned about the window of vulnerability to begin with because about 80% of our strategic forces are deployed on submarines and bombers and really are not vulnerable to Soviet counterforce. For those people who were worried about the window of vulnerability, the President's own Scowcroft Commission several years ago recommended deployment of the Midgetman mobile ICBM. Midgetmen would be deployed in 1992 at a total cost, over fifteen years of actual operation, of about $40 billion. The SDI would not be able to produce an actual operational weapon until 1995, with a development cost of $100 billion alone, and additional tens or hundreds of billions on top of that to deploy the system. For those who are worried about closing the window of vulnerability, Midgetman is the clear weapon of choice.

We could use the SDI to defend against a terriorist attack. But it is difficult to imagine that a terrorist group would try to deliver its one nuclear weapon in the one way that we could thwart. It is far more likely that they would wrap the hydrogen bomb in a bale of marijuana and fly it across the Mexican border.

SDI could guard against an accidental launch, but we could do that equally well by rewiring a few of our Minuteman II ICBMs to intercept the occasional stray missile. But we really have not had very many stray missiles flying around in the last forty years, so it is unclear that this is a real problem that needs a real solution.

THE DANGERS OF LEAKY DEFENSES

Although it is far from clear that less-than-perfect defenses are good, it is all too clear that they are bad.

If both sides were to deploy a Star Wars defense, it would significantly increase the risk of nuclear war. The type of leaky umbrella that Star Wars would provide would be more effective against a retaliatory drizzle than a torrential first strike. However effective an antimissile system would be against a massive surprise attack which was carefully timed and coordinated, including direct attacks on the defense itself, it would be much less effective against a much smaller and badly coordinated retaliatory strike. With both the U.S. and USSR developing counterforce weapons to threaten the other side's land-based missiles, an antimissile system would be the key to a first strike that could completely negate the other side's retaliation.

This would provide incentive to strike first. In a time of intense crisis, both sides would be concerned about the other side's temptation to preempt, and both sides could try to beat the other to the draw. Rather than preventing a war, the defense could ultimately provoke a war.

In addition, "defensive" weapons could be used for offensive missions. It is highly unlikely that space-based weapons would be used to attack targets on the ground, since they are already many cheaper and easier ways of doing this. But space-based weapons could be just as effective in attacking other space-based weapons as they are in attacking ICBMs. Whether space weapons are offensive or defensive weapons may prove to be just a question of who goes first.

The history of the arms race provides numerous examples of new offensive weapons deployed in response to strategic defenses. In the 1960s the United States began deployment of multiple warheads on our ICBMs and SLBMs, in respone to Soviet work on antimissile systems. In the 1970s, the U.S. initiated the air-launched cruise missile and Stealth bomber programs in response to Soviet air defense improvements.

The President's own advisors have concluded that the Soviets will probably respond to the SDI by deploying more offensive forces. The Fletcher Panel, a group of scientists and engineers who designed the SDI program following the President's Star Wars speech, concluded that the Soviets would probably deploy 30,000 ballistic missile warheads by the end of the century if the U.S. went ahead with the SDI. This would constitute a fourfold increase over their present arsenal.

There would be a considerable cost advantage to the offense in its race with the defense. ICBMs are a mature technology, the development costs for which have already been paid. Space weapons still have many years and billions of dollars of development ahead of them. For an equivalent budget the offense could perhaps double the size of its force before the defense became operational.

The SDI will imperil the future of arms control. It will make controls on offensive weapons impossible to achieve. It also immediately threatens the 1972 Antiballistic Missile (ABM) Treaty, the most important achievement of the arms control process to date.

If the Soviets responded to the SDI by major increases to their offensive forces, they would quickly surpass the limits imposed by the SALT II Treaty. The type of deep reductions in offensive forces that are currently under discussion at the Geneva negotiations would clearly be impossible.

With the completion of the ABM Treaty and the interim agreement on offensive nuclear forces in May 1972, the superpowers recognized that limitations on defenses were a necessary (though not sufficient) condition for limitations on offensive forces. The treaty also formally acknowledged the overwhelming strategic reality that defense against missile attack was not feasible because the destructiveness of nuclear weapons gave offensive systems an insurmountable advantage.

The 1972 ABM Treaty permits the deployment by the United States and the USSR of 100 ABM interceptors at one site, the testing of fixed land-based systems, and research on other technologies. It prohibits testing or deployment of space-based, air-based, or ground mobile systems of any type, including lasers. The Soviets are improving their permitted system around Moscow, but it is of very limited effectiveness. The U.S. dismantled its one site in 1975.

The SDI includes a number of prototype demonstrations that are inconsistent with the provisions of the ABM Treaty. These are the same demonstrations that account for the major increases in funding for the SDI.

The issue of most immediate concern is the initiation of testing in 1988 of the Airborne Optical System (AOS), also known as the Airborne Optical Adjunct (AOA). The Airborne Optical System is a modified Boeing 767 aircraft that carries a pair of heat-sensitive infrared telescopes for tracking and identifying reentry vehicles while they are still above the atmosphere for interception by mid-course and terminal defenses. The first flight of AOS is scheduled for 1988. The flight testing of AOS would be inconsistent with Article V(1) of the ABM Treaty banning the development, testing, or deployment of air-based ABM components.

The stated goal of the SDI is to render nuclear weapons impotent and obsolete by erecting a nonnuclear defense. But in fact, the SDI includes several types of nuclear weapons.

The best known of these is the Excalibur X-ray laser, which is powered by a nuclear explosion. Other such "third generation" nuclear weapons include hypervelocity pellet devices, charged particle beams, directed electromagnetic pulse (EMP), and high-power microwaves.

The Excalibur X-ray laser could be used for boost-phase interceptions of ballistic missiles. The interceptor would be forward deployed in a ground-based or mobile sea-based mode (probably on submarines to enhance survivability), with interceptor rockets that would be launched into space on warning of attack. Each nuclear device would have a number of laser rods (perhaps twenty) that would be pumped by the explosion of the device.

The SDI proposes to use nonnuclear warheads for its ground-based terminal interceptor rockets. One potential countermeasure open to the offense, however, is the use of maneuvering reentry vehicles, known as MARVs. By making unpredictable maneuvers, MARVs can greatly complicate the task of the defense in directing ground-based rockets to intercept reentry vehicles.

Defense responses could include use of additional interceptors to cover all possible courses that the MARV might take, or significant increases in the maneuverability of each interceptor, but these would be very expensive. Should the offense resort to maneuvering reentry vehicles, SDI terminal interceptor rockets would probably require the use of an enhanced radiation warhead with a yield in the low kiloton range, of the type deployed in previous American ABM systems.

The SDI is frequently referred to as a $26 billion, five-year program. However, this cost and time frame is a product of the Department of Defense budget process, which only projects five years into the future. With the new 1987 budget request, which gives funding figures through 1991, the SDI is now a six-year $42 billion program.

In fact, the initial development phase of the SDI will run through 1995, at a cost of over $100 billion. The SDI is intended to support a deployment decision in 1991 time frame, as part of the new strategic concept that is the basis of the Administration's current arms control policy. Increases of about $1 billion annually are anticipated each year for the next decade.

The estimate of $100 billion and 10 years assumes that the SDI program proceeds according to the present plan, but this may prove too optimistic. For the most part the SDI consists of development efforts at the very frontier of military science and technology. In recent years similar efforts, such as the new antisatellite (ASAT) weapon program, have been plagued by severe cost overruns and schedule delays. If the SDI encounters the cost overruns and schedule delays that are typical of these high-risk high technology projects, it could become a 20-year $250 billion development effort.

The very rapid growth of the SDI will result in the SDI consuming a rapidly increasing percentage of total funding for defense research and development. Prior to Star Wars, research on strategic defense consumed only a small part of the overall Pentagon research budget. Under the Strategic Defense Initiative, this research will grow to over 20% of the total by 1991, with further growth in the next decade. In the absence of Star Wars, the total military research effort would actually decline over this period. The SDI is also the difference between continued growth and declining budgets in the specialized areas of strategic forces research and military space research.

The cause of this is not difficult to see. Most of the large programs that have dominated the defense budged in recent years are now close to completion. The MX missile, the B-1 bomber, and other are now entering production. No other programs of similar magnitude are in prospect.

In the absence of Star Wars, much of the military research establishment, which grew as a result of these previous efforts, would find itself without a project to work on. Star Wars fills this void.

By the mid 1990s, however, there will be a precipitous decline in SDI funding unless a system is actually deployed. The political difficulties posed by termination of the B-1B bomber program suggest that similar pressures may arise with respect to a future decision on missile defense.

Given the very large budgets projected for the SDI, it is not surprising that defense contractors have expressed considerable interest in this program. Thus far, this interest has taken at least several forms. Many companies are using Star Wars as part of their advertising efforts. Some companies have formed special divisions to consolidate all of their work on SDI-related contracts. In addition, several efforts are underway to increase industrial cooperation in support of the SDI.

Altogether over 500 companies are now doing work on $8.5 billion in Star Wars contracts. While many of these companies are in California, over a dozen other states also are home to companies working on the SDI. As the program grows, new companies in additional states will be added to the roster.

The Star Warriors hope to build an industrial constituency. But today most states have little if any of the Star Wars pie. The B-1 bomber was kept alive because virtually every Congressional district had some company that had a piece of the action.

One way that the SDI is building a political base is by giving research contracts to universities. These contracts fill in some of the holes in the map for the Star Wars largess. They are a means of quickly creating a local political constituency for the program. But this has also stirred up local resistance by administrators and faculty. Thousands of professors across the country have signed petitions stating their refusal to accept SDI money and their opposition to the program.

CONCLUSIONS

The SDI will fuel the offensive arms races as each side adds more expensive weapons to keep the other side's defenses from becoming effective. It will make arms control impossible, because in that type of environment there can be nothing to agree on, except that both sides are going to be building as fast as they can. The SDI will increase the risk of nuclear war, because these leaky defenses are going to be much more effective in defending against small retaliatory attacks than they are against massive first strikes. These weapons are going to be extremely expensive, costing tens of billions of dollars to develop and hundred of billions of dollars to deploy. Although the goal that the President has set is to make nuclear weapons obsolete, it is nonetheless ironic that some of the most promising and certainly some of the most intriguing weapons that are being developed to make nuclear weapons go away are in fact nuclear weapons themselves.

Opposition to strategic systems such as the MX or the B-1 bomber emerged only when the weapon was about to be deployed. By the time opposition was mobilized, these projects had developed massive industrial constituencies. Fortunately Star Wars is still just a research program, and it will be several years before the contractors become overly dependent on it. The SDI poses a unique chance to affect the future of Star Wars before it becomes a jobs program.

Although the SDI probably will work at the gadget level, it obviously will not work perfectly at the system level. Thus as a national strategy, Star Wars is not going to work at all.

An Unanswered Question: At What Rate Should SDI Be Funded?

JOSEPH E. FINCK

Administration officials, members of Congress, and the public at large currently differ in their views on the need and objectives for the Strategic Defense Initiative (SDI). The range of opinion extends from support for a minimal program that adheres to the ABM Treaty while conducting basic laboratory research as a hedge against Soviet breakout, to an accelerated program aimed at development and deployment of a defensive system at the earliest possible time. There are a myriad of alternatives in between. To date, the issue of how the rate of funding specifically relates to SDI objectives has not been well defined.

As conceived by the SDI Organization (SDIO), the research program would cost on the order of $26 billion over a period of five to seven years, leading to a decision in the early 1990s on whether or not to proceed with development. The SDI is organized into five research program elements. The current funding levels for these elements plus SDIO headquarters management are presented in TABLE 1.

Even those opposed to the SDI generally believe that some form and level of research in strategic defense is warranted. Accordingly, even without the SDI program, the funding level in this area would not go to zero. Such a minimum funding scenario would essentially revert to the situation prior to President Reagan's speech in March 1983. It can be argued that for stability to be maintained, this scenario requires that the United States have the ability to monitor Soviet strategic defense efforts to ensure they will not negate the deterrent value of our offensive strategic forces. It presumably also assumes that, for long-term stability, the United States and the Soviet Union must agree to meaningful arms reduction, or the United States must find other ways to resolve the problem of ICBM vulnerability.

The short-term funding request of this "monitoring" scenario appears to be far less than those proposed by the SDIO in pursuit of strategic defense. It can also be argued that if a useful ballistic missile defense should prove technically unachievable, considerable expenditures will have been saved. It would be wrong, however, to assume that because the risks in taking this approach are not readily apparent they are smaller then those of the pro-SDI options. All options include the risk of nuclear weapons for many years.

Joseph E. Finck was an American Physical Society Congressional Science Fellow and Legislative Assistant to Senator Bill Bradley (1985–86). He is currently affiliated with the Physics Department, Central Michigan University, Mt. Pleasant, Michigan 48859.

TABLE 1. Funding Levels for SDI Research Program in Fiscal Years 1985–87

	FY85 Appropriation[a]	FY86 Request[a]	FY86 Appropriation[a,b]	FY87 Projected[a]
Surveillance, acquisition, tracking, and kill assessment	546	1,386		1,875
Directed energy weapons technology	376	965		1,196
Kinetic energy weapons technology	256	860		1,239
Systems concepts/battle management	99	243		273
Survivability, lethality, and key technologies	112	258		317
Total research	1,389	3,712	2,750	4,900
Management	8	9	9	10
TOTAL	1,397	3,721	2,759	4,910

SOURCE: U.S. Department of Defense.
[a] In millions of dollars.
[b] Allocation of the research funds was left to the discretion of the SDIO.

Those in favor of SDI do not all have the same concept of what SDI could or should accomplish. Furthermore, proponents vary in their assessments as to how much funding is required and at what rate to meet their own objectives for the program. In a world of countermeasures and counter-countermeasures, time might be the essential factor in achieving technical feasibility. What follows is a discussion of two different scenarios for the relationship between SDI goals and funding.

If the goal of the SDI is to proceed rapidly with research to achieve the capability to develop and deploy, unilaterally or otherwise, a system that is sufficiently ahead of offensive countermeasures such that it provides an effective defense against the offensive threat that is in place at the time of deployment, then SDI probably must be funded at a high rate, even prior to assessing the program's success.

This scenario places the greatest burden on technological development, especially in the absence of arms agreements or other solutions limiting the offensive threat over time. However, its appeal derives primarily from the possibility it holds for the United States independently to lead the superpowers to a more strategically stable position. This scenario could require an ongoing, fast-paced, heavily funded program for continually enhancing system effectiveness, in the face of presumed rigorous Soviet efforts to counter defenses.

If, on the other hand, the strategic need for some SDI-derived ballistic missile defense exists, but is not imminent (*i.e.,* if strategic stability is not greatly threatened in the near term without such a system), and negotiations with the Soviets can be realized that result in offensive force reductions and verifiable agreements on development and deployment of defensive systems, then the possibility exists for slowing the rate of funding from an all-out pace, limited only by technology. Given the premise that new strategic defenses will eventually be needed for stability, however, it follows that the rate of funding should consider the factors above and should not be slowed by resource constraints alone. If it were, the United States would run the risk of falling behind the Soviets both offensively and defensively, seriously limiting the ability of SDI ever to develop a system that would be effective against an ever-changing strategic threat.

Both of these pro-SDI scenarios seem to dictate the need for large near-term funding to accomplish their objectives. If the assumptions behind these scenarios are correct, then a decision to pursue either option without appropriate funding would likely doom them to failure. Nonetheless, the issue of what constitutes appropriate funding for either case remains unresolved.

Roundtable Discussion

Chair: HEINZ R. PAGELS
Panel Members: HAROLD AGNEW, RICHARD GARWIN, SIDNEY D. DRELL, FRANKLIN LONG, CHARLES H. TOWNES, GEROLD YONAS, LOWELL WOOD, ASHTON B. CARTER, MICHAEL M. MAY, RICHARD SCRIBNER, AND GEORGE F. CHAPLINE

H. PAGELS (*The New York Academy of Sciences, New York, N.Y.*): This is the first of two roundtables that are going to be held at this conference. The second one will be at the end of the last session.

The purpose of this roundtable is to allow the experts present here to comment on some of the thoughts that were expressed in the sessions which took place earlier today.

H. AGNEW: In the discussions today we have heard a lot about mirrors. When I was young we called mirrors looking glasses and there was someone who wrote a book having something to do with looking glasses. I would like to talk a little bit about going through the looking glass.

When the President started this initiative he mentioned that if we were eventually successful we were going to make the results available to the Soviets and we would share the technology with them. Let me back up. What I am going to do is go through the looking glass.

Most recently the people involved have put on a real effort to get our allies to join with us, particularly West Germany, France, the U.K., and Japan. In the last couple of days I was at a meeting where some of these representatives were present. Their complaint was they would would like to get involved primarily for the reason that they believe if they don't the technical spin-offs which may occur as a result of this R and D could greatly influence their competitive positions in the nondefense field. So, they are very much interested in getting involved. If indeed there is some direct spin-off in the defensive sense against missiles which perhaps threaten them in Europe or wherever they are that is somewhat secondary, but as it is they are frustrated because of security issues.

They simply aren't given access to the things which are presently considered secret. Gerry Yonas has alluded to some of these this morning. So, here we are again. We are working hard, spending a lot of money and trying to work closely with our allies, but we don't want to give them what they perceive as necessary classified materials. Yet at the same time when we really get all done and have all of this then the President says it is his objective to make it available to the Soviets. I'm not certain which side of the looking glass we are now on.

Sid Drell says, and Edward Teller says he agrees with him, that this is really unusual, this is a double looking glass. You can't ever do anything in space because one nation will shoot down the other's systems. It is a very, very unstable situation, but it is certainly true what you do on your own land should be allowed as a national endeavor and one should be allowed to do these things on and over one's own territory. I would suggest that there is one way of having an effective system, assuming any system can be effective, and having it in space, especially since the President said that eventually he is going to give it to the Soviets anyway, and that would be to agree with the Soviets that we will have a cooperative system in space. This system would be jointly manned, or manned by them if it is over the U.S. and manned by us if it is over the Soviet Union. Since it will actually be over the territories it would be much more effective. You don't have to have pop-up mirrors and go a long way away. It would operate in space over our respective territories and control would switch to the other party when it is over one's own territory.

Because it would be in space, if you use the proper weapon systems, namely nonnuclear and by this I mean any of the laser systems, any of the kinetic weapon systems, any of the neutral particle systems that will not penetrate the atmosphere, you could shoot them all whenever you wish and you would not bother anybody on earth.

This has an advantage when you worry about being able to operate these systems in fractions of a second. You can exercise them all you want. All you do is expend some consumables. Therefore it really doesn't matter that you are actually firing the systems. The weapon systems mentioned cannot penetrate the atmosphere and therefore will have no effect on earth.

The point about the difficulty of getting systems on line is certainly true, but if you can exercise them all of the time there is no start-up problem. That's no longer an issue. You can exercise the system whenever you want. People worry about false alarms. It doesn't matter if it is a false alarm because if you shoot at objects, if they are there you destroy it. If they aren't there it doesn't matter. It doesn't bother anybody on the ground and all you have done is waste some energy or projectile.

The advantage of all of this, and I will come back through the looking glass, is if you are going to spend all of this money, develop these systems that both we and the Soviets are going to be able to use to shoot down anything that comes up, that shows the futility of having the missiles in the first place. Doesn't it seem strange that you are going to spend all of this money through technical means to get rid of something and if you really want to do that and believe that you can, why don't you just get rid of the objects and save all that money and effort? Perhaps you really can't in which case it's back through the looking glass.

R. Garwin (*IBM Thomas J. Watson Research Center, Yorktown Heights, N.Y.*): I really admire the attitude and the imagination shown by the previous speaker, which competes with that shown by our President on March 23, 1983, but I have to point out to him that defensive weapons over the territories of the U.S. or the USSR don't stay there unless they are at geosynchronous orbit—in which case it will take an awful long time for a kinetic kill vehicle to get down to boost phase.

Further, if the defense is jointly manned, obviously it must not rely on the Russians to defend the U.S. against Soviet missiles in boost phase. Otherwise they just need not do their job and our defense vanishes. We must not rely on the Russians to defeat Russian missiles in boost phase. So, the joint manning really doesn't work.

Let's talk about the SDI program for which people are spending billions of dollars a year. There are some problems there as you may have noticed. The purpose, "to strengthen deterrence," is totally different from what the President had in mind, his dream of a defense so good that we could abandon our own strategic retaliatory force. Now we have to keep all nuclear weapons and we have to ensure that they penetrate to their targets. That means the Soviet's SDI can't work very well. Otherwise we have lost our deterrent.

Even in this SDI research program there is no general understanding of its criterion for success, which was defined by Lieutenant Colonel Worden (special assistant to General Abrahamson) on April 9, 1986 in a debate with me at Johns Hopkins University as allowing the Soviets to kill up to 3000 military targets in the United States by the use of nuclear weapons. That's *success* for the SDI!

We are not sure whether we can do even that, but in any case the decision has been made and enunciated by Caspar Weinberger and by Fred Ikle, the Deputy Secretary of Defense, that we will have in the future a larger component of defense per se in our security posture.

We've made that decision; we don't know whether we can do it. There is something wrong. The three general counters to this system are fast-burn boosters, space mines, and antisimulation. We can have great fun with these things, but they are very serious. Antisimulation in mid-course means that you dress up your warheads to look like cheap decoys rather than the other way around.

Antisimulation in boost-phase intercept means that you can use cheap boosters. You put them on the ground outside of silos. If they are assumed by the defense to be decoys and ignored, you have a surefire way to penetrate the defense, because you include among the "decoys" some real boosters with a guidance system programmed with a little initial apparent stagger, and it gets through to its target.

This is a very difficult question. We will not succeed in protecting cities. We are not even trying. As Lieutenant Colonel Worden says, "it is not a military goal of the Soviet Union to attack U.S. cities," So, it is not up to the defense to defend against it.

What we are going to get in the case of success, in my opinion, is not worth either the money or the risk to our security and the ABM Treaty.

S. Drell (*Stanford University, Stanford, Calif.*): I will comment about another part of what Harold Agnew said. Harold started out in his remarks commenting upon how the Europeans were coming in because they were afraid of being left behind technologically.

That argument has always interested and surprised me. Last year some of you may have noticed that a Presidential Commission on Industrial Competitiveness chaired by John Young, the president of Hewlett-Packard, issued a report which I have seen discussed only once in a newspaper, in this past December's *Washington Post* in a full-page article. This got me to read the report which says that the Pentagon has now become a net user of commercial technology, the point being that military systems have become so exotic, so slow at reaching fruition, that to look to them as a way of stimulating advanced technology is out of kilter and is the wrong direction. In fact, the countries whose economic productivity is growing at the greatest rate among the Western democracies are those who are devoting the smallest portion of the GNP to the military.

I therefore do not really understand that argument for our allies coming into SDI. In fact, it seems to me that one of the important issues that we face right now for the future of the United States is that with an increasing portion of the federally supported R and D in this country being tied to the military at the expense of the civilian sector, we will end up hurting ourselves economically; and I think the Europeans are using the wrong argument when they allow themselves to be brought in this way.

H. AGNEW: Actually, the Europeans said just what you said. They viewed with great alarm that we were having a higher and higher fraction of our R and D, basic R and D, being done on basic military pursuits.

On the other hand, they said since so much is going in there must be a pony someplace.

F. LONG (*Cornell University, Ithaca, N.Y.*): I think one must give the Europeans more credit. As far as I know all that SDI-related research will be paid for by the United States. So, they can make a reasonable gamble. The benefit to their civilian efforts is either zero or positive. It seems to me it is not negative.

C. TOWNES (*University of California at Berkeley, Berkeley, Calif.*): I would like to make quite a different point on this technological question. It hinges on the fact that the total amount of money we put into real science and research is such a small fraction of the total national product. It is of the order of 1%. If we put into research 1% of our total effort, and if it affects the total effort in any appreciable way, it is easy to see how one could argue that we might well double it. We might even be a little wasteful and triple it and still have be a good buy. Why don't we do that?

Well, the trouble is that you never can predict the outcome of research. You can't go to Congress and say, look, if you give me this money I will discover these new things and it is going to produce this new industry.

So when dollars are short we always concentrate on what is predictable. I think the country characteristically simply doesn't put enough overall effort into research.

That means that even some not terribly efficient efforts can in the long run be worth it to the country. Hence, I would not write off the SDI.

I remember once I was coming into Washington on a plane; I ran into an engineer whom I knew and asked him, "What are you coming here for this time?" He said, "Well, I am going to the Pentagon because I want to try and get a contract for our company to do some research on integrated solid state circuits." This was a time when there was no such things, and I said, "Oh, do you think they are promising?" He said, "Well, not very promising. We certainly wouldn't spend our company's money on it, but the Pentagon is willing to spend some money and we would like to have some of that."

I think one has to say that solid state circuitry was really initiated by governmental effort, and would not have been investigated nearly as soon by private effort.

Every once in a while something like that happens. I don't think it is particularly because of great virtue in the Pentagon. I think there are ways the Pentagon could cut down on spending. Nevertheless, I believe it is important to recognize the potency of general technical effort. Even when inefficient it can be of value to the country.

G. YONAS (*SDI Organization, Washington, D.C.*): I have spent some time discussing SDI with Europeans over the last year and a half and I find that their interest is real and is widespread, but it has many reasons.

One aspect that I think is inescapable is that this program has a different flavor than the average developmental program in the Pentagon. Because it is emphasizing providing the basis for a future decision, it is to a large degree looking at a tech-base effort across a very broad front.

Some of the areas that we are pursuing that would require very large advances are in compact power supplies, advanced lightweight strong high temperature materials made out of advanced composites, low-cost electronics that are fast and require low power requirements that are radiation hard, software that is to a great degree automated and flexible and expandable which has tremendous implications for robot manufacturing in advanced factories, electro-optical techniques across the board, advanced sensors, space transportation. They see this very large fraction of our budget going into these areas that have implications across the board and of course they are interested.

We are looking to them because we see that they are making advances in these areas also. We don't have a monopoly on advances and technology. We think together there could be some synergism that allows us to achieve our goals faster at a lower cost, but there is another issue that I think also has driven their interest in the SDI and that is believe it or not they are interested in defense of their people and their military sites, their airfields, their command posts against Soviet short-range ballistic missiles, and they say this is a case where our emphasis on technology may allow them to get something they want militarily through the development of space-based sensors, low-cost interceptor missiles, possibly airborne sensor platforms, something that they worry about militarily, and they see that our joint programs could solve an important military problem.

I think that there is this mixture of interest and even if there were no SDI we would see a European development and possible deployment of a defense against short-range missiles.

H. PAGELS: One question I would like to ask that came up in Professor Drell's talk is, How can SDI research proceed in order not to violate the ABM accord? Is this possible? Would you like to comment on that Dr. Yonas?

G. YONAS: From the very beginning we have had clear instructions from the President to pursue the program in compliance with the ABM Treaty and we have a mechanism to have oversight from the Executive Branch and from Congress and from other branches of the Pentagon to act as the judge and jury over the various programs that we would propose, to assure that we are in compliance before we can proceed.

I think we have had and will continue to have a great deal of public oversight over this process. I doubt very much if Congress would appropriate funds for activities that would be in violation of our treaties.

L. WOOD (*Lawrence Livermore National Laboratory, Livermore, Calif.*): If I could interject a point there, Congress in the authorization for the current fiscal year's funding of the Strategic Defense Initiative specifically said that no funds would be obligated or expended in violation of any treaty of the United States. So, it is just not a matter of stipulation or inspection or whatever. It is a matter of law.

A. B. CARTER (*Harvard University, Cambridge, Mass.*): Just a small comment following up what Gerry said about the technical content of the program. Much of what is in there are things that we are doing anyway and would continue to do whether there were an SDI or not. So, I think when we are talking about the program very specifically that's a margin added on to a lot of research efforts that were underway for many other missions as well as generic purposes before SDI got under way. We should bear that in mind as we are trying to assess it as a research program.

R. GARWIN: Professor Townes's remarks about the general applicability of high technology, and of broad efforts in research and science, might have merit if it were *additional* money, but, it doesn't seem to be additional money. We haven't created any more scientists or engineers. We are taking them from someplace else. We are taking them from other programs.

I think if we wanted to have the greatest impact on science and technology, on air traffic control and safety and public welfare, we would have a program which was focused with our allies to do something about conventional weapons. I would find it bizarre to find our allies developing and deploying a short-range ballistic missile defense system in Europe when we don't have an air defense system that is worth anything. It would be very remarkable.

H. AGNEW: On that point, the Europeans whom I have talked with recently said the first step would be applications for air defense systems. Then, they could see this leading on.

They also made the point, coming back to the funds, any funds that they would expend in this endeavor, these are private companies, would be only those funds in areas which essentially fulfilled their long-term company objectives anyway.

L. WOOD: Professor Garwin's suggestion that increased R and D funding would not be followed or associated with an increase in the number of scientists or engineers doing R and D seems absurd on its face. It certainly flies in the face of all previous data associating increase in scientific manpower in this country with increase in the R and D funding available to support effort by that manpower.

R. GARWIN: I didn't say that wouldn't happen. I said this is not an increase in R and D funding. It is a diversion of R and D funding from other programs.

L. WOOD: Both the absolute fraction and the absolute amount of the Department of Defense budget devoted to R and D has been rising for the last five years. That's a matter of record.

R. GARWIN: That has nothing to do with SDI which is only two years old.

L. WOOD: I just pointed out that during the 1980s the Department of Defense R and D budget has increased about 65%. Obviously there are going to be more people doing defense R and D. Salaries have not risen 65% for defense R and D researchers. So, the points that there will not be more scientists and engineers absolutely and that there will not be more doing defense R and D and there will not be more doing SDI R and D are all manifestly absurd.

F. LONG: It is not quite that simple. This was analyzed by economists for the big push of the Apollo program and the conclusion was reached by serious economists that, in fact, the major impact of the Apollo program was to push the price, the cost, of an engineer to an industrial company very substantially upward, and therefore cut down on the available market.

L. WOOD: The law of supply and demand says that when the price goes up the supply goes up.

C. TOWNES: The Apollo argument has been used many times. I know a very distinguished person who at a time of debates about initiation of that program gave public testimony to Congress that the Apollo program was very unwise because it would rob all of the rest of the U.S. science and industrial base in order to get this landing on the moon.

I think the history is simply not that. It surely must have increased the salaries of engineers some. That happens in any period of prosperity. If we had a deep depression, that would decrease their salaries and make them more available to any small company that wanted to hire a good engineer. However, in terms of the overall effort in the United States in the general development of science and technology, I am quite convinced that the space program really substantially helped. I would, in fact, like to see some good hard studies on this broad question.

However, my judgement is that it's pretty evident that the total technological development during that period was very rapid.

H. PAGELS: I can't resist commenting. A few months ago I met with Si Ramo and I asked him about this question of technological fallout from the SDI and how it compared with the Apollo program. He commented that one of the things that resulted from the Apollo program was heart monitoring stations in hospitals where patients could have their hearts instantaneously monitored as they were for astronauts. He said that on the other hand, you don't pay $52 billion for heart monitoring stations.

With regard to SDI it was his opinion that no one had examined the problems of the managing of the SDI project. No one had ever attempted to organize that many human beings together for a common purpose. He went on to say that the managerial technology for such a system does not at this time exist, least of all in the military.

L. WOOD: In a document which was put out before the Defense Appropriations subcommittee of the U.S. Senate last year by the Department of Defense and accepted and published by the subcommittee, it was stated that the Apollo project in its third year of endeavor spent nearly three times as much as the SDI in its third year of endeavor proposes to spend. That is to say, the Apollo project in 1985 dollars spent nearly $14 billion dollars. The Strategic Defense Initiative proposes to spend, if they are fully funded, in the fiscal 1987 period $4.8 billion.

So, Dr. Ramo's comment, if it was related correctly, surely was wide of the mark because Apollo in its third year of endeavors spent nearly three times as much as the SDI hopes to spend in its third year.

Where did all the managerial genius come from that spent that three times larger amount of money so well?

M. MAY (*Lawrence Livermore National Laboratory, Livermore, Calif.*): Just one brief comment to return to the question of technological fallout from defense R and D generally, not just SDI, but defense R and D in general, either for the civilian economy or for other defense programs. The answer to that question depends on a number of criteria, in particular, for instance, on how broad the military R and D is.

It is quite true that in the early days the Department of Defense played an important role in pushing more advanced transitors, but that was the purpose of their funding. They weren't putting the money into specific end products. They were putting the money into fairly broad research.

To the extent that military R and D has been focused on narrow end-use objectives for things which really only the military and possibly the space programs can use, to that extent it has not had a major fallout for the civilian economy.

In particular, we have been outdone in the past decade or so in taking something that was originally invented here and translating it into something that was useful in the marketplace. What was done for military was developed for military uses, while the production research and other research for the civilian sector were not funded.

SDI is really too new to have a track record. If we do want technological fallout, and of course by itself that's not a reason to pursue SDI, but if we do want that as a side benefit, then a significant part of the R and D funds have to be expended on a broad front so as to bring about advances in knowledge that are not just focused on getting the end products that would be useful for the defense application.

R. SCRIBNER (*American Association for the Advancement of Science, Washington, D.C.*): I am going to shift the discussion and pick up some of Sid Drell's remarks. I want to emphasize that offensive arms control will still be needed even as SDI proceeds, that we haven't given careful enough attention to the possibility that our present preoccupation with strategic defense could lead us to a less secure world, and that the notion of sharing strategic military technology with the Soviets is unrealistically idealistic.

I would guess that most people on the panel and most in the room would agree that proceeding with SDI research per se is a prudent thing to do. We disagree about what levels of funding and what emphasis to place on different program areas within SDI, but not that the U.S. needs a healthy, thoughtfully carried out ballistic missile defense *research* program as a hedge against changes in the future. We disagree strongly over the necessity for and strategic implications of the proposed "ramp up" rate of the SDI budget and the timing and need for the engineering development and testing aspects of SDI. The question emphasized throughout the debate is a question of how far and how fast should the U.S. proceed with the SDI. Does this approach truly serve U.S. national security interests?

As Sid indicated, it would seem that in the planning for any development of a defense-dominated situation, some kinds of limits of offensive weapons are required. Many people, including Paul Nitze, the President's advisor on arms control matters, have emphasized that the transition period will be tricky to say the least, and that arms control will be needed. So, a BMD system such as the President envisions would also require arms control agreements limiting offensive nuclear weapons in order that it be judged as capable of working effectively.

As one looks ahead, it is a serious question whether the SDI program is going to include tests in just a few years that would violate the ABM Treaty as it now stands. I don't know whether the plans have changed, but reportedly there were plans to run tests which might violate the ABM Treaty. If that were the case, we might lose the substantial benefits of the treaty unless we were able to negotiate satisfactory modifications of it. Since at least in the short run the Soviets could better exploit a situation in which there was no ABM Treaty than we could, it would seem to be clearly to our advantage to do nothing to jeopardize it.

The Soviets themselves have repeatedly stated that the United States musn't try to predict what they will do, and that, in fact, their responses to our pursuing the goals of SDI will be both offensive and defensive. There is certainly some bluff in that. There is certainly some propaganda in that. There is also more information to add to the reasons to pause and consider carefully how best to proceed. If we need limitations on offensive weapons in order to have ballistic missile defense work, is the way we are proceeding now likely to get what we want?

As Sid mentioned, the current arms control regime, including the ABM Treaty, and the conditions of nuclear deterrence may not be the best of all possible worlds. On the other hand, before we shift to something else, *i.e.*, a defense-dominated world, I think we had better take a good careful look and be very sure that what we are shifting to is a better world, more secure from the threat of nuclear war.

As has been pointed out, there are ways other than strategic defense to work toward discouraging the tendency toward a first-strike attack, *i.e.*, setting up regimes that would make it more costly for a possible belligerent to use nuclear weapons. We are not putting very much attention into those alternatives at this time.

We've heard today about "mirrors" and "in the looking glass" with regard to the unreality of the possibility of sharing strategic defense technology with the Soviets or the joint management of satellites. If the day comes that we could share state-of-the-art military technology with the USSR, we will no longer have an adversarial relationship with the Soviet Union but rather a much more friendly and cooperative relationship – a relationship in which neither nuclear weapons nor strategic defense is needed. It is reasonable to assume, however, that we will have an adversarial relationship with the Soviets for the foreseeable future. In that case, negotiating some sort of sharing of sensitive technology (where now we don't even share oil drilling equipment or fairly ordinary – to us – computers with them) will be far more complicated and less likely to succeed than negotiating a nuclear arms reductions agreement.

L. Wood: I would like to just very briefly offer an example of the more general points made by Charles Townes and Mike May with respect to what the technological fallout is and might necessarily be to DOD-type initiatives.

As Charles Townes pointed out, DOD effectively brought into existence the modern integrated circuits through sponsorship of solid state electronics for various DOD purposes; however, the development of exceedingly fast circuitry, solid-state circuitry, was not seen as very important for DOD purposes in the last decade and a half. As a result, the technology has not only been very effectively picked up by the Japanese, but developed by them at least one full generation beyond the comparable level of development in the United States.

As a result, at the present time not only the fastest integrated circuits with respect to doing digital logic, but the highest performance digital circuitry with respect to storing information and retrieving it are available exclusively from the Japanese, and indeed you can't even buy that circuitry from the Japanese these days. You have to buy it in the form of Japanese computers.

The second tier, the previous generation of digital circuitry available from the Japanese, is nonetheless the highest performance that can be purchased anywhere in the world on the open market, that is to say, Japanese hand-me-downs, the type of circuits that they are willing to sell one by one rather than packaged in computers, are still the highest performance ones that you can buy. This is because the market was not perceived as being substantial in this area either by U.S. companies or the military need was not perceived as substantial by DOD, as a result of which the U.S. technology effort faltered in the last decade and the Japanese are at least one and some people might say two generations ahead.

With respect to the issue of how much, how well, and how quickly money gets spent by the Strategic Defense Initiative, I would just like to offer some specific numbers associated with this situation.

The Apollo program in the 1960s on the average doubled its budget every year for the first five years. That program grew extremely rapidly to a program which in present dollars, you know, dwarfs by roughly threefold the total amount which the Reagan Administration proposes to spend on the entire Strategic Defense Initiative.

There weren't a great deal of complaints in those days that the money was coming too fast or that it couldn't be spent efficiently. People were mostly concerned with how in the world we could spend enough in order to get to the moon in this decade, but the average rate of growth was over 100% for each of the five years.

I would like to invite the attention of those of you who have read the newspapers for the last three years to the essentially reactionary nature of the opposition to budget growth in the Strategic Defense Initiative. When the Reagan Administration first proposed growing it up from about $800 million to $1.7 billion in the first year of the Strategic Defense Initiative, people who opposed the whole idea said it was much too much, that it should have been $800 million.

Nonetheless, the Congress appropriated $1.4 billion and the following year when the Reagan Administration proposed to very greatly increase that the response was no, $1.4 billion is the right level. You should hold it at this level.

Nonetheless, the Congress appropriated just shy of $2.8 billion. This year in testimony in the last two months people such as Sidney Drell and former Defense Secretary McNamara have said, and you heard Professor Drell repeat it today, $2.8 billion is about the right level. You should show that you can use that well before you ask for any more. Secretary Brown said you really shouldn't have more than 25% growth a year above this level. Therefore, you should probably make do with three and a quarter or three and a half billion dollars.

If the Administration gets, and who knows what it is going to get, $4 billion this year, I strongly suggest to you that the reactionary nature of the opposition to budget growth will say next year that $4 billion is just about the right level, we definitely shouldn't go above that level. But the striking thing is the opponents of SDI research are not saying that it should be $800 million or $1.4 billion or $2.8 billion. They are trying to hold the line somewhere around $4 billion and I predict that this will be the way that they will go indefinitely. Always the previous year's level is the right one.

R. Garwin: $1.4 billion is my number and that is plenty.

L. Wood: I apologize to Professor Garwin. He is one year more reactionary than most of his colleagues.

G. Chapline (*Lawrence Livermore National Laboratory, Livermore, Calif.*): I just wanted to mention one amusing example of fallout from the SDI program that's apparently going to take place. As you heard from Gerald Yonas, one of the main focuses of the SDI program has been to develop very high power free electron lasers. It turns out that free electron lasers are a marvelous way to heat plasmas and probably most of you also know that one of the fallouts from the Geneva Summit was a proposal for the Soviet Union and the United States to build jointly a Tokamak.

It is my understanding that the United States contribution to this will include a free electron laser heater for the Tokamak which will incorporate the technology developed under the SDI program.

H. Agnew: In reference to Professor Pagels's conversation with Si Ramos relating to the inability of an organization to handle such a large amount of R and D funds, I think Lowell Wood rebutted that and made some comments. I would like to mention that there is a firm that handles at least a thousand times whatever we are talking about now. To me it is a big R and D program. It is called the United States government and senior officials say all kinds of things: raise oil prices, lower oil prices, quit smoking, but let's support tobacco. It is covering all of the aspects. Kill the cows. We have too much milk. If that isn't a big R and D program I don't know what is and they seem to handle it and all of its constituency doesn't seem to matter.

S. Drell: The Apollo program was mentioned as one that built up much more rapidly. Indeed, that is true because the Apollo program was not a reasearch program. It was a directed effort initiated by a President of the United States to put a man on the moon within a decade.

I have not heard that the United States, through its Congress or through its people or through the President, has made a decision that we will *deploy* the SDI by a given year. Therein lies the fundamental difference. We are told when we complain about the way the SDI program is going (emphasizing demonstrations), or rapidly increasing its budget, that a good research program is being developed. I repeat that when you are talking about a research program designed to try to find out what technologies might be made available and what kinds of systems can be developed against what kinds of countermeasures, you don't compare it with the Apollo program. As to the rate of build-up, I stand by my statement that 30% a year is the maximum rate of budget increase that can be absorbed efficiently into a research program which hasn't already signed on the dotted line to the effect that we are going to deploy a system which we don't yet know how to design.

As far as what budget levels one supports, the figure I used last year when testifying before the Congress was that I thought a $2 billion a year budget was about right. I still think that is true, but you have to be realistic. The FY86 budget for DOD now is $2.75 billion, and I think it would be inefficient to sharply cut that down. You are quite right; I have changed my figure. I would like to see SDIO show that it can carry out a good research program at $2.75 billion. It is more than enough money.

P. SPRAGUE (*National Semiconductor Inc.*): I wasn't planning to say anything today until Mr. Wood launched forth on his thumbnail sketch of the history of the semiconductor business which I disagree with from beginning to end.

L. WOOD: Are you making lots of money at National Semiconductor these days?

P. SPRAGUE: No, sir. I am actually going to bring that point up. The situation in terms of the Japanese is not a failure by the American industry to recognize the significance of the integrated circuit or the fast memories or memory circuits. I would say the industry has lost probably half a billion dollars pursuing Japanese pricing which the Reagan Administration has allowed to exist at below cost and in pursuing it we have all collectively lost enough money that we have collectively pulled out of it, not because we didn't believe it is a driving market and critical, but because in a marketplace economy we wouldn't have survived.

We actually asked a high official in the Defense Department how he felt about the fact that now the entire memory business with the exception of one small company, Micron Technology, is located in Japan and that includes Texas Instruments which does its manufacturing there.

His response was the Japanese are our allies and we are not worried about it. So, I am glad they are not worried about it, but, as far as we are concerned we were driven out of that business. We were driven out of it by unfair pricing and by the fact that the DOD buys its parts from its low cost suppliers. If you like to get them from the Japanese, you have created that particular problem and that's where you are going to have to buy them now.

L. WOOD: The problem was that your company never had a substantial presence in the technologies that I referred to, specifically the fastest circuitry and the fastest RAMs. You weren't in it at all and no one else was either and that's why the Japanese got it. They got it by default not by unfair pricing.

G. YONAS: Well, having seen how a name can adversely effect the difficult task of public diplomacy, by that I mean the appellation Star Wars, I would like to ask you all to drop the terminology "technological fallout" and use "technological spinoff."

The second point is in response to Sidney Drell's comment about the need within the government for a red team and a high level review committee. We have both of those functions under way and I would certainly appreciate whatever advice anyone can give in terms of how we can improve that process.

In terms of Harold Agnew's description of the managment process and Si Ramo's suggestion that it is a difficult management team, we have announced the intention to form a new institute somewhat such as Rand to give us additional managerial support, top level technical advice and review in an independent and noncompetitive mode in order to help us facilitate the management of this complex program.

Finally, in terms of arms control I have heard people say SDI requires arms control, but SDI prevents arms control. So, it is a self-contradiction. My question there is: Arms control compared to what?

Until the SDI came along it wasn't clear we were proceeding with an effective arms control process. There was no evidence that our entire strategy based on offensive deterrence was leading us anywhere in terms of reduction.

We are now sitting down with the Soviets and engaging in discussions where we clearly have their attention and we have at least a scenario in which the technology proves to be sufficiently convincing that we can enter into a jointly managed transition, but if you don't believe that will work I think there is very little evidence that the previous approaches would have taken us down a beneficial path.

The Impact of SDI on Defense Technology Perspectives

SIR JAMES BLYTH

May I begin by expressing my appreciation of the honor that you do me in inviting me to speak to this distinguished audience today on a subject of such great moment.

It is an irony that another speaker this morning is Dr. Pierre Aigrain, the eminent scientist whose wise council has for so long steered the policies of the French government and the Thomson Group in France, since only half a year ago his company and ours were engaged in a struggle to secure the contract to supply army tactical communications systems to the United States Department of Defense. Much to our chagrin, it was his colleagues who won and we who lost on that occasion, but the point of greatest significance, perhaps, is that this was a competition between two European systems deemed better able to satisfy a need of the United States than anything indigenously available. The proposition that the United States can no more pursue policies of splendid isolation in the field of military technology than in the realm of politics and diplomacy seems to have received powerful practical support.

I shall argue here that it is essential in our present epoch, when the battle for supremacy between military research laboratories can dominate the outcome of any subsequent physical conflict, that the West should confront possible opponents united in its technological strength, just as for a generation its military power has been brought together through the agency of the North Atlantic Treaty. Although we see signs that this is already starting, it seems to me very likely that the Strategic Defense Initiative (SDI) will greatly accelerate the trend, if only because the magnitude of the scientific and technical challenge which faces us appears so very, very large.

General Fuller, in his great book *The Conduct of War*, stated more succinctly than anyone else ever did the present military condition of the world. He wrote: "So it comes about that the two great camps into which the world ... is now divided are, as in trench warfare of former days, separated by a no-man's-land which neither dares to cross, and we arrive at a stalemate which both fear to break, and which, through fear ... leads to both sides frantically multiplying their nuclear armaments in order indefinitely to postpone the Crack of Doom."

This eloquent picture of world nuclear stalemate describes a system which has given us four decades without a world war, and for that we must be for-

---

Sir James Blyth is Managing Director of the Plessey Company plc, London SW1P 4QP, England.

ever grateful. The strategy of mutually assured destruction, fraught with great dangers and unattractive in many ways though it may be, has in fact given us a kind of peace in our time, and has for a long time seemed the best, and perhaps the only, policy open to us. Even so, it has been an uneasy peace, scarcely indeed to be dignified with that title, lived as it is under the shadow of universal destruction.

Now, at last, an alternative has been presented to us, and the crucial question which we are now obliged to answer is whether President Reagan's Strategic Defense Initiative constitutes a genuine opportunity to break with this pattern, or is merely, as some still claim, an illusion. That crucial question is a highly technical one, which I do not propose to attempt to answer today. I will restrict myself to one observation: the historical record has invariably been much less kind to those in the past who have propounded the impossibility of suggested technical developments than it has been to those who took the contrary view.

Nor do I wish, on this occasion at any rate, to give my attention to the delicate diplomatic and political problems of transition that may arise in getting from here to there, from a world of mutually assured destruction to a world of effective strategic defense. Others will be all too ready to explain how fraught with danger such a transition must necessarily be, and it cannot be denied that serious consideration has to be given to what must be done if the world is to pass through this dangerous place without disaster. Let that, however, be a discussion for another speaker or another day, although I must say that I do not see SDI as an isolated technical challenge.

My main concern is, however, different. I shall consider the military problems which may follow the implementation of SDI, problems which, as I hope to demonstrate, are with us now, but will move from the periphery to the center of military thinking as the nuclear threat recedes. It seems to me neither premature nor unrealistic to consider this issue, for two reasons. First, the condition of the world we are likely to have to face after successful implementation of SDI is something which we should legitimately consider as part of the debate about whether this is a road we want to take. Secondly, there is much in common, I believe, between the demands of SDI technology and those of the "conventional" defense technology which could follow, so carefully laid plans may succeed in addressing both together.

Before the first half of the nineteenth century technology was not perceived as an important factor in war, causative of defeat or victory, and indeed it would have been inconceivable to von Clausewitz and his contemporaries that the outcome of battle might be determined solely by a decisive technological superiority.

Even at the time of the American Civil War it would not be easy to argue that technological factors played a dominant part in the outcome. Yet only a single year after the peace at the Appomattox Court House, the Prussian total defeat of a larger Austrian army, and a few years later the unexpected outcome of the Franco-Prussian conflict, demonstrated the dominance of technology on the battlefield. Above all, nineteenth century colonial wars confirmed in the most dramatic way the total superiority of technological armies.

In the two world wars things advanced still further, and it would not be fanciful to claim that the struggle between opposing technological innovators was just as important as the conflict between armies.

One of the lessons of history is that in each epoch, nations quickly learn to exploit for purposes of war such new technology as becomes available to them. Furthermore, each use of new technology is pressed into service to address the dominant question of the conduct of war in its day, to be answered by another generation of military.

The late nineteenth and early twentieth centuries can legitimately be represented as a period in which it was the new chemical energy sources, and the mechanical engineering needed to exploit them effectively, which dominated military technology. The key to the conduct of war in that time was advance in the technology of explosives and chemical fuels, the latter making tanks, flight, high-speed warships, submarines, and rockets practicable. However, as the twentieth century wore on, another technology, electronics, was more and more often called in to answer pressing military needs.

It can hardly be denied that electronics has now become the new dominant technology of our own time, and like all its historical predecessors, it has received the call to arms. Beginning as a mere adjunct to the established energy-based developments in defense, it soon began to take on a life of its own. SDI is thus one, but only one, fruit of the military information technology revolution. It is not the destructive power of our weapons, nor yet the sources of energy which propel them to their target, that give us hope that the threat of the ballistic missile can be contained. Rather our expectation of success comes from our new-found ability to detect the threat at great range and to direct our counterattack against it effectively, with a speed and accuracy which are literally superhuman.

Three categories of things have changed, transforming all of our military perspectives with them: we have new sensors with which to detect and identify friend and enemy, new means of communications and control within and between our military installations, and now, most recently of all, machine intelligence (in the broadest sense) comes to supplement the understanding and reasoning powers of the human combatants.

Military communications have been participating in the general revolution in communications technology of which we are all so well aware. We have coined a new jargon, speaking of C^3I – communications, command, control and intelligence – as the means of coordination and coherent military response to an extended, fast-moving situation, on land, at sea, or in the air. What it comes down to is that the conventional "fog of war" is at last showing signs of being dispelled, and increasingly commanders can conduct battles with an accuracy of information and directness of command to their resources on the ground unparalleled in past history.

The sensor revolution embraces almost the whole electromagnetic spectrum, from the visual through infrared and radar. All of these means of detecting possible threats have undergone remarkable advances in recent years. It is now possible to "see" targets in virtual darkness, thanks to image intensification techniques, and infrared imaging systems have a resolution and sensitivity far beyond the expectations of a couple of decades ago. As for radar, the use of various frequency agile techniques, of new coherent sources, synthetic apertures, electronically steerable beams, and new types of modulation have yielded radars capable of a remarkable combination of flexibility of response, range capability, and fine resolution.

In addition, there has been a rapid increase in the resolution and complexity of "pictures" of the surroundings which can be formed, using the so-called ESM techniques, which depend on the electromagnetic radiation emitted by target objects, whether their radar equipments, their radio communications, or indeed other electrical equipment. This could be thought of as a military and terrestrial counterpart of radio astronomy!

Even acoustics was pressed long ago into the military service for image formation, particularly at sea. Here too, improvements in both the physical understanding and the engineering of transducers has brought about revolutionary advances.

Important though all of these advances are, they are however less significant by far at least in their potential, than the breakthrough which has been achieved in the ability to interpret the patterns which the sensors record. It is in the processing of the images by complex computer systems which exhibit the beginnings of intelligence that the past is likely to be most sharply differentiated from the future.

In favorable circumstances, for example, it is possible to discriminate between a target and extreme surrounding clutter, even although the physical effect of this perturbing phenomenon is many thousands of times greater. Moving targets can be distinguished from their background, even when the observing vehicle is itself moving at high speed. Most importantly, the images "seen" by a variety of sensors can be compared in a manner which draws on recollections of similar occurrences in the past. Targets are thus distinguished from nontargets with ever greater certainty by virtue of the wealth of additional intelligence made available through this fusion of multiple observations.

Whether we speak of sensors or of communications, the vital factor which has revolutionized both of them is the almost explosive development of microelectronics over the last three decades, making it possible to put undreamed of computing power into military systems of all kinds, and endowing them with a complexity of response that verges on the intelligent. This is the fact that changes all. It is not so much the improved ability to see, whether by light or radar, but rather the newfound virtuosity in interpretation of what is seen, and it is not the ability to communicate, but the power to adapt, shift channels and propagation paths, code and decode, interpret communications and infer their significance, all without human aid, that constitutes the revolution in military engineering of our time.

Nor is this all that machine intelligence is potentially able to do: there are many other possibilites. Autonomous defense systems, capable of conducting the active defense of limited sectors or military assets for substantial periods without human intervention, are to a limited degree already with us. This technology will become widespread first in the defense of surface ships against missile attack, where the necessary rapidity of response means that human intervention is no longer possible. All of this leads on yet further, in fact to military robotics, which is a fascinating prospect that could easily absorb all the rest of the time at my disposal.

Rationally considered, the battlefield in space or indeed on earth is altogether too difficult and hazardous an environment for human beings to survive in for long. I suppose at some level we have always known it, but now at last it becomes technically possible to contemplate the early prospect that our fighting might be done for us by robots. Guided weapons are already, in a sense, an example of this, but the military applications of robotics are likely to multiply and spread far beyond present practice before very many years have passed. The political, economic, sociological, and perhaps even ethical implications of this new phase of conflict would be a study in themselves.

The revolution in military information technology is driving towards its apotheosis. Only because the technical advances I have described are now a reality has it become possible to speak with any degree of credibility about the Strategic Defense Initiative. Drawing on the arsenal of new technology, SDI uses all of its principal elements (new sensors, new communications, vastly enhanced computer power, and ultimately artificial intelligence) needed to make the whole quasi-autonomous defense system function. The space technology needed for SDI has largely been in place for some considerable time: it is the advance in microelectronics which has finally dropped the starting flag on this awesome development.

The U.S. Administration has, very wisely, worked very hard to cast the whole program into the form of a cooperation between all of the Free World allies. So vast is the project, and particularly so large is the scientific and technical input which will be required in its early stages, that it would be both difficult and unwise for the United States to seek to shoulder this burden alone. Just as the great enterprises of peace, such as the design and launch of new major passenger aircraft, as a matter of economic necessity increasingly become projects for international cooperation, so also must the front-rank programs for defense.

But just as the new microelectronics has made the SDI something more than a mere dream, so also one can be certain that it will radically alter what we please to call "conventional" warfare. This matters profoundly, because a perfect defense against nuclear attack, when at last it is in place, will remove the threat of nuclear retaliation from those who contemplate conventional aggression. President Reagan has spoken of making nuclear weapons "irrelevant": to the extent that this happens the relevance of conventional defense will be all the greater. Indeed, this has even been cited by some as an argument against the future deployment of the Strategic Defense Initiative.

This is not my position. For myself, I take the view that mutually assured destruction is a far from ideal posture, if only because the cost of any failure would be so unacceptably high—and surely it is hardly possible to guarantee that no failure could ever occur. It seems to me, therefore, that SDI is both a necessary and a desirable development, if only in the interest of the long-term survival of the human race. Enhanced risk of conventional war may be an inevitable consequence, but history teaches that all advances in military technology bring their consequent new problems, and the need to achieve an alternative deterrence for conventional attack I see as in that category, and not a particularly alarming burden, or even a radically new one.

After all, let us speak plainly. The nuclear stalemate only deters certain categories of conventional war, in which the armies of the major powers take the field in formal battle array. It does not deter the peripheral wars, such as Korea, Vietnam, and Afghanistan. Nor has it in any way impeded the development of the bloody and terrible war which we in the West are fighting this very minute, whether or not we realize it. Ranged against us in mortal conflict right now are not one but several of the Islamic states, together with a number of Middle Eastern nongovernmental groups, and their mode of attack is through guerrilla actions of a particular type which we choose to call terrorism.

It is, to be sure, a curious type of conflict, a war counterfeiting peace, so that we retain economic and in some cases even formal diplomatic links with those who, nonetheless, make their clandestine attacks upon us. All of this is only made possible by the very technological revolution in military energy sources, the new explosives and compact hard-hitting weapons, which transformed more regular forms of war in the first half of this century.

To counter it we have called in aid the military information technologies. New means of detection and sensing, improved communications, not least by satellite, and increasingly machine intelligence are our leading counter terrorist weapons now. Thus the very techniques, the very silicon chips, if you will, that make the President's Strategic Defense Initiative feasible are also those with which we seek to build our defenses in warfare at its lowest level. Such is the universality of the new microelectronics, the new military information technology. "Conventional" war of the SDI future might, I suspect, have much in common with counterterrorism.

After all, let us consider its likely shape. The new "smart" electronic sensors will detect very easily anything large or at a temperature elevated above its surrounding, will identify and target anything that moves, and will effectively direct against these things homing weapons of unparalled (because of the accuracy of their guidance) hitting power which will guarantee a hit every time. Modern explosives will do the rest.

I see, therefore, a war in which the conventional platforms (with the sole exception for the present of the submarine) will be extremely vulnerable, and will therefore have to move very fast, or be very heavily defended, or both. This makes them extremely costly (as we are already becoming painfully aware), so while they will be important they will also be few. What we are left with is essentially an infantry war: the soldier on his own or in a small group, using concealment and deception to make his own way across country in order to strike at vital targets, then withdrawing to friendly territory. The parallel with terrorist warfare is uncomfortably close, and it may well be that we are already fighting the wars of the future today, without realizing it.

What moral do I draw? Only that in the age of SDI we will need, and desperately need, a new "conventional" military technology in order to defend ourselves against the threats that will then confront us. The ability will be essential to fight peripheral actions, such as the one thrust upon the United Kingdom in the South Atlantic a few years ago, and also the guerrilla and terrorist wars in which we are already engaged, and which are likely to grow in scale.

But shall we be adequately prepared? For example, the United States action, made at the request of certain members of the Caribbean community, to liberate Grenada was on the whole an admirably successful exercise, because the technical means required for its effective discharge were available. By contrast, in the recent strike against Libya, the United States armed forces were obliged to achieve what they could despite the fact that their technical resources were not ideally matched to the task confronting them.

The defensive technology for both subsidiary theater and guerrilla forms of engagement has much in common with that for SDI: the new military information technology is at its heart. The basic and strategic research needed for SDI may therefore be close enough to the needs of "conventional" defense for there to be no initial competition for resources, but in the longer run, and when the decision to develop operational equipment is taken, should resources then become stretched, the temptation to neglect "conventional" defensive military technology must at all costs be resisted.

Above all, the international cooperation which we are so laboriously striving to put into place in two quite separate initiatives to support SDI on the one hand, and the struggle against international terrorism on the other, ought to be seen as two facets of the same task.

If we will SDI we must also will the means of conventional defense which complement it, the need for which is with us here and now. The Strategic Defense Initiative is a great opportunity for international cooperation in the West. But let us also ensure that it is the beginning of a new level of cooperation in all the areas of threat which menace the free world, and not only in one of them, however important.

SUMMARY

We presently live under a nuclear stalemate, which preserves peace by the threat of universal disaster. Does SDI offer a way out of this situation? Each epoch uses the technology at its disposal to solve pressing military problems, but this creates new problems in turn. In our age electronics and information technology play the central role, and on them SDI depends. The implications of the use of information technology in war have been considered, and likely "next generation" military problems to which it will give rise are reviewed. With an effective SDI the risk of major nonnuclear wars could return, however they would be quite different in character from wars of the past, as would the defensive capability needed to deter them. The SDI program challenges the West to act in a concerted manner. If international cooperation can also be carried over into the approach to "conventional" defense of the next generation, technical problems should not prove intractable.

DISCUSSION OF THE PAPER

R. GARWIN (*IBM Thomas J. Watson Research Center, Yorktown Heights, N.Y.*): It seems to me that you have it backwards. I would have absolutely no objection, in fact be a strong supporter of a program of this magnitude as a conventional defense initiative because we could use that now. We could do it incrementally. We would not delude ourselves as it seems to have deluded you that we will avoid the position of mutual threat because the SDI doesn't promise to have us escape that condition. What it promises is to eliminate the benefit from a military attack and it defines the attack on cities as non-military and does not propose to defend.

So we will continue to be in this business of mutual assured destruction. We will have wasted ten years. We will have put our heads in the sand and as Dr. Wheelon I think so frankly said yesterday about the monoply grant to NASA, it would be a policy of national tragedy for the nation. Unless we look at whether we should do an SDI, which has not been looked at, we will be in the same condition.

Why not do it now, conventional defense. I mean, why be in the position of St. Augustine who asked the good Lord to make me chaste, but, not just yet?

SIR JAMES (*The Plessey Company, London, England*): The only serious point in that particular context I was trying to make was that if the SDI program is to proceed by political initiative, then, it would be folly indeed not to consider trying to meet the initial demands, particularly the technological and research demands for the SDI program with what might already be happening and what might happen after SDI.

What I didn't try to address, I think, was should you do SDI per se. I made the assumption that SDI was a political initiative. Therefore, how can you better utilize that technology? Secondly, what technologies will be needed in order to counter what happens after SDI?

C. SCHMID (*ASA Congressional Fellow*): I share your opinions about science and technology, but also I would like to bring your military history up-to-date in that we are really in this first strike mode right now, whether it is real or perceived, so we really have to think about first strike and we have to think about errors in technology and what they might lead to, and having an SDI system we have to worry about false alarms and short times like we are talking about our timeless responses. We are talking about short times, minutes, to make up our minds and what might happen should the Soviets perceive that we are in the first strike mode, that is, all of a sudden we make the decision to shoot one of these various technologies we are talking about. That's perceived as the beginning of the first strike, and then all of a sudden the Soviets launch into the MAD situation. What do you think about first srike and SDI in the role of not MAD, but in first strike?

SIR JAMES: I think you are in that situation now. I don't actually see that SDI per se alters that. My personal view is that the problem with SDI is not what happens when you have it in place. It is not what happens when you have, if you can achieve it, 100% cover. It is what happens when you have 50% or 60% cover and while you are putting that in place. That is why I said there is this very dangerous time. There is this very dangerous place when you make the transition to having any SDI capabilities in space. That I believe to be the time of greatest danger. It is also why I believe that when you come out of the research and development phase that we are presently in and you start to move towards what inevitably will be a testing phase, and I don't know whether you touched upon this yesterday, the possiblity of how you test, the fear of how you test without causing anything that moves towards first strike is going to be a very, very interesting diplomatic task indeed. I wouldn't like to have to handle it.

V. Wolk (*Private Consultant*): Sir James, since you brought up Clausewitz my question may apply more to the afternoon than now. Therefore, if you wish to defer to the afternoon I will understand. Clausewitz said the objective of war is to impose one country's will upon the other. Now, we can understand how this is happening in the peripheral wars that you have mentioned, but what would be the objective of a war between the United States and Russia? What do we want that they've got? What do they have that we want?

Sir James: I will try and answer it for you, albeit imperfectly I suspect. My own view, is that we have arrived at a situation where the ideology has become irrelevant. We are not talking about imposition, I certainly believe in the case of the Soviets. They are talking about the very peripheral imposition of ideology. They have long ago given up the sort of world domination of the Communist ideology.

So we come then to what our friend was asking about, which is what is liable to cause first strike. You actually are in a precipitation argument. You can actually hypothesize the situation where something like Chernobyl can cause a series of consequences that are likely to cause such strike. I can easily get my head around to that situation, and therefore the attraction of SDI it seems to me has always been if it can be made to work and if it can be made to work at a high enough statistical probability rate it can be worthwhile.

That attraction is the one I think the President seized on. It removes, if you can do it, the situation that mere chance can influence that sort of nuclear conflict and not decision at all and not imposition and not the desire to impose your will.

G. Yonas (*Strategic Defense Initiative Organization, Washington, D.C.*): My question is speaking to your past experience as a military historian. Many people tell me that there is ample evidence that offense has always been able to overcome any conceivable defense. Do you see any historical perspectives that would indicate that there is a basis for a different point of view, one for instance that says there is going to be an ebb and flow between offense and defense and that it's only normal for some period of time to have defense be superior?

Sir James: I think of a historical example easily. I think I am right in saying that Château Gaillard in Normandy was never broached as a castle. It sits there today as an enormous ruin, the society that built it having decayed and passed away. I find that a much more worrying consequence than the thought that the SDI can be psychologically aversive.

H. G. STEVER (*National Academy of Engineering, Washington, D.C.*): I am surprised you didn't speak of the Battle of Britain.

H. FRIEDMAN (*University of Connecticut, Waterbury, Conn*): You said history seems to suggest that those people who oppose a particular strategy are in the wrong and those people who are for an innovative strategy generally are correct, yet at the same time you said that what we have now is unparalleled developments, communication, direction of combat, and the rest. If we have now what we might say is a unique situation, how can you justify on the basis of past experience?

SIR JAMES: I think what I said was that those who claimed that a particular initiative was impossible because of the technological achievement required have generally been proven to be wrong historically rather than those who said it could be done, and therefore, I just don't see any lack of continuity in that argument. All I am saying is don't believe, or it is risky to believe, that a particular defensive posture cannot be achieved because you believe that the technology is too difficult. That's the only fundamental.

C. TOWNES (*University of California at Berkeley, Berkeley, California*): Well, I am quite convinced about the power of technology and I see a number of virtues in the SDI program. Nevertheless, I would like to pose this problem. With respect to realization of a breakthrough or overcoming a technical problem there are after all two technical problems involved. One is to overcome the offense and the other is for the offense to succeed.

So one has really a contest between technological developments on the two sides and it seems to me that's what makes this quite different from solving some arbitrary and very difficult technical problem. It is rather a contest, not solving a problem of nature.

I wonder if you would like to comment. Isn't that really rather different from the kinds of breakthroughs that we have previously experienced?

SIR JAMES: I don't see it as different. I see it as more difficult because I would have thought that the combination of different types of defenses from different types of offenses is something that has always gone on and we can all think of an enormous number of examples.

Where I would agree is that if you are going to try and conduct that in the sort of environment in which we are describing conducting it, then the problem is infinitely more complicated, and again I come back to what I said earlier. I think if SDI is willed politically and if SDI commences technically, then I suspect the thing that will stop it actually being implemented will be that a political realization comes about that says you cannot fit those two things together, you cannot fit the time over which you can put the defense in place against the time that has already been consumed in order to put the offense in place.

My personal view is that if SDI doesn't occur that's what will stop it happening. It wil be the political realization that you cannot make it work in time frame.

N. LONG (*University of Missouri*): I wonder if you could put on the hat of the leader of the "red team" and suppose you are in a company employed by the Soviet Union and you are a very optimistic believer in technological potential, why you would regard the technological problems of overcoming SDI as insuperable in the sense that you don't regard SDI itself as presenting insuperable problems? You took the position that anybody who bets against the possibility of technology developing in a particluar way was historically proven wrong except perhaps squaring the circle.

On the other hand, if you put on the hat of the red team and you look at this as a technological problem of overcoming SDI and you were to take in reverse the position that you said about the impossibility, then if your company were employed by the Soviet Union I assume that you would be thinking about ways to deal with Dr. Yonas's capacity and presumably if technology provides no limits you will find out how to deal with SDI.

Sir James: Again, the answer to that is the time frame argument because in large part he starts with one singular advantage. He starts with a system that is in place and is now going and will need to be adapted to cope with SDI. What he probably won't do is scrap what he has, although I can think of a couple of ways for that argument to be a trifle flawed. In the main he will adapt. What we are talking about here is not a single leap. Again, it is more of a continuum, but to take your point it is a very significant jump in order to prevent that. How he gets beyond it is going to be another very significant jump once it is up there, and therefore, what we are talking about is how much preservation can you achieve.

What would be extremely dangerous to believe is that if you put SDI in place and you have some very, very cast iron probabilities of success attached to it it would be extremely difficult and extremely dangerous to believe that in twenty years time it would still be in place and it would still give you the probabilities of success. That's one of the greatest weaknesses of SDI, that having made the investment and getting it up there that you can believe that we can now forget about that because you cannot. All you can do is say that you have achieved as much as you can if you take a photograph at this point in time.

U.S.-Soviet Relations: Out of Sync?

MARSHALL D. SHULMAN

In the course of preparing myself for this morning I found myself surprised by the conclusion to which I came and I advance it to you as a provocative notion. Perhaps it will stir discussion.

I am going to broaden the assignment. The title of this session is "Perceptions of Soviet Policy," but I am going to put it in the context related to the general theme of the conference, which is "The High Technologies and Reducing the Risk of War."

The thrust of what I propose to say is that we are in what seems to me a new period both for the Soviets and the U.S-Soviet relationship, and we in all probability have passed the point at which those who have sought to reduce the risk of war through arms control negotiations between the two countries can any longer expect that to be a productive way to approach the problem. That time may have passed if it hasn't already passed.

Whatever effort we may make in the future to try to reduce the risk of war will need to address itself to a different agenda than what it has been in the past.

You may remember in the old animated cartoons the figure who is running and he runs off the edge of a cliff and he keeps running and it is not until he looks down that he realizes the ground is not any longer underneath him, and then he falls. I think that is the situation that we are in. We are still running. We don't realize that the ground is no longer beneath our feet.

There are many reasons for this development, it seems to me. The main reason is that the two countries are so out of synchronization with each other. This is a period in which I believe the Soviet Union has come to a point of greater readiness for serious arms control negotiations than at any point in the past, whereas the U.S. political system has passed beyond whatever readiness it may have had for such arrangements.

This appears to hold for the foreseeable future. I see no signs that this is likely to change while in the meantime the technical characteristics of weapon systems, including the Strategic Defense Initiative (SDI), are passing beyond the point at which any regimen for the rational management of nuclear weapons is likely to be feasible. It will certainly be even more difficult than what we had to deal with in the past and it may pass beyond the point of feasibility.

I am going to deal with this in three parts. First I am going to deal with the Soviet side of the equation, secondly with the U.S. side, and then I will

---

Marshall D. Shulman is Director of the W. Averell Harriman Institute for Advanced Study of the Soviet Union, Columbia University, New York, New York 10027.

talk about the direction in which events seem to be moving as a result of the interaction between the two.

On the Soviet side of the equation it seems apparent that the Soviet Union is entering what may turn out to be a new historical stage in its development. It is quite obvious that the new and more vigorous leadership in the Soviet Union is at least making an effort, a very serious effort, to address the fundamental problems in its economy as a main priority, that the first stage of its efforts as were outlined in the new party program in the twelfth five-year plan presented at the 27th Party Congress is to address in the first instance the problem of work discipline: alcoholism, absenteeism, and corruption. Then what seems to be on the agenda for possible follow-up would be somewhat more fundamental efforts to overcome the dysfunctional effects of the present system as it is now constituted that work against innovation and initiative in the system.

It seems clear to me also that on the basis of the information that is available to us we can only give an agnostic answer to the question of whether the Soviet leader, Mikhail S. Gorbachev, will be able to achieve anything like the very ambitious goals he set out for himself in whole, in part, or perhaps not at all, and we simply do not know how formidable are the problems that he faces in overcoming the bureaucratism, the lethargy in the system, as well as the potential political opposition from those who seek to preserve their perquisites and express what is basically the impulse of a very conservative society.

The logic of this priority of trying to modernize the industrial economy is that by its inexorable logic it leads the Soviet Union, against its inclinations, to seek a stabilization with the U.S. and if possible a reduction in the military competition in order to avoid having to increase still further the flow into the military sector of resources that are most needed for the modernization of its industrial economy.

This is not just a question of the aggregates of the total flow of rubles into the military sector but a qualitative problem as well. That is, it is very clear that the electronics, the computers, the alloys, the scientists, the labs, the skilled labor, everything that is needed in order to keep pace with the United States in the new weapons systems and those that may be required in response to the new systems are also the same advanced technology items that they most desperately need to apply to the industrial sector in order to modernize their economy, which has been the recurrent theme in everything that Gorbachev has been saying.

This has been reflected in the unaccustomed flow of new arms control initiatives that have come from the Soviets beginning about eight weeks before the summit and continuing through the statements of the leadership on 15 January 1986.

Normally, as you know, the Soviets have been reactive. They have tended to wait until the U.S. makes a proposal and then they react to it, usually negatively. Now for the first time they have been showing an extraordinary number of initiatives in this field.

It is quite clear that Gorbachev may have made a mistake in addressing these, in the first instance, in a public way which, of course, encouraged a response from the West that this was primarily intended for propaganda purposes. I think this was a mistake on his part. It seems the reason why they did it in this way was that they felt from observing the United States that they were in fact engaged in a public relations contest with the United States and it was part of the game that was then going on. Secondly, they felt that if it only produced a negative response from the United States they would gain whatever advantage there might be in bringing to bear world public pressure on the U.S. to move in these matters. Regardless of the way the proposals were initially advanced, they reflected a serious intent which was bolstered by the logic of their situation, which I discussed earlier.

It was also clear that what the Soviet leadership was seeking to do was to address itself to what it understood had been the previous U.S. objections to the Soviet positions at earlier stages. Thus came the offer to reduce offensive missiles substantially to make possible a deterrent balance at lower levels.

There also came an offer to reduce the Soviet heavy missiles, which they understood had been the major U.S. concern. Then came an offer to meet the U.S. objections regarding verification, including the willingness to go in the direction of on-site inspections, the full measure of which remains to be tested. There came the offer to meet the U.S. position on the theater nuclear forces by accepting the U.S. zero-zero position, by detaching these negotiations from dependence on the prior resolution of the SDI issue. There came the offer to break through the deadlock on the Vienna and MBFR negotiations on conventional weapons in Europe by proposing asymmetrical reductions of a somewhat greater order than had been proposed earlier with verification of withdrawals, and there was also the effort to expand the discussions in Stockholm of confidence-building measures that had been going on.

It also seems interesting, but I advance this somewhat more tentatively, that there were a number of what I would call "tender shoots," that is, little buds appearing above the ground that may or may not be significant, but nevertheless are worth our attention whether these come to flower or not. There has been in Soviet writings, discussions, and speeches a somewhat greater attention to the factor of stability than in previous periods. Not altogether a new theme, it has had a somewhat new and interesting emphasis.

There has been a recognition in the Soviet utterances, including the speeches of Gorbachev, of the importance of mutual security. It has always been said that the conception of Soviet security that they have is that everyone else should be insecure. They sought to meet this argument by indicating that they now understood that they could not be secure if the United States felt insecure, and this approach to mutuality in security was at least a step towards the recognition of the arguments that had been made against them in the past.

In a related point, there has been a greater degree of recognition of the Soviet involvement in the world economy. The language in which this is expressed is that of international economic interdependence, which simply recognizes as a fact of life that when the U.S. is in trouble internationally and economically, whether in the monetary system in 1974 with the oil crisis or in subsequent developments, whatever tendency they might have had in the past to rub their hands in glee and say "good, the worse the better" is no longer appropriate because they themselves are so deeply involved in the world economy that these crises affect them adversely. This shows a formal recognition of that reality.

I think it would be premature to say that these represent a start towards accepting the arguments that have been made by us to them for many years or that these are going to be the ascendant line of thought. That is why I call them "tender shoots." At this point I think that's all they are, but they are interesting.

Bear in mind that in the past what we have seen is that ideas, especially about political strategy, have had a long germination time. The negotiations that took place in 1972 that led to the signing of SALT I date back at least to 1955 and the first groping efforts that Khrushchev laid out against opposition and against cross-cutting developments for almost twenty years. It is therefore characteristic of the process that ideas do emerge. Some survive and some do not, depending upon external events and internal policies.

Relations with the United States now present a dilemma for the Soviet Union, and the most interesting thing to me was the tactic that Gorbachev chose after a summit. Had he been working in a way that was characteristic of earlier Soviet leaderships he might have come out of the meeting and shown a little muscle and said the United States isn't interested because there simply was no progress on what was the main issue, the effort to control nuclear weapons. Instead, what he said in essence was "We have begun civil dialogue and that's good. We've had some good talks. It is true we didn't make progress on the most important thing, arms control, but we started a process and we hope it will continue."

It was, as I said, an uncharacteristic Soviet response. It is clear why he chose that tactic, but the problem is since that time he and the other Soviet leaders and their analysts have been puzzled and surprised by the lack of effectiveness of what they had thought were efforts to meet the U.S. positions, and this was complicated by their uncertainty about how to interpret the series of actions that have taken place since the summit. The Soviet interpretation saw a provocative pattern in a series of actions that included the warships probing in the Black Sea, the warships in the Gulf of Sidra, the charges in our Nicaraguan debate of Soviet efforts to take over Latin America, the demands for the reduction in the Soviet United Nations personnel, the response to the Soviet offer of a moratorium on nuclear testing by continuation of U.S. nuclear testing, the discussion of the sending of Stingers, the shoulder-held antiaircraft weapons to Savimbi in Angola and to the Afghan insurgents, and finally, the U.S. attack on Libya and the nonresponse of the United States to Gorbachev's offer in his speech on international cooperation on terrorism.

As I said, the Soviets are uncertain about whether this is a deliberate effort to signal a more forward U.S. policy or represents a somewhat random pattern, but there are clear signs of debate in the Soviet Union about this. There may be opposition, although I don't think we know enough to say that it is organized opposition, but nevertheless Gorbachev has held to a muted response through all of this. On the Soviet scale the decibel rating has been very low in their response to these events, when it might under other circumstances have been at a much higher decibel rating than it was.

Gorbachev is still clinging to the idea of the importance of a civil dialogue and continuation of a process of contact to hold tensions within moderate range, although with evidently diminishing expectations of productive negotiations.

Probably the reason he is doing that is that the Soviets recognize through their greater depth of understanding of Western policies that a muscular militant response, which would have been characteristic of earlier periods, would be dysfunctional, that it would have the effect of strengthening the right wing in American politics. Whatever tendency there might be in this country to reduce military expenditures for budgetary reasons would be lessened in the face of evidence of further Soviet militancy.

Whether he will be able to continue to hold to this position is uncertain.

On the U.S. side of the equation, briefly, it is apparent that the U.S. is experiencing a conservative swing of domestic politics and a resurgence of nationalism in its foreign policy, in part as a reaction to our experience in earlier periods (and part of that experience was Soviet behavior in earlier periods). This has had a cumulative effect and a residual impact on American popular feelings and on the actions of the government.

The dominant view in the government as it appears to the Russians is to carry forward only some symbolic and marginal elements in the U.S.-Soviet relationship so as to keep going with the summit meetings, despite some right-wing opposition. To some extent these are felt to be of value in domestic politics, and perhaps, of some value in influencing European public opinion.

Examples of these marginal elements are the consulates, the Aeroflot and Pan American flights, the cultural exhibitions, and the museum exhibits, exchanges which are called the President's Initiative and which are explained domestically here as one of the steps in undermining the Soviet system. In this category we can also include the possiblity of some marginal small steps in arms control: possibly some of the confidence-building measures, perhaps bits and pieces of the mutual balanced force reduction, the upgrading of the hot line, the discussion of the crisis centers that Richard Perle is now negotiating with the Russians, and the discussion of regional questions at the assistant secretary level. But the dominant view is not basically hospitable to substantial arms control beyond these marginal elements.

The dominant position regards some arms control as not in the U.S. interest. It regards the U.S. security as better advanced by trying to regain or to gain superiority in significant ways. The SDI is clearly going to be budgeted at a substantial level, although lower than what the Administration has requested. At any rate, it is approaching a period of development and testing. It is not just a matter of research. It has generated a very large and important interest group in the American economy and in American society.

There does not appear to be any politically effective constituency in the U.S. at the present time or foreseeable future that opposes this view or other views dominant in the Administration such as the holding down of trade (except for grain, which has its own motivations) and the need to apply pressure to seek a contraction of Soviet positions in Afghanistan, Angola, Ethiopia, Vietnam, Kampuchea, Central America, and Cuba, but especially in Eastern Europe.

The expectation is that the effect of these pressures will be perhaps to bring about a roll-back, perhaps concessions, perhaps changes in the system.

Now to the last point: the direction in which the events are moving as a consequence of the interaction between these two positions. As for the military dimension, it seems to me that one can have very little expectation that there is any prospect for substantial arms control in the foreseeable future, but that does not mean that the level of military competition will go through the roof. Obviously it is constrained by important limits on both sides: by resource limitations on the Soviet side, by budgetary constraints on our side, and perhaps there may be some movement towards flattening of the curves of military expenditures.

Nevertheless, there are new systems in both countries that are already funded and being developed (and oddly enough there is a fair degree of congruency between the kinds of systems that are now coming out of the pipeline on the Soviet side and the American side, which hasn't usually been the case in the past): new intercontinental bombers, new submarines, new intercontinental missiles, and new cruise missiles, as well as a new phase of the military competition on the U.S. side, the Strategic Defense Initiative.

Meanwhile it is quite evident that as a consequence of these systems there will be less stability, less verifiability, and a new phase of military competition in space.

As to the level of tension it is clear that this is likely to be in the middle to upper range subject to external perturbations, that is, external events in the Third World which by their nature have a high degree of unpredictability. We can see fairly obvious candidates for trouble (the Persian Gulf, Iran). Others may just take us by surprise by leaping out of nowhere into tomorrow morning's headlines and may present us with situations where there is a direct conflict of interest. Despite the caution on both sides against getting involved with each other there is always the risk of a lack of control in such local conflicts.

In the Third World competition generally, there are indications of a reduced commitment on the Soviet side to active prosecution of targets of opportunity, for they have learned from their experience in the seventies that it doesn't pay (as other empires have learned before them), and also that contrary to their expectations they could compartmentalize their efforts to pick up pieces of change from the Third World without impairing their relations with the U.S. They now understand that isn't so and that if they seek to improve their relations with us they cannot pursue these targets of opportunity. In any case their economic constraints make it less interesting, but there is a question of whether that will continue if it is challenged. One of the test cases will be in Afghanistan, which is currently under negotiation.

The background of all of this is that because of the resurgence of nationalism not only in this country but in every major industrial society in the world today (which has occurred for a variety of reasons that reflect to some extent local particularities), there has been and there is likely to continue to be a weakening of the international system and its codification of constraints on behavior of nations in the world.

There are likely to be strains in both alliances, NATO and the Warsaw Pact, despite the harmony of the Tokyo pronouncements. There are also likely to be domestic effects in both countries. Within the Soviet Union, the effect of mobilization under circumstances in which the military competition increases and impairs their primary effort to improve the economy is likely to mean a higher rather than a lower degree of repressiveness and control in the society, a movement in the direction which we would prefer not to see.

In this country, obviously, it means a continued military emphasis, a warping of societal needs, probably a weakening of scientific research in its direct bearing on the current nature of the competition in industrial technology, which has some relation to the last part of the earlier panel discussion.

All this means that we are going to have to think somewhat differently than we have in the past about conditions to maximize security and reduce the risk of war.

We cannot expect to proceed in the traditional ways we have been talking about for forty years now about the kinds of agreements that may be possible. It may depend upon the rationality of unilateral decision-making on each side under conditions of a dynamic deterrent balance, regulated not by formal agreements but by domestic constraints and by the further development of tacit practices between the two countries.

This may have some bearing on what we do in this country within our own study groups and what we say to the Russians in this period. Particularly, in the agenda for our own study, it seems to me it ought to concentrate more on the degree of rationality of the decision-making process with regard to defense policy. It clearly seems to be not a very rational policy and not well designed for a rational consideration of overarching national interest in regard to defense policy.

In regard to what we discuss with the Russians we now have a number of groups, governmental and nongovernmental, that seem on the whole not to be very effective. At the government level it is clear that there needs to be some form of responsible communication between competent people who can go through an exploratory phase in a knowledgeable way and then, perhaps, influence their governments accordingly. That does not exist.

Among the many nongovernmental channels we have, for the most part there has been a degradation in the quality, the knowledgeability, and the responsibility of the participants in dealing with the Russians. However friendly may be the atmosphere in those discussions, they are not really competent, for the most part, to perform that exploratory function.

There are matters that can be usefully discussed with the Soviets: the question of stability, the interaction of their strategies dealing with theater warfare and ours, the interaction of the tendencies both countries have had to move toward an offensive theater strategy.

We must seek a greater degree of balance and stability in the military competition by a better understanding of the way in which their decisions and ours interact, in the hope this will lead to more rational and enlightened decisions on both sides.

At the very least, by not preserving the illusion that we are moving towards formal agreements we at least remove the rationale for bargaining chips as a way of justifying additional military programs in the name of arms control negotiations, however speciously applied.

DISCUSSION OF THE PAPER

A. GLICKSMAN (*United Nations Association, Arlington, Va.*): What I would like to question you about is your preliminary statement concerning what Mr. Gorbachev is up to. It is very clear that Mr. Gorbachev sees what he needs to do is to make the Soviet Union enter the third technological revolution, the third industrial revolution in technology, but at the same time it also seems to me he is a man of the system. I think it was Seweryn Bialer who described him as a technocrat. He is a man who is committed to the system. What he wants to do is streamline it. He doesn't want to change it. He is not a radical or revolutionary. He is a product of the Soviet system.

The thing about this revolution that we are seeing is that it is very different from any of the revolutions in industry before. It is information based. It is a revolution in which the free flow of information determines the pace and the expertise of the acquisition. Is Mr. Gorbachev going to make those radical changes required?

M. D. SHULMAN (*Harriman Institute, New York, N.Y.*): Seweryn Bialer is my valued colleague, but we differ on this point. The question is whether or not Gorbachev is going to be able to go beyond the rather limited effort to change work discipline, but will stop short of addressing the fundamental characteristics of the system that are needed in order to raise the levels of innovation and productivity and so on.

Now we don't really have the evidence for this to be able to say yea or nay to that proposition. What we do have have been extraordinary discussions of the structural problems in the Soviet economy coming out of the comments of Novosibirsk and elsewhere. The proceedings over the past year in their professional journal are really breathtaking in the radicalness with which they address these fundamental problems in the economy and they are formidable and it is interesting to me that Gorbachev has brought Agabenyan, the head of that institute, the publisher of that journal, to Moscow to an important place in the party.

He is a shrewd politician. He would be out of his mind if he would announce that that is what he is going to do now because he would make the same mistake that Khrushchev made, which is to get all of the organized elements of bureaucracy mobilized against him. He has begun very cautiously. He has begun by efforts to address things that are relatively more manageable and that will within the space of a year or a year and a half, if he is lucky, begin to have some palpable effects on the consumers, which then will create the political base with which he may, if he chooses to do so, address more fundamental reforms that will challenge the privileged positions of important bureaucracies.

The answer to that seems to be not yet apparent to him.

M. MAGE: I would like to ask Dr. Shulman and also Dr. May: In view of your very pessimistic assessment of the chances for arms control, do you think there are any conceivable circumstances under which the United States atom bomb community would be willing to go along with a complete test ban treaty?

M. D. SHULMAN: Well, my subject and my competence, such as it is, has to do with the Soviet Union. With regard to American politics each of you in the room is as well qualified as I am to speculate about that.

My answer would be, however, that I do not see presently any signs of a politically effective constituency that would support a movement in that direction.

The Contradictions of SDI

DAVID AARON

Professor Shulman has given some perspectives on the current scene in Moscow. I will try to illuminate something even more enigmatic than the Kremlin: the contradictory perceptions of the strategic defense planners and policymakers in Washington.

General Abrahamson recently reiterated that the purpose of the Strategic Defense Initiative (SDI) is to affect the behavior of the Soviet Union. Taking that as a starting point, I would like to examine the judgements and assumptions about the USSR that underlie planning for our strategic defense program.

First, what developments in the Soviet threat are seen as requiring strategic defenses?

Second, what assumptions must be made about Soviet behavior and capabilities to realize other objectives claimed for SDI, including the President's vision of making nuclear weapons obsolete?

Finally, given the strategic and human realities on both sides, what is the most promising application of "Star Wars" technologies to the subject of this conference, reducing the risk of nuclear war?

The first question may appear simple but is the most complex. U.S. defense programs are designed, theoretically at least, to respond to a military requirement, which is usually stated in terms of a threat by the USSR, present or projected. The Strategic Defense Initiative is no exception.

Soviet doctrine, strategic force deployments, and research programs have all been cited by government officials as justification for strategic defenses. What have these changes really been, however, and is SDI the proper response to them?

In the Pentagon's publication *Soviet Military Power*, the statement is made that "in a nuclear war, Soviet strategy would be to destroy enemy nuclear forces before launch or in flight to their targets." The report goes on to point out that the USSR has "developed extensive plans either to preempt a nuclear attack or launch a first strike."[1]

The publication also enumerates the impressive array of Soviet hardware being developed and deployed to support such a warfighting strategy—in particular hard target ICBMs that could destroy Minuteman and MX-Peacekeeper missile silos, antisatellite weapons, hardened C-3 facilities, reload missiles, and other paraphernalia of protracted nuclear war.

This most recent authoritative Adminsitration document claims that "Soviet leaders since the 1960s have followed a relentless and consistent policy

---

David Aaron was Deputy National Security Advisor (1977–81). His present affiliation is: D. L. Aaron & Co. Inc., Westport, Connecticut 06880.

for the development of forces for nuclear attack . . . they believe nuclear war could be fought and can be won at levels below general nuclear war."[1] Their "grand strategy" is to exploit "the coercive leverage inherent in superior forces, to instill fear, to erode the West's collective security arrangments, and to support subversion."[1]

"Thus, " it concludes, "the primary role of Soviet military power is to provide the underpinning for the step by step extension of Soviet influence and control."[1]

Describing the need for SDI in this context, arms-control negotiator Paul Nitze last March expressed the Administration's "disappointment in the deterioration of the strategic balance," pointing particularly to the deployment of large numbers of MIRVed ICBMs which, he said, are "posing a real threat to the survivability of the entire land based portion of U.S. retalitory forces."

Mr. Nitze explained that "our work on SDI is, in large part, a reaction to the unabated growth of this threat," and he expressed the "hope that new defensive technologies can mitigate [such] adverse developments in the area of strategic offensive weaponry."

In short, the USSR is perceived as a relentlessly expansionist power, building first-strike nuclear forces to coerce and intimidate the West and others. Soviet warfighting strategy and offensive nuclear forces threaten the stability of any deterrence based on devastating retaliation alone. SDI is a response to this threat, promising a safer and more reliable means of assuring deterrence.

The question is whether these perceptions of the Reagan Administration are supported by the facts and the hoped-for capabilities of the SDI.

For many years, Soviet strategy clearly did conform to these perceptions. Nuclear war was considered inevitable and winnable. What the Soviets call their military technical strategy, their operational doctrine, emphasized preemptive nuclear attacks by Soviet forces at the outset of any major hostilities.

However, in contrast to the Administration's view, most experts on Soviet doctrine and strategy believe that the declaratory policy and operational planning of the Soviet Union has evolved away from such "warfighting" concepts.[2]

The process started in the early 1960s, and by the early 1970s top Soviet political and military leaders stopped calling for military superiority and began calling for parity and equality, especially in the context of SALT negotiations. They also stopped saying nuclear war would be a catastrophe only for capitalism and started saying that it would be a "danger for mankind."[3]

In 1977 then Soviet leader Leonid Brezhnev himself outlined a new doctrine in his now famous Tula speech. He said:

> Allegations that the Soviet Union . . . is striving for superiority in arms, with the aim of delivering a 'first strike' are absurd and utterly unfounded . . . Our efforts are aimed at preventing both first and second strikes and at preventing nuclear war altogether . . . The Soviet Union's defense potential must be sufficient to deter . . . [and] not a course aimed at superiority in arms.[4]

Later, on the sixtieth anniversary of the Bolshevik Revolution, he went even further and renounced superiority for any purpose including deterrence.[5]

On the military operational level, Marshal Ogarkov, chief of the Soviet

General Staff, wrote in the most authoritative Soviet military publication in 1979:

> Soviet military strategy, as Soviet military doctrine as a whole, has a deeply defensive orientation, and does not provide for any kind of preemptive strikes or premeditated attacks . . . It does not pursue military-technical superiority . . . but any potential agressor must know that in case of a nuclear missile attack . . . it will receive an annihilating retaliatory strike."[6]

Finally, in 1982 Brezhnev formally stated that the Soviet Union would not be the first to use nuclear weapons. That pledge has since been reiterated by General Secretary Gorbachev.

I go into this at some length not because I believe we can base our security on what Soviet leaders say. I do so because some of the strongest critics of deterrence and détente, who are also ardent supporters of SDI, have always maintained that we must pay attention to what the Soviets say about their strategic plans.

What they have said in recent years does not justify the adoption of a totally new strategy based on defense. What they say does not suggest that the USSR cannot be deterred by the threat of retaliation, and that instead the U.S. must deploy major strategic defenses in order to try to fight and somehow "prevail" in a nuclear war.

To the contrary, Brezhnev's expressed view was "Should a nuclear war start, it could mean the destruction of world civilization, and, perhaps, the end of life itself on earth."[7]

But what of their secret plans? What if this public talk is window dressing or even a deception? Perhaps their real intentions are unchanged from the days of Stalin and Khrushchev. What about the growth in counterforce capabilities pointed to by Mr. Nitze?

There is no doubt that the Soviet Union has deployed major forces capable of attacking our fixed ICBMs and bomber bases. These capabilities are growing. In the next decade all of the USSR's currer t crop of formidable strategic ballistic missiles will be replaced by new even more capable systems now in development or testing.

In my mind there is also little doubt, despite Ogarkov's writings, that the Soviet Union has plans that would enable it to carry out a preemptive nuclear strike on U.S. forces. The question, however, is whether the capabilities envisioned for SDI are the appropriate response to this threat.

It is important to recognize that a dedicated defense of ICBMs is possible and potentially cost-effective. A point defense based on existing technology when combined with a shelter mobile basing system would require the USSR to attack all our shelters while we would only have to defend those hiding our ICBMs. That was the leverage behind the Carter "race track" in the desert, which was killed by President Reagan for political reasons and for which he has never found a satisfactory substitute.

Needless to say that is not what the President is talking about now. In fact, he has said repeatedly that SDI is not intended to protect missiles. The facts bear him out. Insofar as any concept of SDI exists, it is for a layered area defense.

Still the President and General Abrahamson insist that such a system will discourage Soviet first-strike proclivities. Even if it's not perfect, they argue, a space shield will introduce uncertainty into the calculations of any aggressor and thus discourage a first strike.

Cutting through all the possible scenarios, the first strike they are trying to deter is the one in which the Soviets, in a crisis, might attack our ICBMs and bombers yet seek to ward off retaliation by sparing our cities.

This is an interesting perception of both Soviet and U.S. behavior. It has been estimated that 40 million Americans ultimately would die in such a "surgical" nuclear attack. Is there some profound tradition of American restraint that would stay our hand from retribution? Is there some gambler's streak in the Russian character that would count on it? Nikita Khrushchev lost his job for miscalculating an infinitesimally smaller wager in the Cuban missile crisis.

Bear in mind that the President's own Scowcroft Commission has said that no such "window of vulnerability" exists. Even if the USSR attacked first and destroyed much of our ICBM force and many of our bombers, they would still face overwhelming retaliation. The additional uncertainty provided by a trillion-dollar area defense would not add much, if anything, to the effect of that deterrent.

In my view, instead of reducing whatever Soviet inclinations exist for a first strike policy, strategic defenses are likely to encourage them.

This judgement is based on one cardinal strategic fact: The best opportunity to beat a strategic defense is by striking first. This is so for several reasons. Striking first makes it possible to (1) deploy countermeasures to the best advantage, (2) concentrate the attack in the hope of a breakthrough, (3) gain tactical surprise, (4) ensure the maximum scale of the attack and thus exhaust or overwhelm the defense, and (5) coordinate the assault so as to exploit one's strengths and the adversary's weaknesses.

This is a variation of the answer to what is sometimes called Napoleon's dilemma. He would ask candidates for command a simple question: Faced with two hostile forces, one larger and one smaller than your own, and no avenue of retreat, which do you engage first?

The correct answer is that you should attack the larger force. You may gain the advantage of surprise, and with luck, if you succeed, you may frighten away the smaller force. If you attack the smaller force, you are more likely to win, but you will be diminished for your encounter with the larger force and will more surely be beaten.

The only time that a second strike is preferable is when there is a perfect defense or no defense at all. In both cases, of course, a secure second strike capability is required on each side.

To put all of this in less esoteric terms, if the President is right and the Soviets would have to worry about getting a first strike through, they will be even more worried about getting a retaliatory strike through.

In addition to the strategic rationale we have just considered, there are powerful historical reasons to believe that, confronted by the prospect of possible American superiority, the Soviets will return to a reliance on preemption.

The lesson of Hitler's invasion is indelibly etched on the Soviet military consciousness. They believe that lesson is that they should have struck first even though they were weaker. It is a lesson clearly applied in the early days of the nuclear era. When confronted by American nuclear superiority, at a time superiority really meant something, Soviet doctrine stressed preemptive nuclear war.

A more sophisticated version of the President's argument is that the re-emergence of American nuclear superiority as represented by SDI will induce more overall caution in Soviet behavior. There would be fewer crises that might grow into war.

A member of the Joint Chiefs of Staff once conceptualized it for me this way. He said one should think of the strategic balance as a teeter-totter. To be most stable, it has to have equal weight on both sides, right? Wrong: That's too delicate. Much better, he said, is the stability that comes when our side is so heavy we're resting on solid ground and the other guy is up in the air.

Unfortunately, our historical experience during the late 1940s through the 1950s right up until the Cuban missile crisis, when the Soviets were strategically inferior, was not one of tranquility. There were repeated crises, particularly over Berlin, where the USSR used its geographic and military advantages to offset our nuclear strength, and perhaps even to prove that such strength was politically meaningless.

In sum, the idea that SDI is required to offset developments in Soviet strategic doctrine and weapons is contradicted by the logic of nuclear strategy as well as the historical record.

The second question is whether SDI will advance other possible U.S. objectives vis-à-vis the Soviet Union. Some see the program as an opportunity to win or at least to make a major advance in the historical struggle between capitalism and communism. The Strategic Defense Initiative is a way to exploit our technological advantages: spend them into the ground, break their economy, and shatter party control by forcing them into a costly defensive arms race.

The principal problem with this approach is that it is based on wishful thinking. Clearly the Soviet Union would prefer not to spend resources to cope with SDI, but there is little doubt they have the wherewithal to do so. Recent testimony before a joint economic committee by both the CIA and the Defense Intelligence Agency (DIA) makes clear that strategic forces get top priority in the USSR, and that there is no short-term conflict with Gorbachev's efforts to modernize the economy.[8] If there is a "crunch" in the future, the military will still get first call.[9]

The CIA has also testified before Congress that by the early 1990s the USSR could deploy 20,000 strategic missile warheads.[10] A recent Senate Armed Services Committee staff study reports that each time the SDI office defines the Soviet threat it gets worse, and the weapons labs have developed threats "ten times larger and more complex."[11]

There is also the question of who is going to spend whom into the ground. Most analysts believe that it will be cheaper to thwart the defense than build it. This is subject to controversy of course, but the strongest sign that it's true is General Abrahamson's recent efforts to wiggle out from under the injunction that SDI be cost-effective. He wants that criterion changed to "affordable."[12]

I can't help wondering what affordable might mean in an era dominated by the deficit, and the Gramm-Rudman deficit-reduction bill, and the collapse of federal efforts to educate our young, rebuild our infrastructure, restore American competitiveness, protect our environment, and deal with the time bombs of an aging society and a growing permanent underclass.

In sum it would be folly to pursue SDI on the easy assumption that the USSR, for technical or economic reasons, cannot compete.

Indeed, one of the more recent arguments advanced for SDI is that we have to respond to their vigorous ABM program. The Pentagon talks anxiously about how the Soviets have modernized the ABM systems they have deployed around Moscow, and worries that they may be getting ready to deploy it nationwide. The Department of Defense suggests that may be the reason they are violating the ABM treaty with their missile warning radar at Krasnoyarsk.

In the advanced technologies, the Pentagon points to the vigorous Soviet program of research in lasers, particle beams, and directed energy. The Secretary of Defense has even gone so far as to say that they are "years" ahead of us in some areas.

All this has to be kept in perspective. The radar at Krasnoyarsk is a clear violation, but Undersecretary of Defense Fred Ikle has stated that none of the Soviet infringements on the SALT agreements are militarily significant. The new ABM system around Moscow is the technological equivalent of the safeguard system which we abandonded 15 years ago as ineffective.

According to the Pentagon's Defense Advanced Research Projects Agency (DARPA) and the intelligence community, we are equal to or ahead of the USSR in every critical ABM technology. The only sense in which they could be "ahead" of us is that they started before we did. That is analogous to claiming the Portuguese are 300 years ahead of us in developing a global navy.

Nonetheless, the Soviet ABM effort is impressive. It is estimated they spend at least as much as we do on strategic missile defense. They have top scientists and design bureaus working on the problem. While they criticize SDI they refuse to admit the existence of their own efforts.

What this adds up to is a justification for a prudent research program to hedge against Soviet ABM activities. It does not justify pursuing SDI on a crash basis on the contradictory theory that the Soviets are ahead but they will never catch up.

But what of the President's positive vision of a world of secure defenses on both sides, where offensive nuclear forces are reduced to little or nothing? As appealing as this dream may be, it founders on the most obvious contradictions of all.

I am not talking about the problem of sharing our SDI technology with the Soviet Union. The idea that an administration that embargoes Apple computers would transmit our most advanced nuclear and electronic secrets simply lacks credibility. It is also doubtful future administrations would be willing to share this information, because even if SDI never succeeds in defending us against ballistic missiles, the technology will have widespread applications to conventional weaponry.

That issue aside, the world the President envisions requires that this relentless and implacable adversary, the locus of evil in the modern world, will suddenly become more cooperative and congenial than France or Britian, as close to us as Canada.

We would have to negotiate the most profound and sweeping arms control agreements in history, demanding the most intrusive inspection of each side's territory. In implementing his vision, we would have to go through a period where each side would have a devastating first-strike capability against the other.

I should note that it is not just the President's political vision which would require such cooperation. Scientists considering the problem of how, technically, to protect the space-based weapons needed for "boost phase" intercept—the crucial and most vulnerable component for any SDI—have concluded that there must be a U.S.-Soviet agreement not to deploy space mines or other antisatellite systems. One has even gone so far as to conclude that SDI's inherent vulnerabilities could only be overcome if we and the Soviets jointly build and operate it.

This is the deepest contradiction of all. The policies of the USSR are judged so aggressive that ordinary deterrence is no longer viable and must be supplanted by massive strategic defenses. But for this defense to work, politically or militarily, the Soviet Union would have to become the most cooperative enemy in human history.

In my judgement, these contradictory visions of the Soviet Union and SDI suggest that the real impetus for strategic defense lies deeper than our hopes and fears about our principal adversary. I believe that SDI seeks to repeal the realities of the nuclear age. I see it is a nostalgic effort to recapture the freedom of action we once enjoyed. It is an attempt to go back to a future where we can safeguard our security by our own efforts alone.

The most profound truth of the nuclear age is that the world's two great antagonists must cooperate in order to ensure the world's survival. Their security is interdependent. All contrary instincts, dogma, and ideology must bow before this reality. The inevitability of war, the class struggle, and the concept of security through superiority all founder in the vast sea of violence promised by nuclear war.

The Strategic Defense Initiative is a fantasy clutched at by those who chafe under the restraints imposed by this reality. For those who feel the Soviet Union has taken advantage of mutual deterrence to expand its power and influence, it promises a way to strike back.

To others, it is a technological solution to the threat to mankind from nuclear weapons, a fix that does not require facing the painful fact that traditional concepts of state sovereignty and nuclear weapons cannot forever co-exist.

This brings us to the final question: Is there another way that the advanced technologies of SDI *can* contribute to reducing the risk of nuclear war? The answer is yes—by using the political potential of SDI to achieve more meaningful and effective arms control arrangements and concomitant political accommodation.

The Administration boasts that SDI has already brought the Soviets back to the bargaining table. Now it is incumbent on our negotiators to use that leverage, not to legitimize a defensive arms race, but to stop it. At the same time, SDI should provide a powerful incentive both to reduce strategic offensive arms and halt their accelerating sophistication.

Many say that the President will never bargain away SDI, and that may be true. But in approximately two years, the Reagan era in American politics will come to an end. We need to begin now in our national debate to define America's national security strategy for the next century.

Even in the last two remaining years of this Administration it may be possible to reach an interim accord that reinforces the ABM treaty, defines more sharply permissible research, and sets objectives for a permanent agreement. This too may be difficult for the President to accept, but it would preserve some research, which has been the cardinal demand of his Administration.

I want to stress that the burden lies not only on the United States to negotiate in good faith. The Soviet Union bears an even greater responsibility.

First, the Soviets must satisfactorily clear up all of the serious questions concerning compliance with the SALT agreements, in particular the violation of the ABM Treaty represented by the Krasnoyarsk radar.

Second, it is time they got down to business at Geneva. From all reports they have been unwilling to engage in serious dialogue and persist in a definition of "research" that would entirely exempt their own ABM efforts.

Finally, the Soviets must take some concrete action to improve the political atmosphere. Let us not forget that it was the Soviet invasion of Afghanistan that dealt a crippling blow to the arms control process. There is a need for genuine confidence-building steps by the Soviet government, and not just public relations campaigns and peace offensives.

There is nothing in the likely characteristics of strategic defenses or in Soviet history and behavior that inspires confidence that deployment of strategic defenses will do anything but undermine our security and jeopardize nuclear stability. As we have seen, realizing SDI will place an inordinate premium on cooperation and self-restraint far beyond what is required for more modest, realistic, and practical measures to reduce the risk of nuclear war.

Irrespective of our fears, dreams, and differences, the overriding nuclear reality remains. We share a common fate. If we apply the political potential of SDI technology in the light of that truth, we can build a more secure future.

REFERENCES

1. Department of Defense. 1986. Soviet Military Power. p. 22
2. Garthoff, R. L. Detente and Confrontation: American-Soviet Relations from Nixon to Reagan. The Brookings Institution. pp. 768–785.
3. Brezhnev, L. I. 1977. Pravda. Nov. 3.

4. BREZHNEV, L. I. 1977. Outstanding exploits of the defenders of Tula. Pravda. Jan. 19.
5. GARTHOFF, R. L. Op. cit. p. 772.
6. OGARKOV, N. V. 1979. Military strategy. *In* Soviet Military Encyclopedia, vol. 7. pp. 563–564.
7. BREZHNEV, L. I. 1982. New York Times. June 16.
8. THE SOVIET ECONOMY UNDER A NEW LEADER. 1986. (Report presented to the Subcommittee on Economic Resources, Competitiveness, and Security Economics by the Central Intelligence Agency and the Defense Intelligence Agency.) March 19, pp. i–ii.
9. GATES. R. M. & L. K. GERSHWIN. 1985. Soviet Strategic Force Developments. (Testimony before a joint session of the Subcommittee on Strategic and Theater Nuclear Forces of the Senate Armed Services Committee and the Defense Subcommittee of the Senate Committee on Appropriations.) June 26, p. 9.
10. IBID. Fig. 5.
11. WALLER, D., J. BRUCE & B. COOK. 1986. SDI: Progress and Challenges. (Staff report submitted to Senators Proxmire, Johnston and Chiles.) March 17, p. 1.
12. NEW YORK TIMES. 1986. May 1, p. A20.

DISCUSSION OF THE PAPER

G. CHAPLINE (*Lawrence Livermore National Laboratory, Livermore, Calif.*): Given the reluctance of Congress to modernize our offensive nuclear forces, it seems to me one of the most serious problems faced by the United States is how to respond effectively to Soviet violations of arms control agreements.

Wouldn't you agree that the SDI is the most effective means yet found for responding to those arms control violations?

D. L. AARON (*D. L. Aaron & Co., Inc., Westport, Conn.*): I think it can be an effective means to get them to stop the violations. If the thought is that carrying out the SDI program will respond to it, I doubt it, because I have profound doubts as to whether SDI is in our long-term strategic interest.

I think the prospect of SDI has caused the Soviets to say and to admit that Krasnoyarsk is, in fact, a violation. They came back to us and said, if you will stop Pave Paws we will stop Krasnoyarsk. But that is clearly unacceptable, because Pave Paws is perfectly legitimate under the ABM Treaty. But their gambit recognizes the fact that they have done something wrong, and I think part of their incentive for rectifying it is the SDI program.

M. M. SHERRY: Ramifications from the Chernobyl catastrophe are not yet completely apparent, but apparently the Soviet Union that had in the past, as Marshall Shulman related, to choose between guns and butter may now actually have to choose between guns and the essential human nutrient of water.

With that reality, and an earlier speaker today alluded to the fact that a scenario like that of Chernobyl could lead to a first strike, do you think the Soviets may ever judge that our public talk is window dressing and if they fear that an American first strike is forthcoming might attack from that perspective?

D. L. AARON: That's always been the great fear of the nuclear age, and there is no question that the Soviets have said that they fear that's what is behind SDI. If you get into a situation where both countries fear a first strike from the other, that's the definition of the instability we have sought to avoid since nuclear weapons and ballistic missile delivery systems were invented.

PART V. INTERNATIONAL SIGNIFICANCE OF THE NEW DEFENSE TECHNOLOGIES

The Politics of SDI

McGEORGE BUNDY

The problem we face today is the requirement of coexistence with a government and society which are deeply different from our own, and which have standards of behavior that most of us would regard as minimal in international affairs. We are required to coexist with the Soviet Union by the existence of shared thermonuclear danger, by the existence of the fact, so well expressed by one of the greatest of thermonuclear physicists, that "mankind has *never* encountered anything even remotely resembling a large nuclear war in scale and horror" and that "it is meaningless to speak of victory in a large nuclear war, which is collective suicide." I am quoting from Andrei Sakharov.[a]

This is our common condition. Our differences as large organized societies are deep and varied. The intrinsic disposition to "lie, cheat, and steal," in the President's words, in the Soviet Union is very high. Our own capacity for candor and fairness and argument is limited, but the difference is a very large one. In approaching the question about what we ought to do about major new enterprises of changing or adjusting or reversing the thermonuclear balance, it is a mistake to take the Soviets to be anything but what they are. Fortunately—and this I think is shared ground between Dr. Teller and myself—they are extremely careful, cautious people. They know as well as we do, they know as a government as well as Sakharov knows as a physicist, what a thermonuclear war would be like.

The reality over the forty years we have existed together with this capacity—for the first four years as a monopoly, but since then together—is that each side, for its own reasons and by its own perception of danger, has in fact been extremely careful about coming anywhere near the brink of large-scale superpower nuclear war.

It is in that context that I would like to talk about the emerging technologies and especially those which relate to the Strategic Defense Initiative (SDI).

There has been a great deal of confusion about what the SDI is and what it aims to be, most of it created by the Administration itself. It is at least four things. It is, indeed, Mr. Reagan's "dream" of a "strategic space shield" that

[a] Andrei Sakharov, "The Danger of Thermonuclear War," *Foreign Affairs*, pp. 1004, 1006 (Summer 1983).

McGeorge Bundy was Special Assistant to the President for National Security Affairs during the Kennedy and Johnson Administrations. He is currently Professor of History at New York University, New York, New York 10003.

can make nuclear weapons "impotent and obsolete." All of these are the President's own words for what he has proposed.

This dream will not happen, and I think no speaker at this meeting believes it will. Its true believers are exactly two, Ronald Reagan and his loyal cheerleader, his lawyer Caspar Weinberger. There is no prospect in the generation ahead of us that either of these great societies will abandon its reliance on the capacity in some measure and by some means to retaliate, when it is sufficiently aggrieved, with nuclear weapons.

There is no defense ministry on either side which is currently planning or has any expectation of planning on the abandonment of ever more modern offensive systems. Each great society as it observes the preparations of the other for defense is driven to reemphasize its own concern with maintaining and improving an effective penetrating offense.

This is the position of the Soviet government announced by Andropov within days of the President's speech of March 1983. This is the position of the United States government announced by Secretary of Defense Weinberger in a message to the President of the United States to warn him against the dangers of concession just before the summit of last fall. What actually happens, operationally, in the current condition of the two countries is that evidence about defensive efforts in one country merely stimulates offensive reinforcement in the other.

The hardest question in operational terms which the advocates of the Strategic Defense Initiative have to address is the ways and means of making the reversal of attitudes which is required by their desired shift from emphasis on an offensive retaliatory capacity to emphasis on a defensive capacity. They need to tell us, which none of them has done so far, and perhaps we can do better as this session wears on, how they plan to persuade the Air Force and the Navy that they should not have new offensive systems because of reports of increasing defensive capability on the other side. My own belief is that the reason that question has not been addressed is that there is no good answer to it.

The second kind of SDI is a determined effort, by technological enthusiasts and also by people who believe there is a great and present danger from Moscow, to find reinforcement to American nuclear deterrence.

This is an entirely different thing from making nuclear weapons obsolete. These believers in reinforced deterrence do not all believe in the same solutions, and as in the current issue of *Commentary*, just to give one example, they tend to make verbal war on one another. There will be no early resolution of these differences because, in fact, people preach their own solutions to this problem, but not all of them are going to happen.

Third, in the form expressed by such members of the Administration as Gerald Yonas and Paul Nitze, for each of whom I have great respect, SDI is a research program and so far *only* a research program, designed to learn as much as we can, with full respect for existing treaty obligations, about possible ways of improving the strategic nuclear balance by defensive systems which must be both reliably survivable and also cost-effective at the margin. For a program thus defined, and it is a definition very different from the one that still comes from the top of the Administration, there is general political and technical support. Debate is mostly about its size and shape.

I find no significant nationwide opposition to a research program that remains strictly limited to research, and I think it is important to remember that a real national decision on going beyond that stage will not come in Mr. Reagan's term, and perhaps not in that of the next President either.

Fourth, the SDI, more precisely the President's dream of SDI, nourished and reinforced by very skillful people within this Administration, is a clear block to new arms control agreements while he is President. To many in the Reagan Administration that is really one of its advantages. For others, and I must tell you for me, this is its most obvious present flaw because I believe that there is available to a President who would grasp it an opportunity of historic importance for a major trade of their fears for ours, their fear of what we might do somehow with strategic defense against our fear of what they have done and may still be doing in the multiplication of excessive many-warhead land-based missiles of very large size as a threat to at least a part of our strategic deterrent.

I think that a president who wanted to do so could make a SALT III agreement of very large and constructive importance on precisely this basis, and I think it will not happen under Ronald Reagan.

Now, when we think about all of these many different SDIs, one is capable of having many different reactions. One could wish, and I will come back to this point in the end, one could wish that it had not been presented in a fashion which its own most ardent supporters do not, in fact, defend: as a way of making us all safe under some kind of magic umbrella from the nuclear danger with which we have all lived for forty years.

One could wish that the program were not characterized more by salesmanship than by analysis. This is conspicuously not true of what Dr. Yonas did yesterday, and we are all in his debt for that careful and honest exposition.

One could wish that we had been more careful with ourselves and with other countries in the way in which the program was launched without effective consultation, even within the United States government, let alone with dispassionate and independent scientific analysts within the United States and still less in conversation or consultation with those who are partners with us in the great alliance of the West. That was bad.

It is more important now to examine the decisions and the opportunities and the dangers that are ahead of us. We have time. That is one of the most important things to be said about the Strategic Defense Initiative. Large-scale decisions going beyond research can be kept years ahead of us. We can, I think, be careful about the authorization of kinds of testing and development which might be taken as violations of existing treaties. Against the desires and hopes of many of the advocates of SDI, existing treaties have public support in the United States. I don't know of anyone who is able to say publicly that he would like to test an X-ray laser in space.

Let me say, about this question of defending existing treaty arrangements, that it is a nontrivial matter and that we should all be honest with one another about the point at which we would be prepared to abandon existing treaty obligations.

It is important to observe that the President himself has so far understood that there is both national and international political importance in not being the first to abandon even an expired unratified treaty. This is not an entirely one-sided matter in public opinion, and it will not be so as the argument continues. Honesty in exposition and recognition of difficulties will be enormous contributions from whatever side they come.

I believe that this is a time for reflection. One of the things we should reflect about, which was suggested this morning by David Aaron, is whether there is really current or prospective strategic nuclear danger that makes improved defense a very high goal. Do we now have a state of danger in the thermonuclear balance between the United States and the Soviet Union?

I think not. What we have seen demonstrated over the last twenty-five, perhaps thirty years—if asked to name a single date, I would say what we have seen demonstrated since 1955—is that in terms of what each country would have to fear from general nuclear war there is stable and deeply rooted deterrence between the Soviet Union and the United States.

This has been demonstrated by history, and I think it is demonstrable also in the logic of what a general nuclear war would mean for each country. At each moment of danger, whether in Berlin in the fifties or Berlin or Cuba in the sixties, it has turned out that the existence of this danger has been sobering to both sides. In fact, neither one has ever ventured to challenge by force a vital national interest of the other, an interest to which one might be led to respond by resort to nuclear war, so that the reality of our situation with the Soviet Union is one of mutually recognized coexistence in *behavior*, constantly punctuated by verbal nonsense on both sides.

This stable nuclear deterrence is something we should treasure, and we should examine measures which are intended to improve it by asking with the greatest care what kinds of consequences they may have upon the behavior and the reaction of the other side. Over the last forty years we have been too much given to excessive fear and we have repeatedly overreacted to real evidence of Soviet achievement. We did so when we moved to the development of the H-bomb without considering the possibility of an agreement to avoid that excess. We did so when we found a missile gap where there was none at the end of the 1950s. We have also done so in the last few years in creating out of the obsolete design of a single element of our deterrent, the land-based ICBM, a "window of vulnerability" through which no one has tried to come.

It is as important to seek agreement as it is to seek technological advancement. It is unwise always to seek to do new things instead of asking which ones may be unwise or unnessary or expensive or even dangerous.

I believe that we have been victims of repeated worst-case analysis and that we can predict that in the event of deployment by one side or the other or both of defensive systems, worst-case analysis will continue to govern in both great capitals. An American system which is large enough to scare the Russians will not be good enough to reassure us and the same thing is true the other way around, and the predictable reaction will be that of Andropov in 1983 and Weinberger in 1985. We should be extremely careful before we move in that direction.

Finally, I think we have given altogether insufficient attention to the question of the kind of regime we wish to see in space through time. The deployment of multiphase systems, whatever it may be, will require very substantial space-based components. Those space-based components will necessarily become attractive targets from the point of view of military planning in Moscow.

I ask you to think what we would do if we were to see large-scale space-based deployment of instruments threatening the reliability of our own deterrence. Moreover, the question is not evenly balanced because our dependence upon space for secure and reassuring deterrence is much higher today than the dependence of the Soviet Union.

I remember myself, as I was in government at the time, the reassurance that came to us in 1961 from the evidence provided by the first effective space satellite about Soviet ICBM nondeployment. It was enormously reassuring. Ever since then information from space has been absolutely indispensable to American self-confidence.

Gradually and incompletely, but in a very impressive and satisfactory way so far, we have been able to achieve international acceptance of this use of space. It is even agreed on in the SALT treaties. National technical means are protected by treaty. How long and how far would that protection last in a world in which either side felt genuinely and gravely menaced by a new space capability?

Let me remind you that while it is possible to argue with innocence that defense is not as threatening as offense, the President himself said in March 1983 that the combination of defense and offense could properly be understood as threatening and that is precisely the combination on which each side is working today. So, we need the time to reflect.

DISCUSSION OF THE PAPER

UNIDENTIFIED SPEAKER: The President obviously considered the pieces of his original proposal carefully before he announced it. What is your analysis for his including the sharing with the Soviets of the SDI information?

McG. BUNDY (*New York University, New York, N.Y.*): I have to reject your premise. I don't think that was the best considered speech of this President, and I don't know what he means by sharing with the Soviet government because there have been no public discussions really of the serious ways and means of doing that. It is a subtle, complex question.

I believe that the President's readiness to state that objective is encouraging and that while there are obviously great difficulties in the ways and means by which you communicate on matters which in another mode are extraordinarily secret, one should not knock that particular proposal. One should encourage real attention to its implications.

G. Mayer (*Los Alamos National Laboratories, Los Alamos, N.M.*): How do you see the role of the intermediate-range nuclear forces in Europe which in the opinion of many Europeans is a threat for the Soviet Union. How do you see their role in combination with the SDI? There was a lot of discussion in 1983 about the intermediate-range nuclear forces as a direct threat for the Soviet Union. How do you see their relation to the SDI program which has been started right now?

McG. Bundy: I think that both we and the Europeans—perhaps in the first instance one of the wisest Western statesmen, Chancellor Schmidt—overreacted to the deployment of the SS-20 and in particular I think we found a rather bad solution in the cruise missiles and the Pershing. I think seaborne missiles are better and that we could, indeed, have dealt with this as we dealt with earlier concerns about missiles by a clearer and sharper commitment of the sea-based resources already in existence and in prospect.

The problem of the political relation between SDI and Europe is an important one. We heard serious comments on that this morning from two people with whom I could not contend on these questions.

I believe myself that we will have very serious questions as we go along in the SDI, not only with allies, but within our own country. It is not possible, as we come to the consideration of development and deployment and the abandonment of existing and much approved treaties, that we can avoid a national debate and that is one reason the more for thinking it important now that we have less salesmanship and more analysis in our discussion of these issues.

N. Zumbulades: You mentioned the worst-case senarios. Isn't it true, perhaps, that in an offense-dominated world worst-case scenarios rest with the potential victim while in a world where there is a mixture of offense and defense the onus of worst-case scenarios shifts to the potential attacker?

McG. Bundy: I don't know that I know the answer to that. The existential deterrence, that is to say the deterrent effect of what *can* happen, quite aside from what will or will not be decided, is going to be very strong for a long time to come.

What fragmentary and partial defenses are most likely to do—but on this there could be argument and there should be analysis and for that there is time—on the evidence we have before us of our behavior in the past, is to stimulate new and better offensive processes.

One of the weapons that most of us like least among the current deterrents is the MIRV. We owe the MIRV largely to the ABM.

M. Sherry: In your opening statement you mentioned that our President has told us that the Soviet Union is to be viewed as liars and cheaters. You have spoken about the inconsistency of President Reagan's gesture after his 23 March 1983 speech of saying that he would share the technology with the Soviet Union. You spoke about the later proved inaccuracy of our window of vulnerability of the seventies, of our bomber gap of the fifties. Do you feel that we may have some of the faults that we attribute to them and it may not be black and white as we are picturing it?

McG. Bundy: If I painted the United States as white I picked the wrong brush. I didn't mean to do that.

The Necessity of Strategic Defense

EDWARD TELLER

I like to agree with the person who talked ahead of me, and I am grateful to McGeorge Bundy for making this possible. I agree with him wholeheartedly in his respect for the man who made the Soviet hydrogen bomb and who had the great courage to stand up against his government. If Sakharov is permitted to go back to Moscow, there will be much more reason for us to cooperate with the Russians.

In respect to the danger of Soviet preparations for defense, McGeorge Bundy and I are in obvious disagreement. Soviet preparation for defense against an American retaliatory blow is real.

The defense of Moscow is a hard fact. The radar in Krasnoyarsk has not yet been completed, but will be ready in the near future. Furthermore, the Soviet Union has spent at least a billion dollars per year for several years on high intensity lasers. These can be used against satellites and possibly against missiles at a distance of 100 miles.

The Soviets may deploy instruments of defense against retaliatory missiles from the United States. In case the Soviet Union should ever attack us, they may have means to make sure the destruction shall not be mutual. We are now engaged in research in order to find out to what extent defense is possible. Not to pursue such research would result in continuing ignorance concerning a real danger.

McGeorge Bundy and I are also in disagreement about X-ray lasers. This laser is a truly novel initiative. In practice it may not be effective, or it may be more effective than all the other defenses put together. It is a necessity for us to find out which is the case.

It is clear that X-ray lasers cannot penetrate the atmosphere. A mistaken statement was quoted by Soviet representatives at an international conference. The Soviet representatives protested against X-ray lasers as a means to strike the Soviet Union from space. This, you know, is an absurdity. X-ray lasers will not penetrate the atmosphere.

The story of Soviet defensive efforts is too long and too complicated to be repeated here. I would like to give you a sample of Soviet activities because the proposal is ingenious and thoroughly worthy of attention.

It is an old idea to use a high-energy electron beam against a missile. This

---

Edward Teller is Consultant and Associate Director Emeritus, Lawrence Livermore National Laboratory, Livermore, California 94450. He is also a Senior Research Fellow at the Hoover Institution on War, Revolution, and Peace, Stanford University, Stanford, California.

appears to be impractical because the beam would be deflected by the earth's magnetic field and this field is varying and unpredictable. But there is a trick that can get around this difficulty. The trick was discovered in the Soviet Union and after the initial publication nothing was heard about its development.

The trick is to use a moderately strong laser beam with a sharply defined direction. The laser beam ionizes the air. From the low-density ionized tunnel, the electrons diffuse out and a positively charged track is left behind. The high-energy electron beam is then injected into this tunnel and the beam is kept on a straight line because the electrostatic forces confining it to the tunnel are much stronger than the forces due to the earth's magnetic field. The trick works in the high portion of the atmosphere but not in outer space nor in the denser part of the atmosphere.

This happens to be one sample of many technologies where we are following up a Soviet initiative that was published in their literature many years ago. Our efforts should not be called SDI, but rather SDR, for "Strategic Defense Response."

When we talk about an American advance, there is evidence in all too many cases that we are repeating what the Soviets have accomplished many years ago. This is one of the reasons why we have offered full cooperation to our allies. We need their help just as badly as they need ours. I would like to talk specifically about our latest partners, the Israelis.

All over the free world SDI is hotly debated. In little more than a year, I traveled across the ocean nine times to discuss SDI and I found in every country a division between right and left. The right is for SDI; the left against it.

Last August I visited Israel and found something peculiar. In Israel I found a different attitude. Right and left did want SDI and they told me why. It was clear and simple and unanimous. They want defense against short-range missiles from Syria. They cannot stay mobilized all of the time. Their mobilization sites are known. They fear, and I believe very rightly so, that the rockets which the Soviets have already delivered and are still delivering to their opponents will keep Israeli mobilization sites under bombardment. Without a mobilized army they will be helpless.

We have talked a lot about defense against long-range missiles. They are particularly vulnerable in their boost phase. The Israelis are vitally interested in defense against short-range missiles and the prospects for that are not poor. Short-range missiles have difficulty in carrying decoys and rise above the horizon very quickly. There they can be attacked by an intense laser beam on which the Soviets have worked and on which the United States is now working. Such lasers are impeded by clouds. There are few clouds in the desert in the southern and western portions of Israel.

I returned to Washington and expected difficulties. The negotiating team was going over to Israel a few days after I arrived back from the trip. I reported what I heard. I thought it would be difficult to include Israeli initiatives. I found that the Washington office was willing and eager to accept the emphasis proposed by Israel. We need their work and we need their constructive criticism.

The safety of Israel is not only their safety; it is also our safety. Just as the safety of Czechoslovakia was, in fact, the safety of France. We need defense against short-range missiles because of the menace of Soviet submarines off our coast.

On a recent visit a very eminent physicist, whom I shall name on request, expressed his admiration for the progress we made on X-ray lasers and then warned that we must stop or else the Russians will copy us. The fact is we have plenty of evidence from Russian publications that they had the basic ideas first.

We need underground testing to verify the behavior of X-ray lasers. Such lasers could become one of the methods to make weapons of mass destruction impotent and obsolete. We know the Soviets had tests of the appropriate kind and after a crowded test program they stopped and asked us to stop.

I remember the years when the West underestimated Hitler. I don't want to underestimate anyone.[a]

Today it is very expensive to go into space. What we have to do is make defense easier and more effective than offense. We are looking for methods of getting into space more easily, more cheaply. It might be done by using very high intensity lasers that can heat hydrogen with a little carbon-black in it. This way one can obtain very high specific impulses. As a result, launching of rockets could become much less expensive.

There is another daring proposal of which you have heard: the transatmospheric vehicle. We could construct a plane that actually can get above the atmosphere. The proposal is made much more difficult by the needless requirement that this vehicle be manned. At least during tests, robotics should be used.

By developing robotics, we could use space in our defense more effectively. In the meantime, we should emphasize defense based on the surface of the earth, which is more realistic.

The President has repeatedly emphasized that eventually we should cooperate with the Russians. Indeed, we ought to find the means to make mass launching of rockets difficult. For that purpose we should cooperate and we are trying to cooperate with everyone. If defensive methods are developed in the free world, I hope that the Soviets will eventually sit down at the conference table and discuss cooperation.

[a] EDITORS' NOTE: At this point during Edward Teller's presentation at the conference, the following exchange occurred between Dr. Teller and the previous speaker in this session, McGeorge Bundy:

TELLER: I would like to talk about what may be the most important, a more general kind of cooperation and one more thing, space, very briefly space. I don't recall our president ever emphasizing a space shield.

BUNDY: He said it. He called it a "strategic space shield."

TELLER: He talked about shields.

BUNDY: "Space shield" was his word.

TELLER: In his talk of the 23rd of March space was not mentioned.

BUNDY: He is not a single speech president.

TELLER: Thank you for having interrupted me twice. You are now one up. Shield yes, space maybe.

We have tried disarmament. Our negotiations have led from danger to greater danger. We must negotiate with the Soviets. But to repeat the same ineffective methods of arms limitations in the same hopeless manner is not necessarily the right way. We have neglected too long the obvious possibility of defense.

Thirty years ago I did not believe that defense against rockets was feasible. Twenty-five years ago I started to think about it in a detailed manner. Now I believe it is urgent.

The President heard about the possibility of defense for the first time in January 1967. It is obvious that he considered defense for many years before he spoke about it. That cooperation on defense with the Russians must be left to his successors is quite clear.

I hope that we will all support him and his successors as they work toward cooperation and peace.

DISCUSSION OF THE PAPER

R. GARWIN (*IBM Thomas J. Watson Research Center, Yorktown Heights, N.Y.*): First, let me agree with Professor Teller about the transatmospheric vehicle and it is hard enough without people insisting it be manned, but Dr. Wheelon said the same thing, I believe, about the space shuttle. You say the missiles are extremely vulnerable while they are accelerated and I hate to have repetitive criticism, but, I do insist that two plus two equal four and the Soviet missiles accelerate in the Soviet Union. If you say we cannot have defenses in space because they are vulnerable, how will we be able to see let alone destroy the missiles while they are accelerating in boost phase in Siberia?

E. TELLER (*Lawrence Livermore National Laboratory, Livermore, Calif.*): I am worried about Soviet defensive measures that could destroy our retaliatory missiles from a distance of 1500 miles. We ought to know whether and to what extent this is possible.

I am trying to provide inexpensive means to get into space. I also am trying to cooperate with everybody and make sure that not the Chinese, not the Russians, not the people from Luxembourg, and not the United States will launch a thousand missiles.

This is something in the common interest and if everybody agrees maybe the Soviets will agree. If the Soviets don't agree maybe their neighbors will agree and maybe there will be a way, not a short miraculous way, but a long hard way, in which peaceful defense can be made possible. I am not claiming it is easy.

F. LONG (*Cornell University, Ithaca, N.Y.*): This is a plea for help. All of us have heard now a great many times of the progress in the Soviet Union in many of these technologies. The normal statement is that enormous progress has been made, but it is impossible for people to give details because it is all classified, and therefore you will have to simply take peoples' words.

Now, for those of us who don't have clearance this is really pretty unsatisfactory and what I would ask is, Couldn't you help to see to it that the information in detail and in specifics is made available?

E. TELLER: Thank you for your help. I have made this plea for nearly forty years consistently, repeatedly in a boring manner on every level. I have succeeded in one case. I have succeeded in getting research on controlled fusion declassified. I was given permission to disclose our effort in the Atoms for Peace Conference II in 1958 in Geneva. Ever since, I have been working on that same thing. I want no technical secrecy. I want as much disclosure of facts concerning Soviet progress as is ever possible. I am very sure that lots more could be disclosed.

For instance, I have personally gone and argued with the head of the CIA for disclosure of what we know in a positive way about Soviet civil defense. The answer was, we have disclosed enough. I beg to differ. We know and the Soviets know that we know. They know how we obtained the information. There is no reason why we should not publish it. Every one of us should protest against unnecessary secrecy. You don't need to plead with me on that score. I am doing, I believe, as much as anyone else.

M. STENZLER (*Discover Magazine*): Dr. Teller, you said in your talk that you were concerned that a possible strike of short-range missiles from Soviet submarines off the U.S. coast or from Cuba could prevent us from making a satisfactory retaliatory strike, thus making MAD ineffective. I assume that those strikes would be against land-based targets and my question is: Would or would not our sea-based missile capabilities still keep the concept of MAD intact?

E. TELLER: The question of sea-based retaliation is much more involved. We know the Soviets are working hard at detecting our submarines. I do not know with what success. I do not know both because it is secret and because the people with whom I talked don't know either.

The Soviets may have methods to neutralize our submarines. Also, they do have a terminal defense over Moscow that could be expanded in a short time to cover a lot of the Soviet Union.

I do not know what the dangers are. I do know that we are engaged in finding out how effective various kinds of defense can be. This research is belated, badly needed and starved for ideas and for the cooperation of our very best people.

S. C. COMAN: I would like to know whether there has been in the defense budget, either known or unknown, any planning for high-level prestigious, perhaps secret, conferences with leaders of Soviet science on things like conflict resolutions and changing the propensity of the human being toward aggressiveness?

I know Dr. David Hamberg who's a past president of the AAAS and the president of Carnegie Corporation is very interested in that possibility.

The second thing I would like to know is whether anybody here has read the book called *The End of the World* by Otto Friedrich which is a remarkable book detailing some of the disasters of the past and showing how people did not understand what was happening. They missed the signals at the beginning, middle, and end.

The third question is, Does anyone know about Dr. Robert J. Lifton's talk on the new psychology of human survival at the Ethical Culture School on May 14th?

I feel fairly strongly that the question of human survival is not just technolgocial, but really is a question of changing people, and I wonder if our defense has looked at that question carefully enough. I mean, maybe we should be doing subliminal messages to the Soviets or whomever.

E. TELLER: There has been a lot of talk about the end of humankind. When the First World War started I was six years old. I know from various perspectives what war is and how terrible war is. I do not think we will avoid war by exaggerating the dangers of war. By exaggerating dangers you don't avoid them.

The question of human survival has nothing to do with new psychology. It has to do with common sense. An answer has come from my good friend, Freeman Dyson. He acknowledged that the question of the survival of humankind is a difficult one. He said that the greatest danger of a big war, a nuclear war, is that the survivors will be mad and in their madness will repeat the war. These repetitious blows may be more than humankind can take. What is needed now is to avoid a third world war.

These are the arguments that have led us to cooperate with the British, the Germans, and the Israelis. I hope that agreements with the Italians, the Japanese, the Chinese, and, in the long run, even with the Russians will follow. The ultimate purpose is to make defense more effective than offense.

Roundtable Discussion

Chair: H. GUYFORD STEVER
Panel Members: PAUL DOTY, PIERRE AIGRAIN, JOHN GIBBONS, McGEORGE BUNDY, FREDERICK SEITZ, ROGER L. HAGENGRUBER, CHARLES SCHMID, AND JOHN T. SWING

H. G. STEVER (*National Academy of Engineering, Washington, D.C.*): I once attended an opera fest with many visiting opera singers. After the visiting opera stars had sung beautifully and worked very hard we invited them to a dinner to relax, but then the local folks insisted they sing some more. I thought that was very rough treatment of great stars and now we are practicing it in this roundtable.

P. DOTY (*Harvard University, Cambridge, Mass.*): I have a lot of points, but with Dr. Aigrain here I thought I would go back and ask him and others to comment on the following proposition, that it is announced in many quarters that our present SDI program de-emphasizes hard-point defense. Very little has been said until the last weeks of defense against intermediate- and short-range missiles, and yet there is quite a bit in common between hard-point defense and defense against shorter-range missiles.

Therefore, I wonder how it looks from the European point of view as to whether the SDI program is really committed to a substantial investigation of defense against short- and intermediate-range missiles. If so or if not, do the Europeans expect to undertake an initiative along this line themselves?

P. AIGRAIN (*Thomson Group, Paris, France*): Of course, the nuclear threat for Europe may come much more from intermediate-range missiles or from atmospheric vehicles than from long-range missiles. Even so we should not forget that the Soviets have the option to use more powerful launchers on nonoptimal trajectories if that makes them harder to intercept. This is still an option they have.

Some of these things, for example atmospheric carriers, are really very similar to the defense against airplanes except it would be a little harder, but very similar. Of course, there is a lot of work going on in Europe on that.

My main point is that the biggest fears the Europeans have is not that of a first strike of the Soviets by a nuclear force in Europe because even though this is possible we think it is a completely crazy strategy on the part of the Russians because it would open them to retaliation, immediate retaliation, from the very powerful American strike force. The biggest risk to Europe, immediate risk, is a ground invasion because unfortunately we don't have an ocean between us and the protection we have against a ground invasion right now is retaliation by nuclear ways so that the idea that nuclear retaliation might become if not impossible at least inefficient appears to Europeans, at least to many of them, as a rather unsavory one unless it is accompanied by the development, the simultaneous development, of a high technology system which could compensate for the numerical inferiority of Western European forces on the ground.

The problem of European defense against intermediate-range missiles is important, but I think in second order compared to that. What I would like to see is a greater participation of Europe in the SDI research program. The 1% which has been announced is ridiculous, and in fact has been perceived in many European countries as almost an insult.

Simultaneously I wish that the European countries would team up for a very significant applied research effort on intelligent field weapons with the corresponding large American participation symmetric with Poland so that we each develop a system which can protect us from the first most important risk and the combination of the two will then make the free world as a whole safer.

P. DOTY: You would, then, put antitactical missile defense lower down on the priority list?

P. AIGRAIN: Antinuclear tactical missiles, yes, I would put it lower down.

J. GIBBONS (*Office of Technology Assessment, U. S. Congress, Washington, D.C.*): I do have a question and I am not sure who I am addressing it to . . . perhaps to the panel, perhaps to some member of this meeting. It is a question that has perplexed me for some time: If SDI is not the magic shield as has frequently been described and has frequently, I think, confused a lot of Americans, but if in fact it is a long-term research program to develop, evaluate, and provide new options for future leaders with a goal perhaps better described as being able to introduce greater uncertainty to a potential aggressor and therefore devalue his strategic assets, then it seems to me that SDI becomes a mechanism to raise the ante of deterrence. That may not be the case and I would like to know if people think it isn't.

Also, if SDI raising the level of uncertainty is in and of itself desirable, then what about a comparative analysis of the effects of moving ahead with test limitations or test ban treaties which in turn would raise uncertainty about the effectiveness of nuclear weapons, and therefore might have somewhat the same effect?

I am not sure that such an analysis has been done. I wonder if anyone knows.

P. DOTY: With respect to Jack's first point I would maybe add the answer given by Cap Weinberger at the time of the Geneva summit, in which when asked what the U.S. reponse should be if the Soviets developed SDI it was to increase our offensive forces.

This simple honest reply, I think, is due to some of the discussion today and I wonder if anyone feels that is not the right answer.

McG. BUNDY (*New York University, New York, N.Y.*): Gibbons in his usual way has asked the very hard question which will, in fact, be presented down the road and I think this meeting is not unusual in that repeatedly one speaker or another has pointed out that the actual point of turnover from emphasis on the offense to emphasis on the defense is at the very best in Paul Nitze's words a very tricky matter and in terms of the kinds of reactions we have seen in the past and have heard in messages like Weinberger's at the time of the summit or Andropov's in March of 1983 and our own estimates on the basis of what they have done in the past as to what the Joint Chiefs will think on this kind of issue and what the Soviet Joint Chiefs will think.

I think we have to say that if there is to be a strategic defense deployment that has the consequence of bringing about a reduction of offensive weaponry there will have to be a revolution in the way that the persons most concerned think about it.

Most of the people I have talked with, and I have not been able to improve on their argument, say that you really can't do this if you can't get the offensive reduction first, and that is just one reason the more in my view for thinking that the rational way to proceed now is to trade out the best we can Russian fears for our fears, to get a revised and strengthened ABM arrangement with reduction in big missiles and with a time limit and with a sense that over time one might want to change because there isn't any doubt that if you could *do* it, reliance on defense is better than reliance on intolerable levels of retaliatory destruction.

The problem is how to get there, and there has been a great shortage of thought on that. It is not something that the SDI Organization is equipped to study. They don't have that kind of capability and I don't see it in the Executive Branch. I think we could do better in this room than the United States government could do on this very subject.

J. Gibbons: I have one other paradox I would like to raise, Mr. Chairman. It goes along the following lines: if through SDI we hope to provide a mechanism that will actually help outmode nuclear strategic forces, that is, a very efficient missile defense capability, substantial arms reduction down, for example, to hundreds rather than thousands of missiles on each side would be a very important mechanism by which such high efficiencies might be achieved.

Now, if that is the case it seems to me that one could say that mutual strategic arms reduction is a necessary prerequisite to the transition to an effective strategic defense, so effective that one could then move further toward even deeper reductions.

If this is the case, I wonder if we are giving enough attention to improving the technological options for verification-protected reductions which in turn might make possible defense-protected reductions feasible.

F. Seitz (*Rockefeller University, New York, N.Y.*): Until the Soviets have a much more open society so that inspection is meaningful as it would be in this country where a very large part of the population is prepared, so to speak, to reveal things that they find out one way or another and reveal them publicly, it seems to me it is going to be very difficult for any verification scheme to work.

J. Gibbons: If I might respond briefly to that, I certainly agree with Professor Seitz. At the same time there are some allegations of substantially improved seismic means of detection and more accurate measurements of nuclear explosions down to the subkiloton range. It seems to me that this is one, perhaps, of many means of verification independent of on-site inspection.

Finally, there seems to be a new explicit interest on the part of the Soviets to talk seriously about on-site inspection, not only of missile sites, but of production facilities.

I just wonder if the kinds of resources that we are prepared to commit to arms control measures up to its potential value compared to other ways we are spending money.

R. L. Hagengruber (*Sandia Laboratories, Albuquerque, N.M.*): I wasn't planning to say anything, but that particular question stimulates some response since the laboratories of the Department of Energy [DOE] and its three weapons laboratories are rather extensively involved in research involving verification technologies.

I would simply point out to you that Sandia is not untypical among the laboratories, and at Sandia we allocate approximately 4% of our technical staff to the area of arms control and verification. It is a very significant investment amounting to something in the neighborhood of about $40 million of actual investment each year.

As much as I have looked forward to technologies in verification that will ease problems or act as a catalyst in the area of arms control, I would only tell you that just like this convolution of psychology and technology that exists in SDI, we have even a more potent problem in the areas of arms control of verification. While I think there are areas of promise in verification technology, there is no rabbit waiting to be pulled from the scientific hat.

We are working hard. I think more effort could be put into it. I think it would be great if the scientific community were to add their creative thoughts, cautioned, I think, by the kind of insight that people like McGeorge Bundy and others can offer about the difficulty of dealing with the issue of sovereignty and the realities of actually building or doing things within the Soviet Union.

I think it would be very valuable to do that, but I would like to just simply say I don't believe that there is a rabbit in a hat waiting in this area.

McG. Bundy: The problem of the comprehensive test bans or test bans nearly comprehensive is an old one and a hard one and there is, I am sure, entirely honest disagreement among technical assessors as to whether and how far you can have confidence by seismic measuring means that do not involve intrusive inspection. The laboratories have a point of view and others have a point of view. I don't have a point of view. I don't count myself as a seismologist of standing, but I do myself think that there are political questions here, that you are really not talking just about how certain you can be, but how much it matters and that is in the end a political question.

I think when you get behind the seismological argument you come to a very deep-seated political difference. I don't think the Joint Chiefs, without very dramatic changes in their whole approach to the world, are going to be believers in the abandonment of underground testing. They really believe that that kind of testing is terribly important to their confidence in the capabilities of the United States and their ability to develop with confidence new systems with improved characteristics, some of which can be lower yield and higher accuracy, both of which are different at least from what we found we had in the sixties.

I think the comprehensive test ban is very hard in the politics of both societies, but I think myself that it is, in fact, one of the ways of moving toward a world less driven by technological competition and reciprocal technological fear.

P. AIGRAIN: I think that a test ban may be the easiest problem compared to control of arms production and so on. At least there are, indeed, ways to detect tests, possibly not with sufficient accuracy. I am not sure we have any good way to distinguish between a subkiloton nuclear test and a few hundred ton TNT explosion which, of course, is not banned by anybody and could be very hard to distinguish, but, at least there are ways to check that something is happening and on top of it if the other side does not respect test ban treaties there is a simple answer which is to start tests again. But when it comes to the protection of arms investments, it is much harder to know what they are doing. On top of it, what do you do if they don't respect the treaty?

After all the Versailles Treaty contained very explicit and very easy-to-check provisions that the Germans were not allowed to build any warship of more than 10,000 tons. It is extremely easy to check because ships larger than 10,000 tons cannot be camouflaged and it is very easy to measure the weight of a ship by computing the weight of the water it displaces. What happened when Hitlcr started building ships in the 45,000-ton class? What do you do?

The only possible answer is war, which probably should have been donc at that time by the way. So, you have the problem of detection and you have the problem of what to do if the other side breaks the agreement.

H. G. STEVER: I was very interested in these two days. I think I listened reasonably carefully. We didn't speak very much about the role of the United States Congress in this. We obviously know they have a role, but why is it that they didn't draw any lightning and criticism? They didn't get any great kudos. We have some people from Congress.

R. L. HAGENGRUBER: I was going to wait until towards the end, but I want to do this before Congress acts as a lightning rod. What I would like to say is that during the last couple of days I don't believe I heard anybody oppose a research program in strategic defense. I don't think I heard a single speaker do that. In fact, I have read a lot of work of the critics, and some very thoughtful critics, and in general they seem to say the same thing regarding a research program.

The last two days we talked about the technical challenge of SDI which is what we can do and how much it might cost. We also talked about the strategic challenge of SDI which is the challenge of a safe transition to a world in which you have defense. Would it even be stable at all? Those are the questions that dominate the debate; but it seems to me there are two challenges that are true challenges that ought to be at least brought out before a forum like the New York Academy of Sciences where you gather scientists together in a room.

There are two challenges that we didn't talk much about and which relate to the question that you raised. First somehow we as scientists have to persuade Congress and the public to have the kind of patience that it takes to really do research and thus to free us somewhat from the constant yearly marketing, within the defense complex in the case of defense programs, or within the research complex in the case of academic research programs, that brings pressure for us not to do good science or to go beyond creative truth telling. Hyping programs is not exclusive to SDI. We have tried to sell accelerators in this country and I have listened often to the arguments that involve considerable hype. Good science is esoteric and it takes time. There is a stewardship that belongs to all scientists to honor truth and accuracy in our efforts to educate or persuade Congress and the public and we should avoid the constant escalation of the level of hype that is employed. This is a problem which we all share in, and I think it is an important point.

The other challenge is to convince ourselves as citizen scientists that we, in the defense area, or the academic area, or the commercial area of research and development, can "manage" a large national program to avoid what are basically policy mistakes. That is what we were talking about here, our incapability as a society—Congress is the reflection of us, I guess, as a society—to manage this program to avoid making boneheaded mistakes. I think that we shouldn't be destined forever to believe that a national technology initiative is always going to be an uncontrolled missile capable of doing regrettable damage.

I would say to finish this thought that all scientists are challenged to avoid the black and white trivialisms which have ever increasingly characterized our public positions in these debates and to defend to the extent possible the fact that research is a gray area, that it is simply not given to black and white statements of truth.

I don't remember who said that the first casualty in war is truth, but too often that quote seems to apply to all of our efforts to stimulate some initiative in the area of research, and SDI is not immune to that.

I wanted to make that comment, by the way, before Congress takes too much lightning because it seems to me that we as citizens deserve at least some share of that lightning first.

H. G. STEVER: Let me make myself a panelist for one moment and respond to the business about Congress and their belief in long-term research and so on.

In all of the experiences I have had in government selling science programs and so on I have come to two conclusions. One is that Congress is very good at understanding the importance of long-range research and solving problems that way. Obviously, some of them get impatient on various things.

The second one is I don't believe that our Congress would ever give up periodic review of long-term programs. For one thing it is too much fun to review them if they are going well. It is also too much fun for them if they are going badly, but there are many more imporant reasons. There is a principle of checking up on everybody in our government and so on.

Now, let me go back just to the ordinary moderator here. I think McGeorge Bundy was going to make a comment on my question about Congress.

McG. BUNDY: I was going to make the slightly frivolous comment that we all had larger targets the last couple of days. The advocates of Star Wars or SDI or "Strategic Space Shield" were worried about their critics outside the Congress where criticism so far has really been very moderate and others of us were concerned with what we regard as incomplete levels of understanding and candor in the Executive Branch.

Congress is waiting as I hear it, but let's find out from the people who live and breathe the very different air from Capitol Hill.

C. SCHMID: This year I am serving as a Congressional Science and Engineering Fellow working in a Congressional office. I am usually employed as an engineer, but for the past eight months I have been observing the political process.

The first observation I would like to share occurred two weeks after the Chernobyl nuclear reactor accident at a Congressional hearing. It was interesting to hear Congressman Markey, Chairman of the Energy and Power Subcommittee, ask an official from the Department of Energy about Hanford's nuclear reactor which is similar to the graphite reactor at Chernobyl. His question is typical of a lot of questions used to get just the right answer for their own purposes.

Congressman Markey asked whether or not Hanford could also have a meltdown. I think any scientist at the hearing wanted to say that there is a probability that Hanford could have a meltdown like Chernobyl. But Congressman Markey wanted a yes or no answer. I think the answer should be a matter of stating probabilities, and a yes or no answer will only serve to polarize further the pro- and antinuclear power forces, and not get to the heart of the matter of safety.

In deference to opposing SDI research I will just say that the Congressman I work for doesn't presently oppose a low-level research effort. Support for SDI is also a matter of degree. Funding is going from $2.75 billion dollars last year to a request of over $5 billion this year when you add $600 million in for the DOE's proposal. That's a big jump up too. Just because we don't support $5.4 billion versus $2.75 billon doesn't mean that we totally oppose reasearch or work in the Defense Department.

The other point I've been looking into deals with what kinds of projects SDI is working in. McGeorge Bundy asked about arms control and Mr. Hagengruber said he does some work in arms control. I can't find out what part of the SDI's budget is actually designated for integrating SDI into our present overall defense system, which includes arms control. Proponents are saying it is important to bring SDI into our current offensive-defensive framework, but I can't find out where the dollars are allocated for accomplishing this goal. I am trying to track that down. I don't think the DOE can actually do that and I wonder if DOD is working on it. For instance, if you build a house and you set up all the overall specifications, you are going to try to build that house to those specifications. Where are the specifications?

I was therefore wondering what agency in SDI is actually working on integrating SDI into our overall defense and arms control policy. I realize I am changing the subject a little bit, but I am interested in determining what agency is actually in charge of integrating SDI into the long-term overall process; and it is going to be a long-term process, working on weapons and arms control. A lot of people see weapons hardware differently from arms control. But I am trying to determine where the funds are going and if any is going to arms control based on SDI. Also, is that mostly DOE funds, that 4% for arms control?

R. L. HAGENGRUBER: No, actually the work that we do is primarily limited test ban treaty and threshold test ban treaty or potential CTP verification, IAEA safeguards verifications, some new technologies for monitoring of controls on missiles, limits on missiles that might be used as part of INF-START and there are some arms control studies, but we don't get any SDI money for that.

Now, I don't know where they spend money because I don't track their budget. So, I can't answer your question.

H. G. STEVER: This business of using the SDI as a bargaining chip which would be a way of entering the arms control talks, it always surprises me how late in the kind of discussion we have here that that idea is suggested. For example, in the study that the OTA did, and I was chairman of an advisory committee, we went several meetings discussing the pros and cons of SDI and the research program and a whole lot of things before we started suddenly asking: What about this as a bargaining chip?

Now, I can't quite figure that out and it didn't get a great deal of treatment in this particular meeting here today. Is there some reason about that?

It seems to me that the much maligned president and his top advisers and administrators may be keeping us all in the dark as to what the purpose of this is, what the schedule is and so on so as to magnify that as a bargaining chip. Is that what's happening?

P. DOTY: After the summit the Russians who were there told me that until then they had thought that Reagan was posing SDI as a bargaining chip, but after the summit they felt he believed in it like a religion.

So, in that single evidence they are accepting the fact that it isn't going to be bargained away in this administration.

On the other hand, at the end of David Aaron's talk you could perceive the possibility that bargaining it away or not bargaining it away might be an important part of the presidential elections of 1988.

H. G. STEVER: Yes, that's true. By the way I have seen lots of gamblers who have considered bargaining chips as religious objects.

McG. BUNDY: The number of people who have suggested the bargaining chip approach is very large. I joined with three old friends to say that just after the election or right before the election, but we had that much foresight. But, more importantly and more interestingly the same suggestion has been made by a number of Republican political leaders, the one perhaps best known is named Richard Nixon.

The difficulty is that you have to disbelieve the repeated assertions of the President of the United States, of his principal subordinates, and you have to believe that the distribution of energy and effort and skill and commitment that you can see in the Executive Branch among those with a license to practice in the field of arms control is very different from what it is. I think on the public record, we really don't need Soviet advice on this point. Paul, I do understand why you always check with your other sources, but one government on this point, I believe, is to be believed. That isn't always true about everything that is said about strategic defense by every official, let alone by every advocate of the program, but on this point they really mean it. It is not to be bargained on.

J. Gibbons: I might try to expand on your query, Guy, about congressional perspectives of the SDI issue. The lead for bargaining and negotiating with other nations is in the Executive Branch. Congress wants to be deferential to the President having his options and that's part of the dilemma. Even those who may oppose the implementation of SDI for some reason can be found to be supportive of the present program as long as they think the President will try to use it in some very productive way as a bargaining chip.

So, I believe that Congress is going to tend to lay back on being deeply involved in the international negotiation area and Congress as usual reflects the full political spectrum. There are people who range from total optimism to great pessimism about it.

I think there are two or three areas that I could single out as areas of congressional concern. For instance, in the Foreign Relations and Foreign Affairs Committees some are concerned about SDI not in and of itself, but how it fits into the broader context of national defense strategy and that's an issue, of course, that the Executive Branch has to face. SDI is something that must not be seen in isolation, but as part of the western defense strategy.

Another concern is the offensive capabilities of what is touted as an inherently defensive system. Every powerful defensive system has obvious offensive capabilities that must not be ignored.

There are concerns about the pace of the R and D and the criteria of choice for moving from developing basic scientific understanding, towards field testing of components and subcomponents. The latter activities begin to stress things like the ABM Treaty and also affect the program costs dramatically.

There is concern about momentum, for instance in the Appropriation Committee. Is a program that has enjoyed many years of a very high level of R and D funding able to be abandoned? Or does it gain such momentum that it takes on a life of its own?

There is a concern that if the nation has a more or less fixed real dollar budget, then, what are you not going to do in order to be able to do this even within the area of defense commitments?

There are a number of perspectives in Congress, all of which I think are legitimate. Members certainly represent the full spectrum of American political thought. Someone described the Congress to Will Rogers once as a place consisting mostly of thieves and rascals and Will Rogers responded, well, they are a fair cross section of their constituents.

P. Aigrain: I just wanted to make a remark. I don't know whether the American government or whatever government will be at the head of the United States in a few years will want to use the SDI research as a bargaining chip. It is obvious that research results can be used in many ways. You can decide to apply them. You can decide not to apply them. You can use them for bargaining chips and so on. The point is that it is very treacherous to start bargaining with chips that you don't have yet. Otherwise you may very well get the kind of answer a local banker gave one of my students who was trying to borrow money on his future Nobel prize. He was turned down.

H. G. STEVER: Several of our speakers today and yesterday mentioned that a great deal of this research was the kind of research that we would like to do in connection with other forms of warfare anyway. So, the part that is spent on research, no matter how this comes out, I think is not necessarily going to be wasted. McGeorge Bundy pointed out that perhaps we are spending a lot of money on some other kinds of people in our government who seem not to be concerned with the right thing, but a fair number of the scientists I know actually say that in the beginning the amount of money for some of these research programs was not radically larger than was already being spent and some people even said less, but I guess they are over that hump now about that problem.

C. SCHMID: But the times are changing. I might as well mention Gramm-Rudman because it seems like every discussion I have attended in the past four months has had this subject brought up. I hate to be a bore, but all of a sudden things are getting tighter financially. And when things get tighter, we have to look at the effects on large projects vs. small projects. If anyone has worked on small research projects and seen budget cuts occur they know which ones stay ahead of the game. Generally the large projects have strong representation in Congress, and they are therefore usually the ones that have the least cuts. So, there are going to be proportionately larger losses to small research projects.

R. L. HAGENGRUBER: I would like to add a comment to that because I think I agree. It goes back to the question about managing SDI. Last year because of the way they handled Gramm-Rudman in Congress the cut that got delivered to Dartmouth for the Defense Advanced Research Project Agency was almost 10% which is well out of line, and in fact the Air Force and Navy both took cuts in their research and development programs. They were in excess of the Gramm-Rudman percentages simply because certain parts, in this particular case SDI, were protected, which I think puts a very high demand on the Strategic Defense Initiative program to expend its money in research-type activities that in effect provide at least a level if not increasing base of that part of their work which is called research.

So that makes it a very key question in terms of its management, that the development and engineering parts of the program be done very thoughtfully to avoid an excessive penalty to the area of research because what is in real jeopardy right now I don't think is the issue of whether there will be an SDI or not, but what the cost will be that is paid across the board in the area of defense and research because right now the potential for that cost to be extremely debilitating exists if the program is not managed well. Dispatching SDI won't change that. Managing well could do that.

I would only add, by the way, that I don't believe that it is obvious that the Congress has exercised and exercised across the entire group of congressional people the same level of insight into these very sensitive questions of research that some people might perceive on the basis of what has been a traditional yearly pattern of review in research.

We get contact with a great many of these people and I find that most of them are very thoughtful people and very conscientiously committed to this area, but I find that a great many of them have become very highly politicized about this issue and not altogether without the aid and comfort of the people in the technical community on both sides of this issue. It is a very, very volatile situation for research in the national defense area.

H. G. STEVER: We are coming close to the closing time and may I ask any of the panelists if they have a final word that they would like to say on this subject that may tie together their own thoughts or some other thoughts they have heard at this time?

J. T. SWING (*Council on Foreign Relations, New York, N.Y.*): I just wanted to add one footnote about McGeorge Bundy's remarks about the bargaining chip theory. I really do agree with him that you have to believe what this Administration says about not wanting to bargain it away, but there are two small footnotes worth noting. One of them we have already noted earlier today. The bargaining chip is not likely to arise in this Administration. It has been said before, but it is worth remembering.

Second, even if it were to arise in this Administration it is worth remembering that this particular president is very good at stonewalling all the way along until the very end, and then when you hardly believe he is going to do it he will compromise as he recently did in the budget which has some tax increases which he said would never happen.

McG. BUNDY: I would like a side bet with Mr. Swing.

H. G. STEVER: Very good. I have a side bet on that same subject by the way with Mr. Yonas.

It has been very interesting to me that in the two years that I have been involved in SDI activity, the nature of the debate has changed. Initially, opinions went off in all directions, but with the discussions that have taken place since that time in many different kinds of meetings and forums, almost everybody, as you pointed out, now believes that a research program should be carried out.

I have often wondered whether the motivation of those who really didn't want a research program was that they ought to give a little in compromise or whether there emerged a powerful logic when they put together everything, our relationship with the Soviets, the intelligence information about what they have done, and so on. Has this almost unanimous opinion come from a pure logic of discussion or is there another explanation?

P. DOTY: It is a matter of degree and for you it must be whether the annual research SDI budget is going to be larger than the National Science Foundation budget or not.

I think that point is worth just a moment, that if it did grow at anywhere near the projected rate it would involve the dislocation to that effort of the order of half of the science and engineering that is going on in military R and D. It is not so much money bounded as it is technical manpower bounded, and is that the optimal mix? We have to face that question if it does continue to expand.

F. SEITZ: It is perhaps worth pointing out again, which someone has already done, in the first two years General Abrahamson's main job has been to pull together things which were already going on and in many cases trimming them to try to fit them into some rational mold.

H. G. STEVER: Paul, I heard you on the business of the manpower situation, that's not on the money side, but I am not sure that we have a manpower squeeze at the present time. We have much manpower in our national laboratories, where, in fact, they are being squeezed on their manpower slots.

We will not have time to consider this important aspect of the SDI program further, much as we would like to. We did in my estimation treat many important questions very well, and I would like to conclude this roundtable discussion with many thanks to all of you participants.

Concluding Remarks

HEINZ R. PAGELS

The New York Academy of Sciences
New York, New York 10021

As I listened to the deliberations of various experts and scholars on arms, arms control, and the relationship between sovereign national states during the last two days, I could not but be reminded of the ancient Greek myth of Hephaestus. Hephaestus was one of the lesser gods in the Olympic pantheon. He was the armorer of the gods. He manufactured their swords and shields as well as other weapons: a prefiguration of a modern arms technologist.

Hephaestus was the cuckolded husband of Aphrodite, goddess of Love. I also remember that Hephaestus walked with a limp. According to myth, Hephaestus had come upon his wife and Ares, the god of War, making love, and Ares was so outraged at the intrusion that he broke Hephaestus's legs. This explanation for Hephaestus's lameness did not, however, completely satisfy me.

Many years ago, I had occasion to read some of the historical background material on the origin of the Greek myths. According to one historian, Hephaestus's limp has an entirely different origin. The early Bronze Age Greek kings, in their conquests of the Hellenic Peninsula, travelled with their armorers. These individuals were considered so valuable by the Arcadian kings that their legs were deliberately broken. This ensured that the armorers could not run away and defect to a rival. The myth of Hephaestus reflected this historical reality.

The ancient Greeks already correctly saw the power relationship between the political leaders and the technologists who supplied them with weapons. It might be argued that political leaders have traditionally crippled the scientific and technical establishment. Some people support this viewpoint; others are not as certain. Regardless of one's feelings on this matter, it is evident from what has been said at this meeting that this situation has not changed in the last four millenia. Technologists are still crippled by political leaders.

In the course of organizing this meeting with Dr. Stever, I had occasion to speak with many people in the defense and political decision-making communities. Without passing judgment on the issues of strategic policy that have been discussed and debated here in the last two days, I did find one invariant that characterized the positions of these individuals on strategic policy. Once the person specified a perception of Soviet policy either as rational and simply

---

Heinz R. Pagels is Executive Director of the New York Academy of Sciences, New York, New York 10021.

self-serving or alternatively as ruthlessly domineering and expansionist, the rest of that individual's strategic thinking fell into place. In other words, the underlying reality was emotional, having to do with issues of trust and distrust and the extent thereof. It was not a rational response, although these feelings were held by rational people.

It has been my experience that if there is ever a struggle between emotion and reason, even within rational people, emotion always wins. We owe it to ourselves, and indeed the world, to prevent emotions from overwhelming us, so that we may at least continue our deliberations even with those whose values so profoundly conflict with our own.

Index of Contributors

(Italicized page numbers refer to comments made in roundtable discussions

2818